...ct or
...ication with your child
before birth?
Before conception?

"Yes."
"Yes, of course!"
"I'm not sure. But
there was... something.
Something mysterious."

ALSO BY ELISABETH HALLETT

IN THE NEWBORN YEAR:
OUR CHANGING AWARENESS AFTER CHILDBIRTH

SOUL TREK

MEETING OUR CHILDREN ON THE WAY TO BIRTH

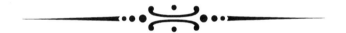

ELISABETH HALLETT

LIGHT · HEARTS · PUBLISHING

Acknowledgements of previously published material
appear on page 321

Cover illustration by Roselyn Hallett, age 4

ISBN 0-9646097-0-3

Library of Congress Number 95-094300

10 9 8 7 6 5 4 3 2 1

Dedicated with love to my daughter, Roselyn Giles Hallett

PART I
MEETING BEFORE BIRTH:
THE VARIETIES OF EXPERIENCE

PART II
THE COOPERATIVE BOND

PART III
DOOR OF DEATH, DOOR OF BIRTH

PART IV
WONDER AND MYSTERY

PART I

MEETING BEFORE BIRTH:
THE VARIETIES OF EXPERIENCE

Something new is in the air. Call it a longing for contact. It almost seems as though the human world has had enough of its splendid isolation, and with a certain humility is learning to listen for voices of other realms.

In popular television shows, a dolphin speaks, angels take a hand in our lives and humans roam the universe, meeting and communicating with any number of life forms. Books about near-death experiences top the best-seller lists; tabloids offer advice on "how to contact your guardian angel." Research that once would have seemed too bizarre is respectable today, with scientists probing interspecies communication, alien encounters, even electronic communication with the dead.

All of this reflects the experience of a great many people whose individual lives have in one way or another been penetrated by something from beyond... something more.

Once a breeze from another world has blown across your doorstep, things are never quite the same. It can happen in many ways: a powerful dream, the touch of a "ghost," a brush with death, a healing presence... Jane Anne Buzana tells how her first encounter with mystery altered her world: "It has opened a whole new realm of learning for me. After this profound and loving experience, there was no stopping me from a never ending journey into the unknown."

For Jane Anne, as for many others whose stories are told in this book, the life-changing experience was a meeting with her child -- before the child was born.

My own first contact with a world beyond the ordinary

happened long ago. It changed me in a moment from a child to a seeker, and started me on the journey that led eventually to the creation of this book.

I was thirteen, and I had just invented the young girl's answer to torrid love affairs. Hero worship!

Handsome, magnetic Dr. Tom Dooley was dead. I had scarcely noticed him when he was alive and at work in the villages of Laos, but by dying young of the most romantic disease possible he caught my adolescent fancy, and a few months after his death I was deep into his last book.

One evening as I sat at my desk doing homework, I was overwhelmed with sad thoughts of the pain my idol had endured. I remember putting my head down on my arms for a moment, full of pity and grief.

I raised my head, went back to homework. And suddenly there was a presence as of someone standing behind me with hands on my shoulders. Happiness and strength, an enormous sense of being comforted, flowed into me from that touch.

I half-turned, looked at the floor behind my chair, not really expecting to see anyone. I got up and walked through the house, smiling, elated. That night I asked my diary, "What does it mean to die? I want to know, but no one could tell me, I'm sure..."

At the time, it seemed a gift too strange and intimate to share. Over the years since then I watched in amazement as "life after death" gradually became something people could talk about -- and by the last decade of the century, something that most Americans claimed to believe in.

It seems odd that I never considered the possibility of contact in the other direction -- with the unborn. But when rumors of such a possibility reached me, I was ready to listen.

✳   ✳   ✳

I was preparing a book on the experiences of new parents when I began to notice tantalizing comments popping up in story after story:

"Throughout the pregnancy I felt we communicated."

"The child's voice came to me often and I knew he was a boy."

These parents were talking about communicating with their unborn children -- and talking about it as if it were the most natural thing in the world!

I was intrigued. Communication before birth seemed a startling new idea. Of course I was aware of projects aimed at stimulating unborn babies by talking to them, playing music -- some even proposed to begin educating in the womb. But here I was encountering something very different. People spoke of hearing from their babies, not talking at them. They described magical, moving experiences of contact that seemed to be initiated by the babies themselves. I wanted to learn more.

I thought back to my pregnancy with my son, several years earlier. Had there been anything like this? Well -- the dreams. Each time I dreamed of my baby, it was a boy. By the time he was born, I was so sure he was a boy that I didn't even think to wonder. And this was a good thing. I never had much to do with little boys, never imagined I could love one of that alien breed. The dreams prepared me, overcame my resistance. I fell in love with my baby boy on the night of his birth.

And how about the way I often laughed in my sleep during that pregnancy? Was my son telling me jokes as I slept?

My curiosity led to a search for stories of other people's experiences. I wanted to know about every possible kind of contact and communication before birth. The enthusiastic response to my request for information told me that I'd stumbled on a realm that had been largely secret, much as contact with the "dead" had once been too private to share.

This book is the result of that search.

Thanks to the generosity of over one hundred and eighty people who have invited us into their lives, there is a wide range of experience here. There are stories of dreams and visions, visitations, inner voices, subtle "knowings" and more. For each person who describes a pre-birth experience, it was felt as a powerful connection with the child-to-be. Some even feel that, as Claire Baiz says, "That pre-natal connection with my daughter is as close as I will ever get to the essence of her Spirit."

These connections and contacts seem purposeful. They appear to come for reasons: to reassure, to announce, to persuade, give guidance or prepare us for future events. Often there is some resistance on the part of the prospective parent, a resistance which the pre-birth connection helps to overcome. Sometimes the pregnancy is actually unwanted or at least unplanned, and termination is being considered.

When there is a crisis or an anxious, difficult time during pregnancy, the contact brings comfort and courage.

There are experiences that seem intended simply as a meeting, a way of forming a bond and making the baby "real."

Sometimes the intent of the communication seems simply to convey love.

*   *   *

Although several fathers will describe their connections with children-to-be, most of the contributors to this book are women. And since most are Americans, with a few Canadians and Europeans, this is clearly not a cross-cultural survey. Nor is it a scientific study or an attempt to prove a position. Instead, my aim is to present people's experiences and their insights and beliefs about them -- and the speculations that arise from the possibility that our unborn children may communicate with us.

Part of the fascination of these stories is in seeing them as evidence for how life may work. They raise many intriguing questions, and hint at possible answers.

Do we come into our physical life from another existence? Do we come randomly, or to a specific family? Do we have any choice in the matter? Do parents have any choice?

What can these experiences tell us about the connection between parent and child? What can we surmise about the child's state during pregnancy -- and before conception? Looking at them from another point of view, what do the stories tell us of the parents' beliefs? What evidence do we see that we, as parents, create these experiences out of our own needs?

It comes down to what may be the most fascinating question of all. Are these experiences really encounters with another consciousness -- a meeting of souls? Or are they productions of our own? Are they "dramatizations" that we create, based on knowledge that we somehow possess about our children-to-be?

Is there another possibility? Perhaps there is a dimension in which we and our children are not separate, and where shared experience is the medium of our communion.

*   *   *

There have been times when I have had to put this material aside and deal with more or less intense reservations.

As records of experience, the stories speak for themselves, but I sometimes question interpretations that are placed on them. With my background in psychology and nursing, I tend to look first for physical explanations and for the possibility of illusion. In Chapter Sixteen I will delve into these issues, and present some caveats which I believe must be kept in mind if we are to balance openness with discrimination.

Meanwhile, I invite the reader to enjoy the stories for the wondrous gifts that they are. Some of these experiences may be the product of a parent's creative imagination; some describe perceptions so far beyond the ordinary that we might be tempted to dismiss them wholesale. But when we look deeper, past the details of each particular story, we begin to see a remarkable consistency. The emerging patterns, which we will explore in Part II, may well reveal the hidden workings of conception and birth.

CHAPTER ONE
COMING TO CONCEPTION

These days, we have a good deal of contact with our unborn children. Through amniocentesis and other prenatal tests, we listen in on their genetic communication. With ultrasound, we hear their heartbeat and even catch shadowy glimpses of them in the womb.

But what if there's more? What if they are talking to us much more directly? And what if this communication is taking place not just during pregnancy, but even before conception?

For some of us, it may not be hard to imagine forming some impression of a child in its mother's womb. But how can we know anything at all about the child who is not yet conceived? One woman's comment may speak for many. Although she sensed communication from her daughter during pregnancy, she says there was no contact before conception, and adds, "I have deep feelings as to why this would be next to impossible."

And yet this seemingly impossible contact is exactly what many parents describe.

Some feel an almost physical presence. Some sense a definite personality, or a warmth, a heart-warming familiarity. It may be a fleeting one-time occurrence, or recurring sensations that amount to feeling "trailed" by a persistent visitor.

For some parents-to-be, an inner voice announces the coming conception or even engages them in conversation. There are mysterious meetings in dreams and waking visions. Messages come in symbolic form, through dream imagery, oracles, odd happenings that don't quite lie flat on the surface of our life...

The contact before conception may be a mysterious meeting with a presence we can't identify, until later when we look back and wonder about it. But often the sense of presence brings with it a strong feeling that this is "my child" coming to visit. A mother recalls:

> There was a very fleeting moment when I felt I met my second child, before she was conceived. I do feel, after this "visit," that children may have some chance to choose their parents, because I think that's what happened that day as I sat in church. I felt her almost like a wind blowing through me, but as a real personality -- a feisty, impish, unpredictable personality.   I conceived her the following month. I felt lucky to have been deemed "qualified" by such an interesting person.

Liz Lipman-Stern recalls an incident one week before her second child was conceived:

> My husband, son, and I were lying in bed. I moved over, leaving a space between me and my son, and felt the presence of our other child there in that space. I knew that the "presence" next to me was my child and that this meant my child was ready to come to my body. I had no sense of the child's sex or any other information, just that my family felt complete there on our bed with my husband, son, me, and our next child. We hadn't yet decided to have another, but that experience convinced us to start.

Some women describe a slightly disorienting impression that another baby is already in the family. Leigh McCune recalls a visit to her father's peaceful rural home, where she says she frequently "gets" things she might otherwise miss:

> My son and I were outside playing and I kept having a very strong sense that I had to go inside and check on "the baby." This occurred many times during the visit. Even at that time "the baby" was a girl.

Not long afterward, Leigh's daughter was conceived.

Perhaps a sudden yearning to have a baby is one way of sensing a contact that we may not consciously perceive, though we may feel it on another level. Does this woman's "craving" mirror her child's desire to be born?

> I am the single mother of Jacob, my son, who is twenty months. I experienced a week of intense craving for a child, where I said

to myself finally, "Okay, I want a baby, I will have a baby, and will go along with this idea the next chance I have." (I had no partner at the time.) Then I felt a presence that was very soothing and loving, and went to sleep. A few weeks later, I conceived my son, and that "soothing" presence has been with me ever since.

The sense of presence is even more definite when it is accompanied by a vision or a voice heard in the "mind's ear." Deborah and Charles Prince had detailed perceptions of their future child. The first experience was during their honeymoon:

> We were staying at a wonderful old hotel which we loved. During dinner, we both saw and heard the spirit of Shawn, and were told we would have her some day. At the time we had no thoughts of another child -- my first child seemed like enough for us. At visits to the hotel afterwards, we always saw Shawn -- that's what she said her name was, and that's what we named her. She told us she would be a good athlete, and so we assumed she was a he!

Their child was conceived over a year later. Asked for more details of the way in which she and Charles perceived Shawn before conception, Deborah explains:

> I first saw her in my mind's eye, and heard her voice. Actually it seemed like a "he" to me, I guess because "it" said its name was Shawn -- usually a boy's name. She had lots of golden light around her, and she only came very close to us that once. She laughed a lot when "talking" to me, and she asked me to tell Charles everything she said -- that she would be our child and would be counting on us to be prepared for her by doing our "work" -- meaning, I think, our spiritual as well as professional growth. After a while, when she appeared Charles could "feel" her too. He "heard" her also one time...

Beth and her husband had tried for two years to conceive, and had almost given up hope when Beth encountered her two future children:

> I was walking on the beach praying for my babies to come to me, and I suddenly felt their presences. "We're coming. Don't worry."
> "Who are you?"
> "Jacques Carroll and Chandra Estelle."

I got pregnant the following month. I had a dream, while pregnant, in which the baby said s/he wanted to do two things -- play football and learn to play guitar. I woke up annoyed! No daughter of mine was going to play football. I eventually had a sonogram, and upon learning I was carrying Jacques Carroll, asked his permission to change his name to John Charles: "Sure, okay mom."

When he was eleven months old, I was giving a client a massage when suddenly Chandra came through loud and clear: "Tonight! Tonight." (I had actually planned on waiting until John was three before trying again.) So I went home and told my husband, "Tonight, tonight." "Sure, love to!" Chandra was conceived.

The questions I asked Beth are typical of those I ask each person upon receiving a story of pre-birth contact. Among them were these:

How did this experience fit in with your ideas about existence before birth and about the connection between parents and children? Did your beliefs change as a result of it?

What "age" did the children seem to be when you felt their presences at the beach? How did you experience their voices? Do the names have any particular significance to you?

I also asked for Beth's thoughts on this difficult question: how can we tell the difference between real communication from another being, and our own imagination or subconscious mind? She replied:

My beliefs did not change because of my conversation with kids before conception. Of course we exist -- always, if not here, then there (wherever). And I believe we choose our families, our parents, our lives. We choose.

What age were the kids when they talked with me? Interesting question. I suppose around three to five years old. How it felt? Wonderful! Awesome (I was in awe). Exhilarating. I heard their voices in my head. Having experienced others' presences before, I know where I end and others begin; I know what is not me.

No, the names were not significant at all to me. Are you kidding? A French kid, and I imagined I'd made up the name Chandra -- never having heard it before. I learned later she/he's an East Indian moon deity.

Ever learning to trust and believe my "intuition," when Chandra called I had no doubts, and I talked with her through the pregnancy. She's a year old and we still haven't made a break from each other.

Another woman who envisioned two children together has given birth to one of them and expects the other to come later. She feels a continuing connection with the child not yet conceived:

> I came to understand that I would have first a boy, then a girl. We had decided to postpone getting pregnant, but still my two yet unconceived children would come into my awareness. I received a strong sense of what they were like, and an even stronger sense of the relationship between them.
>
> I conceived three and a half years ago. I "knew" I was carrying a boy, even without ultrasound or amniocentesis. Though the experiences were different now (the two no longer appeared together), I kept having them and I also began having dreams. In some of these my daughter appeared.
>
> I do not plan to get pregnant again until next spring; however my next child -- a girl (the same one who used to visit along with her brother) -- often visits with me. Sometimes, I swear it is like she is literally in my arms!

CONNECTING WITH FATHER FIRST

Since most of these stories are from women, it is easy to assume that mothers have a monopoly on pre-conception contact. In fact, this experience may be just as available to men -- more so perhaps than connections in pregnancy, when the mother's physical bond with the baby is a factor. The father may be the first or even the only one to feel communication. As one mother says, "My *husband*, not I, had strong contact with our daughter before conception, during our pregnancy, and at birth."

Connecting with their children before conception may be an aspect of fatherhood that men are ready to rediscover. It is an idea with the most ancient echoes: some Australian Aboriginal people are said to believe that conception involves the father's going into the spiritual realm, the "Dreamtime," and meeting there the soul of his future child.

The following stories illustrate some of the ways that men have sensed the approach of their child-to-be.

Kenneth Nova writes, while expecting his first child:

> I believe that I had direct contact with the spirit of our baby-to-be just prior to conception! Last year on May 27,

Wendy (my wife) and I were camping in a cabin near Rocky Mountain National Park. That morning at eleven, a coyote walked past our cabin in broad daylight. We called to it, it stopped and looked at us, and then went on.

Then, on the day before the summer solstice, we were at the Regional Nonviolence Gathering in Nebraska. I went to a men's sweat, led by a Lakota Sioux man. He concluded the sweat with a song to the coyote, during which I had simultaneous visions of that coyote in May and of our baby, being healthy and a harbinger of peace. The song was sung in Lakota language.

The next day, the solstice, we were all together in a large group, sharing songs. This Lakota man said he wanted to sing the Coyote song, and first he would translate it. As if his head was guided by another, he looked right at me (out of about seventy-five people) and said, "Father, I am coming soon" twice, and the whole song had verses like "Father, protect me." Wendy and I were flabbergasted -- the song had a particular meaning for me, beyond the traditional one. We conceived two weeks later!

Kenneth wrote again to announce: "Our baby, a boy we named Max Coyote Nova, is now six and a half weeks old, healthy and very cute."

Susan Bassett says that although her son never "spoke" to her before birth, he did communicate with her husband more than a year before he was conceived:

Samuel had gone to Oregon for his uncle's funeral about one month after we met. When he came back, he asked me, "What does the name João mean to you?" He had no way of knowing it was my grandfather's name. Samuel said he had been on the train coming back from Oregon when a light appeared to him and said, "Name me João." So we did.

In the following story we meet Miriam, a woman who became a mother against enormous odds, and only because the child-to-be made himself known to her and her husband Steven. It was Steven who felt the first contact with their future son. Miriam explains:

Let's start as far back as I can remember. When I was a child, I had no interest in playing "mommy." Although I played with dolls, I always created situations so I would be a teacher or doctor, but not a mama. It wasn't until I entered college and had a health class that I realized my aversion to motherhood went any deeper. One day we were shown a movie on childbirth and

I passed out. The woman hadn't even been admitted to the hospital yet, but I was gonzo.

It became an obsession for me to avoid pregnancy and I sought a surgeon who would perform a tubal ligation. It took me five years, but at the age of twenty-three I had the surgery performed.

Four years after that, I met Steven. He understood that having children was not an option, but wasn't attached to the notion of fatherhood, so there was no conflict.

After three years of marriage, we both started doing guided imagery through music. My sessions seemed to center on past life (I believe) experiences. Many horrible events surrounding pregnancy and childbirth... continual loss through dismal and/or violent means. After each session, the people acting as our guides (we did our sessions individually) had us draw a mandala or some other representation of the experience. My drawings were uniformly depressing. Also, following each session, I would make it home only to collapse on the couch and run a fever of 102 degrees for a few hours.

My final session was much different from all the others. A guide, obviously myself in fairy godmother garb, appeared to me and took me back to several of the key figures I had identified with in my past life experiences. She mediated for me and asked the people from the past to help me out by keeping their fears and sharing with me only their talents and positive aspects. It was an incredibly healing experience, and it prepared me for my husband relating his experience.

Steven's sessions seemed much lighter than mine. He reported Peter Max type visions -- until one day he came home and told me in a matter of fact way that he had seen our baby. I waxed philosophical and reminded him that a "baby" is symbolic of any number of transitions through which we might be going. Then he showed me the picture he had drawn at the end of his session. A blond, blue eyed child was holding out a jeweled box of light.

From then on, we both received visions of this kiddo in our meditations and dreams. He seemed to be continually tapping us on our shoulders, reminding us of his presence.

I was convinced that if I was intended to bear this child, I could "heal" the results of my surgery with my husband's emotional and spiritual support, but he didn't share my faith and I knew that I didn't have enough juice to do it on my own. In 1983, I underwent corrective surgery called tubal reanastomosis. It lasted four and a half hours; Steven observed the entire procedure, standing by my side.

My surgeon told me that I could try as early as one month after surgery to become pregnant, but I wanted to be in top physical condition. I had gone into training before the surgery, but afterwards I really got serious about tuning up my body. I also made a commitment before our Rabbi, family and friends to raise our child(ren) as Jews. Interestingly, that was June tenth and our son, Asher, was conceived on June eleventh.

Once conceived, Asher no longer came to either of us during our meditations or dreams. Mission accomplished, he had other matters to resolve, I suppose. Asher was born on my thirty-third birthday. He is blond, blue eyed and full of light. (There hasn't been a blue eyed critter on Steven's side of the tree in three generations.)

TRAILED BY CHERUBS

Like Steven and Miriam, who felt their future child "continually tapping on their shoulders," many people describe the sensation of a baby spirit hovering near and following them around. Says Trilby Malinn Hanek:

> I most emphatically had an experience of contact with my little darling before he was conceived. In short, I just perceived a *presence* near me (with the awareness centered at my third eye) that always caused me to look slightly upward. (As if I would physically see something!) As I paid more attention to the presence I began to apprehend it as a small flame, similar to what one sees off a lit candle. This "courting" relationship went on for several months before I conceived.
>
> During those months I felt as if I were being tailed, and every now and then I'd be aware that *somebody* was trying to get my attention. It all felt very romantic. Once my husband and I came into agreement about becoming parents (a marvelously romantic experience as well!) our boy came through to us on the first try. Even that summer morning was fecund -- warm, tremendously humid, just at sunrise...
>
> After conception, the feeling of presence intensified (naturally), and instead of perceiving a light near me, the picture changed to what I thought was a baby face. Imagine my surprise when Jack's picture was taken near his second birthday and the little face on the print was identical to the one I'd seen all during

my pregnancy!

Trilby found it natural that the presence would intensify after conception, but in fact it seems more often to be the other way around. The sense of a hovering presence often disappears once conception has occurred. Says Susan Clarke, "It wasn't until I was about three weeks pregnant that I realized I hadn't seen my cherub for a while (but I still didn't even consider the spirit was inside me)!" She recalls:

> My friends looked at me rather askance when I said I *knew* a good eight or nine months prior to my son's conception that I was going to have another child -- and a blond-haired, blue eyed one at that! Even more amazing is that I was a single parent of a five year old girl, Caitlin, at the time and the "baby spirit's" father and I were merely friends.
>
> During the months before he was conceived I could almost "see" this little male cherub floating above my head laughing -- I remember seeing him more when I was alone or working, but I also remember being with Caitlin and saying that the baby was right there with us.
>
> I am convinced that Elliot, our son, was just waiting for his father and me to finally realize what was to happen, because it was only three months after we made the commitment to share our lives as a family that we found out Elliot was on the way.

Becky began corresponding with me while pregnant. In remarkably clear detail, she described the hovering spirit she had sensed before conception:

> I am now in my twenty-eighth week of pregnancy. In November of last year I began to be aware of a little spirit presence hovering around me. At first the awareness was dim, then it became so noticeable that I felt it whirring above my right shoulder. Nothing like this had ever happened to me before -- but I had been having other stirrings about becoming pregnant so I wanted to be receptive.
>
> A month or so after the dawning of this contact, I began to talk about it with people close to me. Several related that this was a common experience for women about to become pregnant. When I heard this, my inner eyes widened.
>
> For a while around this time, my little baby spirit seemed to have wandered away. I wondered if I should have kept its presence a secret.

After the turn of the year, the spirit reappeared, this time hovering in front of my left hip, clearly an animated baby girl. I tried to have dialogues with her in my imagination from time to time. She seemed to be communicating to me that I should hurry, that she could not wait much longer, that I had to heal my wounds in order for her to have a safe home to dwell in.

And gradually she became tinier and tinier. I was still not ready to try to conceive for various reasons -- I assumed she was vanishing from my life. Finally in April, she was a mere dot, still hovering but no longer communicating.

One day, I answered a knock on the front door. It seemed odd that my watchdogs were standing at the front door pointing in silence -- normally they would be barking vigorously. The man at the door was clutching a huge bouquet of balloons. "Are you the new mother?" he asked. "No," I said. Still the dogs were silent. "Isn't this the house with the newborn?" "No," I answered. "You must have the wrong address." It turned out that he did have the wrong address which puzzled him somehow.

The way this incident unfolded shook me a little -- in part because it shadowed both our first serious attempt to conceive and the disappearance of my tiny infant spirit who was no longer even a dot. Within a week I had a positive pregnancy test. I was certain I was carrying a girl and prenatal testing has confirmed that.

We have waited a long time for this child and our joy in her choosing us as soon as our gates were open is immense.

I asked Becky how she perceived that the spirit being was a baby girl, and whether the experience was most like seeing, hearing, touching or an inner impression. She replied:

When I first sensed her whirring above my right shoulder I could not tell her gender, but only had a sense of her infancy. It was only later when she began to hover in front of me that I had a visual sense of her. She looked to be about six months old, dark blue eyes and dark brown hair, clearly an animated little girl.

My impression of her was somewhere between visual and internal. It was never tactile, although I would have loved that, and rarely did I "hear" her, even when we had conversations. Obviously, this is difficult to describe -- my inner sense was quite vivid and sometimes ebbed into my physical senses.

This experience took me by surprise. Yet as it evolved over months, my contact with her affirmed a germ of a belief I was holding that souls choose their bodies and their parents, for whatever reason. I had a very clear impression that this little soul leaped at her first chance to join this family and that she had made a clear choice to wait until I had exited from a previous relationship. I think we have been waiting for one another for a long time and she finally had to beckon me in the startling way that she did. Perhaps she tried at other times when I was not as receptive. Perhaps she is one or both of the babies from two previous abortions. I have an infinite number of questions, more questions than answers from this experience.

After her child was born, Becky added details about the baby and compared her to the pre-birth impressions:

Happy New Year! My baby was born January 8. Labor was very hard but had a glorious ending: Elena emerged rosy and healthy (an unmedicated birth) with a headfull of brown hair and big blue/gray eyes. We'll see what she looks like at six months. It seems, although we hardly know one another yet, that I have known her for a long, long time.

Becky wrote again when Elena was nearly a year old:

Since Elena's birth, my sense of our pre-pregnancy communing is even more grounded, partly because of the perspective of hindsight and partly because she truly *is* the baby spirit who visited me, physically as well as personality-wise. We are, of course, utterly in love with her and are overjoyed to participate in and witness her unfolding. I will never get over how magical it is, from the pre-beginning all the way through and beyond.

THE EARLIEST HINTS

These hints of future children are not confined to the weeks and months just before conception. Some people become aware of their children-to-be much earlier. Seven years earlier, for example, Jane Anne Buzana began to dream of a daughter:

In the beginning I just thought they were like any other dreams, but when they kept recurring, I knew I had to pay attention.

I was always awakened out of sleep in the middle of the night after one of these dreams. They were basically of a mother and baby doing what mothers and babies do, holding, cuddling, and looking into each other's eyes. This child really touched me deeply. I did not know what it all meant, but I knew I would have to listen to my heart. This was not an easy decision to make since I already had two children in school, and was struggling to make ends meet as it was. "Well, God does provide," I told myself. I also knew that this baby was persistent in her quest to be born. The dreams continued, so I decided, if by the time my IUD was to be taken out, I was still having these dreams, then I would allow this child to come. I got pregnant two months after being birth control free.

I had a real intuitive feeling about Christina, and that she was special, and indeed she is. I felt there was a soul connection between us. Because of this soul connection I believe there is the possibility of communication between a child and its parents.

Christina Noelle is now six and a half years old, and we share a close psychic and spiritual bond. She often reads my thoughts, and I am always delighted by this.

Seven years before Debbie Smollen conceived her son, the dream connection occurred. She feels that this dream in August of 1982 put her in touch with her second husband and with the child they would have together. At the time of the dream, Debbie was married to her first husband and already had three of their four daughters:

I was in my living room. The couch was pulled out as a bed and I was lying back in my husband's arms, joyously giving birth at home. I was surrounded by several kind midwives and two of my close friends. As I pushed the beautiful baby out to the midwife's waiting hands, the room filled with the exclamation of "It's a boy!" At this point I turned to my partner to say, "Isn't this wonderful -- we have a son." I remember the strange face behind me. It was not my husband. I didn't know who the man was.

Debbie says that for several years she didn't put much stock in the dream, although she kept thinking about it:

It was probably the most vivid dream I ever had. But after Alyssa was born in the hospital in 1985, I thought I'd never have any more children.

In 1987 my marriage ended in divorce. While sitting in the courtroom I had a vision of the "promise." This promise was that my family would be rearranged in a new and better way and that even though the divorce seemed to be closing a door, a new one was opening. I focused on this for many months following the divorce. One year later, I met a man and knew before I saw him that he was very special (we had a three hour phone conversation prior to meeting).

We had a child together -- our son AJ. He was born at my home, in my living room! We did not open the couch to bed until after he was born. But I knelt against that same couch (now worn -- it's eight years later!) in the same room I had dreamt about. Sitting on the couch facing me just to my left was his father. We joined hands as I pushed our son out to the midwife's waiting hands. As soon as the baby was born I looked up at my partner who was checking the time on his wristwatch. A few moments later the midwife passed our wrapped son between my legs and settled me back on the birth stool. I held this wrapped bundle for a few moments when she said, "Open the blanket -- see what you got." Sure enough I was holding a perfect little boy. The dream had come true.

VISIONS OF UNKNOWN PERSONS

Shortly before conception, some people have visions of a stranger, a distinct "personage." While they may not identify this unknown visitor with the child who is conceived soon afterward, the connection in time is intriguing. Carla Sunderland had a recurring vision about two months before conceiving her first child, a daughter:

> I kept seeing a young Catholic priest with a large wooden cross around his neck. He never said anything, just smiled and nodded at me. I was very frightened of these visions and I still can't understand what this meant to me.

An interesting consideration is that Carla's baby was born "grey and lifeless" with an initial Apgar of zero*, but was revived and did well thereafter. Could this apparition, though frightening, have been intended to reassure her about the outcome of her impending pregnancy?

Lynne Shank describes a visitation that occurred one month before she conceived her fourth child, a girl:

> In the middle of the night, our dog suddenly rushed out of our bedroom, waking me up. I became aware that someone was

staring at me from the foot of our bed. I asked, "Who is it, what do you want?" No one answered so I figured it must be my little girl and again asked, "What do you want?" Still no answer so I said it again, "What is it?" I sat up in bed and looked to where I felt the person was standing. There was silence and no one there.

Then I realized I was perceiving something spiritual so I looked with another perception and felt a little old grey haired woman standing at the foot of the bed and just watching me. I thought in my head, "What is it? Do I know you?" I felt a lovingness towards me but nothing else -- by then I was feeling pretty weird so I covered up my head and buried my head in the pillow and decided when I couldn't see her I wouldn't have to deal with what was happening. I went back to sleep. When I awoke again she was gone. If I had it to do again I would have investigated more. We all said if I had a girl it probably was her spirit.

INTRODUCTION DREAMS

Each of Lucy Kennedy's two sons appeared to her in a vivid dream shortly before conception. She writes:

My husband John and I were planning to have a child after eight years together. I was "working on" my health, trying to overcome allergy problems and some other concerns. Somehow having a baby didn't seem imminent. Then I had a dream that I was standing in the woods, and a little ways away there was a small glade or clearing where the sun was shining on a little child. He was a blond-headed, slim boy, perhaps around three years old. He was just standing there, looking very beautiful in the sunshine. Then along came the doctor with whom I was working on my health issues. He, too, saw the little boy and said to me, "Well, I see you have a fine young son!" It occurred to me instantly that he was mistaken in assuming that the child was mine; I knew I didn't have a child. But I said nothing, letting him believe that the boy was indeed mine. And somehow that set up a feeling of wondering inside me. It reminded me of Mary's reaction in the Bible -- "But Mary kept all these things, pondering them in her heart."

I was sure, when I awoke, that it had been a very important dream. It was, in fact, unforgettable, and after Duke was born and had grown into a slender little boy with light blond curls, it was impossible not to believe that he was the child in the dream. I think that deep down I knew right away that this was my child-to-be introducing himself to me and asking me in this way to "own" him, to accept him into my life. We conceived Duke no more than a couple of months afterward.

I never gave up hope of having another child, even when our firstborn, Duke, was getting close to twelve years old. My husband John had long since given up on the idea and we no longer even spoke of it. In June of 1990 I had a Tarot reading, and toward the end of it the reader just mentioned that "there was another child" if I chose to accept it. I took courage then, because I did believe deep down that it was true, and I simply didn't want to wait any longer. My health wasn't perfect, my marriage wasn't perfect, the house needed all kinds of work -- but it felt useless to wait, to delay what I had been hoping for all those years. I was impatient. My feeling was "now or never."

In July we traveled to Wyoming to live for six weeks while John played at a music festival. On the way, we camped in the Rockies in Montana for a week. One sunny morning I finally was able to tell John what was in my thoughts, and he agreed that he would also like to have another child. I was happy and relieved at his response. Later, as we hiked up to a beautiful lake nestled high among the peaks, all I could think of was my child-to-be. When I was pregnant with Duke, I was hoping for a girl, even though I was certain I was carrying a boy. Now, I again began to think, "Oh, here's my chance to have a little girl."

But then a surprising thing happened. When I let myself imagine having a girl or having a boy, it was clear to me that my heart's desire was another little boy! I saw him so vividly in my mind -- reddish hair, freckles, round cheeks, little nose, smiling, impish -- much like John looked in pictures of him as a toddler. I felt totally in love with this little boy in my heart. He appealed to me, drew me in. He was easy to love; he was what I wanted, finally granted to me. It was an ecstatic, delicious feeling, which I enjoyed secretly all day and which I still can recall distinctly.

As my fertile days approached, I drifted into a frenzy of trying to find out whether John wanted a boy or girl and to figure out how to increase our chances of conceiving one or the other. Duke's wishes were also figuring in: I thought he wanted a brother, although we never told him what we were up to. I felt that the whole situation was hopelessly complicated and I didn't know what to do and couldn't manage to release myself from trying to control the outcome and simply trust Providence to bring about the perfect solution I wanted.

I was pretty well mired in a mind-set of "get a girl or else" when I had a wonderful dream. In my dream I saw enormous green waves leaping on the ocean; a howling wind whipped their white spray into the air. The sun shone brilliantly on the scene out of a clear, intensely blue sky. Then I saw a baby floating in the water. John dove in but soon returned. He couldn't manage to save the baby. I dove right in and swooped up under the child, easily bringing it to the pier unharmed. There he sat like a little Buddha, smiling and happy in his rolls of baby fat.

That was the end of the dream. It had a stunning effect on me. I felt that my Higher Consciousness was letting me know in no uncertain terms that I could rescue this boy-baby that was trying to be born. I stopped trying to get John to commit himself to trying for a boy or girl. I watched my fertility signs carefully and planned to make love right when the egg was first present, which just happened to be the day of the full moon. Our timing was right (if indeed, it had anything to do with the outcome!), because we did conceive a boy.

Not until much later did I make the connection that Danny's spirit wanted to reincarnate through us as a male, and that he was communicating this to me as I hiked in the mountains and he "appeared" to me as a little boy. Now I believe that he was establishing a connection between us so that he could make his desires known and help fulfill them.

When Danny was born and turned out to be a plump, jolly boy just like the baby in my dream, I realized that it was another "introduction" dream. It's too soon to know whether or not Danny will look like the little boy in my original vision, because the "imagined" child was about four, and Danny will be only three in July. However, he's starting to get tiny freckles on his nose and cheeks and his hair is a bit redder each day. We'll see! He has the same wistful, sprite-like quality of the child I envisioned. It's a sweetness and merry appreciation of life (and me!) that feel identical to those of my imagined boy. When I think about it now, there's no question in my mind and heart that they are one and the same, just as Duke and the little blond boy in the glade are one and the same.

I'm glad that my two boys appeared to me in that way. To me, it meant that they had really chosen me to be their mother, and they wanted me to know it!

CHAPTER TWO
CROSSING THE THRESHOLD

We come now to the exciting and mysterious time surrounding the transition into pregnancy -- the days just before to just after conception.

The moment of conception is impossible to pinpoint by ordinary means, and even in retrospect it is often hard to know the exact date when pregnancy began. So if subtle experiences accompany conception, their import may go unnoticed. But some experiences are startling enough to make a strong impression when they happen, and to be remembered later when the pregnancy is revealed.

A French woman describes a strange vision which she later realized coincided with the beginning of her third pregnancy:

> I had been sick during most of the month of June, and so the only time I made love during this month was on June eleventh.
>
> The next night, while I was sleeping and dreaming, I suddenly found myself out of my body two or three meters away from my bed. I had the impression that my dream had stopped at once and that I was very conscious of what was going on. I was looking at my body in the bed and I could at the same time feel and see a tall person, in fact a sort of grey-blue shadow, behind my right shoulder. It lasted a very short time because I was afraid of what was happening. All of a sudden I was thrown back in my body. I awoke with a very fast beating heart. It took me a while to get to sleep again.
>
> Maybe one or two hours later while I was sleeping I suddenly got the impression of having something blown on me or maybe of having the same type of experience again, except I just had the

impression of waking because I was coming back in my body fast. Do you understand? It was very different from what you feel when you wake up in the middle of the night and have the impression you, as we say here, missed a step.

I wanted a third baby but I didn't think of pregnancy because I was sure I had unfortunately missed ovulation. So I realized this experience was linked to pregnancy only when I thought back on it, and because I could be so precise as to the day I had conceived.

Some people describe unusual lights and beautiful colors they have seen around the time of conception. Lynne Shank and her husband shared a vision:

We had made love, and then were lying talking. Suddenly I saw a bolt of multicolored light come down through the ceiling and through the bed under us. As I "see" odd things often, I didn't say anything. But my husband said, "Wow, did you see that!?" He described the same bolt of lightning. I laughed and told him I had seen it too. It later turned out that that day was the conception of our third child.

Each of Susan Bassett's two pregnancies was heralded by a presence that she visualized as light and color:

My husband and I had been trying to have a child for about a year, and were going to an acupuncturist both for health and fertility reasons. He invited us to attend a concert of the Gyoto Monks in Berkeley. During one of their performances I felt my crown chakra* open up (much like a garage door with an opener) and stay open for the duration of the chanting.

I distinctly remember a white sphere with blue around it coming into my head down to my heart, and finally settling in my abdomen. I knew intuitively that this was my son come to be born. All through the chanting I was receiving this light into my body and could feel his presence. It wasn't until after they finished that I learned the piece was called, "The Birth of the Buddha." I went home that night and conceived.

The next morning, a deer came into our backyard and delivered two fawns below the window of our bedroom; that day a friend of mine at work gave me a crystal rooster and said when she had touched it she felt I would be pregnant soon! I mention these occurrences because they just further assured me that in fact I was pregnant.

Unfortunately, my son died when he was twelve days old. He was a very special baby to us because of how he came into our lives and because he was such an old soul. I have done a lot of metaphysical healing around his birth and death and that is another story. I will always remember our first contact with a heart full of mother's love; it was very, very special.

I am not a Buddhist, but after that started being very attracted to Buddha type objects. About six months after his death I had a soul painting done and when the artist unveiled it to me he said that he couldn't help painting another soul that came into the painting with mine. It was the picture of my soul along with the identical blue-white sphere above me that I had seen above my head at the concert. This artist had no way of knowing what I had experienced.

Two years after the birth and death of her son, Susan's doctor mentioned during a routine examination that if she wanted to get pregnant, signs indicated she was at the perfect time of her cycle. Says Susan:

I went home that night prepared to seduce my husband and get pregnant with my child. Well, it was one of those days for him and off he went to sleep without having been "seduced." I prayed and meditated in the bed with him asleep, asking that if a spirit was out there that wanted to come into my body, please come to me.

The room was filled with miniature white lights dancing around. I was sitting up in the bed looking at the mirror of our dresser. I had a bowl of flowers on the dresser, and one particular "light" landed near these flowers and between candles I had lit. Then the whole end of the room became lit as if from a "Hollywood Opening" type of searchlight. The light started as a beam of many colors and kept going back and forth in an arc for at least an hour. Throughout the whole episode I felt such a presence in the room and just knew I would become pregnant with this "being." I told it that even though "her" father was asleep, I was ready and waiting for her. I kept thinking it was my eyes (with tears) playing tricks on me. But I could feel a warmth and a playful presence.

I conceived two days later. I actually felt the sperm and egg go together -- it was wonderful! Now my daughter is nineteen months old and she is the feeling of the spirit I saw dancing in the bedroom. It is a wonderful privilege to be the mother of this child -- she brings me joy every day!

THE WATCHER IN THE BEDROOM

> *When my son was conceived, I felt his presence in a strange eerie way when I was making love with his father. It was as if there was another person in the room.*
>
> *-- Debbie Smollen*

Some parents-to-be have a mysterious impression of a "third person in the bedroom" around the time of conception. The presence can be quite impersonal, or it may convey a quality such as love or joy or a sense of its gender. It may even seem as though it is urging the couple to make love! Mary Halter Petersen describes her experience at the conception of her first child:

> I wasn't consciously aware at the time that I was fertile or that it was conception, I simply remember startling at the feeling that there was someone in the room with my husband and me. I clearly felt the impression of an adult male figure standing at our feet. I jerked up, almost expecting to see someone there. As I felt surrounded by great love, I almost felt it would be like Jesus standing there. Though I'm not religious in the traditional sense, still those figures, images and personages from my Catholic upbringing carry much symbolism for me. To me, this feeling of Jesus was of the love of someone for us as we conceived our son. From later experiences in the pregnancy I came to identify this feeling/person with the being of our son...

Claire C. and her husband Bruce had been together for ten years and had postponed starting a family, as they were young and involved in work and college. After they began meditating, Claire says, her life "took some turns":

> Deciding to quit work was one turn. Thinking about having a child was another. We were taking an advanced meditation course and were spending two to three hours a day in meditation. It was during this period that I had a "vision" in meditation.
> I saw my husband and myself seated at our kitchen table, and sitting between us was a young girl, about eight years old, lying back with her upper body in my lap, blond honey-colored hair

flowing down. I had the knowing that this was something in our future, about ten years ahead.

Several months later we definitely decided we wanted a child. One night, at two or three in the morning, Bruce awakened me and wanted to make love. He said it seemed like someone woke him up and told him to make love to me. We were both sleepy and groggy and we made love. This is so amazing to me, because we just don't do this -- wake up in the middle of the night to make love -- never before, and not in the fourteen years since then! And Bruce doesn't have "experiences" -- he wishes he would, but he doesn't. So it all felt sort of odd to us, but we went with it. It turns out that I conceived that night, and our baby girl was born later that year. And she grew, and she came to have blond honey-colored hair!

CONCEPTION AWARENESS

A surprising number of women claim to be aware of pregnancy's beginning:

"I felt a surge of energy and knew it was conception."

"I have had 'conception intuition' with six pregnancies and knew *that* moment that we were pregnant."

A woman describes her impressions on the night her daughter was conceived:

> As a soft warm August night slipped quietly into the next day, a new life began. I felt in tune with the universe. As my husband of six weeks drifted into a deep serene sleep I became peacefully ecstatic. I was pregnant. We were parents; something we had hoped to be and planned from the day of an engagement.
>
> I knew it. I felt her in the dark safety of my abdomen. Simply the interior feel of knowing my own body and I knew she would be perfect, healthy. She? "Oh," I told myself, "don't be too excited, a boy is possible... you wanted a child, a healthy child..."

Some parents claim to have had a premonition that conception was imminent -- "a strong feeling for the day," as one mother describes it. Another writes:

> I knew precisely when I was going to get pregnant. I remember sitting on the bed talking with John as we prepared to go to bed to make love. I said, "You know this time we'll have our son. Are

you ready for that?" He shrugged and smiled. "Yeah, why not," he said with a twinkle in his eye, "we already know he's on his way." Sure enough, he was.

For me, the moment of conception was "loud and clear as a bell." In fact, with both children, as well as other conceptions which did not come to term, I knew the precise instant the sperm penetrated the egg. It was like a big "pop" inside of my consciousness and a shifting of energy, accompanied by a subtle kaleidoscope of color.

A mother relates her experience at the beginning of a pregnancy that later proved to be ectopic:

It's not something easily expressed in words, but as I was lying there I "saw" a picture of a sperm penetrating an egg, followed by a blinding flash of light and the most incredible sense of awe. I remember turning to my husband and saying to him something about how amazing the beginning of life was. I was actually so moved that I felt tearful.

We might assume that conception awareness is a hormonal signal from within the mother's body -- but what if it's the father who feels it? Tim Richardson recalls:

Mary and I were making love just before Christmas a few years ago and we were aware at the moment of conception that we had created a new child. It was a moment of magic or intuition.

You asked the difference between Mary's experience and mine. That is somewhat obscure given the time lapse, however I'll tell my experience. We were making love one night and on climax I exclaimed, "We just got pregnant." Mary said, "Don't say that." We were a little uneasy about it because we had had an abortion the previous year and had recently gotten back together after a brief period apart. I had made a commitment to myself that if we became pregnant again I wanted to keep the baby. We talked about it at the time, feeling a little exposed about being back together recently, and being young, and what would the family say. I slept well that night. Mary was ill at ease. Many days and hours of mutual reassurance ensued. Conversations with her mother, who knows that babies are the light of the world, and coming to the conclusion that we were ready to do it, led to the birth of Che.

The intuitive feeling came at the moment of climax. I realize that conception can take up to three days; however, you and I know, or think, that there is more to conception than just biology alone. It was an immediate feeling which gripped my body. There is no other way to describe the feeling. Emphatically, we conceived!

As Tim points out, actual conception doesn't take place instantly when a couple makes love. The moment when a sperm penetrates the egg can occur in about thirty minutes, or it may be hours or even days later. Conception awareness may not always coincide exactly with physical conception, but it is a compelling feeling that seems to be experienced by many parents.

For others, the news of pregnancy comes a little later, in a variety of surprising "annunciations."

CHAPTER THREE
ANNUNCIATIONS: "I'M HERE!"

Between the moment when conception may have occurred and the first definite signs of pregnancy, comes an interval of waiting and wondering. I have often loved that time. When pregnancy is both longed-for and possible, it can be a time of exquisite sensitivity, and we may become aware of the most subtle shifts of mood and energy.

It can also be a time rife with signs and hints that *if* I turned out to be pregnant I'd interpret as messages about the baby. Dead relatives appear in my dreams, inspiring hope or anxiety depending on how I feel about them as possible revenants to the family... My small daughter tells me of "seeing" on her window curtain a mother holding a baby... I dream I've had a baby boy, dream his name and time of birth. Then comes the day when I know I'm not pregnant, and I'm reminded that we need to be careful how we interpret our signs and symbols.

Both men and women can be conscious of a change in early pregnancy. This couple had many intimations of their daughter's presence before it could be confirmed:

> Every test I took in the first two months of my pregnancy was negative. Even Planned Parenthood insisted I couldn't be pregnant, but I knew different. We both did; we felt her, heard her, dreamed of her. I had an intense sense of being more than myself, driven to taking impeccable care of myself. I would often hear giggling when I was alone in the house or yard; one night while my husband was sleeping he was tickled awake, but "no one" was there.

Images and symbols appearing in our reveries can give a strong hint of pregnancy. Before she knew she was pregnant, Anne Calajoe caught glimpses of her son during her meditations. "I saw a baby boy waving to my father," she says, "and a day or so later, a small boy carrying a suitcase, and I told him to bring it upstairs."

The "annunciation" of pregnancy can be indirect. For example, the children in our family may be aware of things we do not perceive. Miriam felt ambivalent about her second pregnancy and had not yet told her young son about it, but he said, "Mama, there's a baby girl in our house. Do you see her?" Shortly afterwards, however, the pregnancy miscarried. ("It wasn't easy," Miriam says, "but it seemed correct.")

Ariel's little daughter was twenty months old when Ariel made the following entry in her baby book:

> Tonight, at her bathtime, I was reading a book called *Reading Your Fertility Signals*. Sara, with her sweet eyes looking up and her small but certain fingers and arm pointing to the corner of the bathroom ceiling, said "baby," and lots of other Sara words and sounds many times -- as though she saw a baby, or maybe two up there, like the spirits of babies to be, and she was clear and happy and wanted me to know. When out of the bath she was intent on the book, pointing to the rose on the cover and noticing its center and details, and said "baby." The pictures inside of uterus and fallopian tubes and cervix she pointed to saying "baby." She insisted on holding the book and babbled excitedly, "telling" me.

Though Ariel didn't realize at the time that she was pregnant, it soon became evident that she had conceived just a few days before this incident.

Mysterious "visitors" may bring the message. Diana Lorenz relates that her father had a vision while sitting in church, the morning after her younger sister was conceived:

> An angel came to him and told him he was going to have a daughter. When he told my mother of this she dismissed it as altogether ridiculous. She had no intention of having another child (they had two boys and two girls already), and furthermore her period was due any day. Nine months later, "Angela" was born. As for my mother's period, she passed one drop of blood.

The annunciation can be disarmingly casual, as in Jean Fejes's dream, in which a woman came up to her and simply said, "My mother said to tell you that it's a boy." It may have a touch of ceremony, as this mother recalls:

> Before I knew I was pregnant with my new baby I saw three spirits visit; two were accompanying the new spirit and told me

it was very special and to take especially good care of it. They were very solemn.

ANNOUNCING VOICES

Pregnancy is sometimes announced by an inner voice, as though a mysterious "other" is delivering the information. These transmissions typically have a calm and matter-of-fact quality. A mother relates:

> My husband and I had tried to conceive for a short time -- one month. I was expecting my period, but it wasn't late, just time for it to come. While taking a shower I heard a voice say to me, "It's a boy." It was as though the words were said aloud, but I couldn't tell if it was a man's or woman's voice. So I stepped out of the shower and took a home pregnancy test that I'd had for some time and it was positive!
>
> The sex of our son was confirmed by a sonogram in my eighth month of pregnancy, but I felt confident all along that our baby was going to be a boy. I trusted the voice.

Mucbeah Robinson learned of her son's conception in similar fashion, and the early warning turned out to be providential:

> I waited and waited to meet a mate and marry. At last my yearning got very strong. I prayed for "a baby and a man" every day for about six weeks... Then on Father's Day, I was travelling with a friend I had known for years, a divorced father. That night we had a brief encounter. I had never been pregnant and had tried before in several relationships with no luck, so I thought nothing of it except I wished I had a man of my own.
>
> Tuesday morning twenty-four hours later, I awoke early before the alarm. A voice in my head said:
>   "You are pregnant
>   It's a boy
>   and his name is Kahlil."
>
> For about one week everything looked *so colorful* and bright I called this man and said, "I am either pregnant or ready to ascend." I felt so wonderful -- almost holy. A week later, I was rear-ended in a traffic jam. I needed X-rays but refused pelvic ones. If I hadn't heard that voice, I might have killed or deformed my baby.

Says Candy Wasser, "Never before had I experienced anything even vaguely like the voice announcing my third pregnancy." Although she and her husband were not planning a third child, neither of them was quite ready to say they would not have another. Candy recalls:

> We were driving home at night from a visit to my sister-in-law and her new baby. My thoughts were quite random, my mood of no consequence, when suddenly a voice behind quite clear and simple stated, "Your next child will be a girl who will have much to share with you and your mother." That was it. So *real* it seemed, that tears stung my cheeks and I struggled for understanding and logic. There was none, though a week later my period was missed and the answer seemed simple.
>
> Emily Rose was born into her father's hands too quickly for the midwife to arrive. She has been a treasure all her own.

Perhaps even more amazing is the experience of hearing the child itself announcing its presence. In the following two stories there is an intriguing detail: the background noise "cuts out" and normal hearing is momentarily suspended, as though the child is transmitting its message on an alternate "channel." A mother recalls:

> I had not yet missed a period when my little one made contact with me. I walked into the living room to play some music. As I knelt before the stereo the soul of my child made his presence known. First, the background noise went silent. It was as if I had gone deaf. Then he spoke to me saying, "I'm here." The voice was tiny but clear and it came from below my navel. I remember looking down at my stomach in astonishment... and then the noise of the world returned.

A young woman had just asked her college instructor a question, when her normal hearing was interrupted. "I was very interested in her answer," she says, "yet I couldn't hear her voice:"

> Instead, I heard a voice (which was mostly like a buzzing sound) saying, "The reason you have felt physically burdened and emotionally burdened is because you have invited me into your life. I am here with you. I am here." I felt very warm then, my heart felt warm, as if I had just been hugged by an old friend. I found out the next day that I was two weeks pregnant.

ANNOUNCING DREAMS

Dreams that announce pregnancy are apparently common in various traditional societies. Sheila Kitzinger, in her book *Women As Mothers*, describes how Jamaican women expect a "fertility dream" to occur when they have conceived. The dreams are said to involve symbols of abundance such as shoals of fish or ripe melons.

The frequency of different kinds of announcing dreams varies greatly from one culture to another. According to researcher Ian Stevenson, they are common in Burma and Turkey and among the Tlingit and other tribes of the American northwest. But curiously enough, they have distinctive features in each culture where they occur In Burma, they are more likely to precede conception and carry a request to be conceived. Among the Tlingit, who are said to believe ir reincarnation but only among members of the same family, they tend to occur late in pregnancy and identify the deceased family member who is returning. For further information, Dr. Stevenson's book *Childrer Who Remember Previous Lives* is a gold mine of eye-opening facts and daring speculations.

It's not unusual to dream of babies or pregnancy at times wher pregnancy is possible, when we're considering having a child, or even (as I discover at forty-six) while letting go of our childbearing years. So it's difficult to be sure whether such a dream involves contact with a child-to-be, or whether instead it is our way of mulling over possibilities, or even of symbolizing something else we are bringing to birth.

When the dream turns out to have identifying features of a child who is really on the way, we may take it at least in retrospect as an announcing dream. For example, on the night she conceived her son Sean, Cathie Morales dreamed of a male child about two years old who told her she had conceived. "The child in my dream looked exactly like Sean," says Cathie.

Wendy's announcing dream was the first time she remembered ever dreaming of being a mother, and though she was two weeks pregnant at the time, she didn't suspect that she had conceived:

> Our firstborn son was a happy accident, conceived aboard a ship bound for Alaska. We know almost the exact moment of conception, but since this date was well before my date for ovulating, I did not expect to become pregnant.
>
> About two weeks after our ship-board experience I had a wonderful dream about holding my son on my lap and explaining that "the trees with the red leaves are maples," and in the dream he was a sweet, happy child with the name "Bridger."

I told my husband about my dream in the morning. He said he liked the name "Bridger," which neither of us had heard anywhere before, and "if we ever have a baby boy, we'll name him Bridger."

Two weeks later I found out I was pregnant. There was never any question in my mind that the baby was going to be a boy and he would look like the baby in my dream. He was born two years ago and looks very much like the child in my dream -- same eyes and shape of face. His hair isn't as curly. He is the kind of kid who would ask about the trees as you were driving along a mountain road. And yes, we named him Bridger.

A mother writes, during her third pregnancy:

This pregnancy was unplanned and a great surprise, but right around the time that I missed my period, I had several dreams about being pregnant. I decided to wait a few more days before I would do a pregnancy test. That night I dreamed of the baby telling me to go ahead and do a test so I would make the pregnancy official, tell my husband and quit being all tense and worried. The test was positive and I told my husband who was elated that I was pregnant, which surprised me and laid my worries to rest.

It is not always the mother who receives the message. Kristine Kovach had been without menstrual periods for over two and a half years and had been told by doctors that her chances of conceiving without hormonal assistance were slim. As she and her husband were in their early twenties, they were in no hurry to have children, but had used no birth control for nearly two years. Kristine writes:

In March, my husband had a very strong feeling in a dream that I was pregnant. He recalled no detail or series of events in the dream, but awoke urging me to have a pregnancy test done. Two weeks later, tired of his constant concern that I was pregnant (I did not feel in any way that I was carrying a child), I saw my doctor who confirmed that I was nearly four months along.

In addition to their announcing role, dreams play an important part in connections throughout pregnancy. In the next chapter we will explore the dreamworld, a virtual place that often seems like a space station where beings from different dimensions can meet and communicate with one another.

CHAPTER FOUR
IN THE PREGNANT DREAMWORLD

The world of dreams is a good place to begin exploring contact with our child during pregnancy. It encompasses the whole range of experiences; all the connections and communications that we sense in other ways may also be felt in dreams.

More clearly than our waking experience, dreams present us with the mystery of inner versus outer reality. When a dream seems touched by the child-to-be, we have a chance to consider whether we may really be contacting another consciousness. Dreaming of a baby or a child, we may wonder whether it is a symbol of our own "child self" or a dream about the baby within.

In this chapter we will tour the pregnant dreamworld and discover the ways we may connect with our child-to-be through dreams. This will be only a sampling, for significant dreams are part of many people's pre-birth connections, and they will be described throughout the book.

DREAM THEMES OF PREGNANCY

Dreams of contact need to be seen in the context of the "normal" dreams of pregnancy, with their special qualities and typical themes connected with each stage. Even women who don't usually notice and remember their dreams are apt to have a rich dream life while pregnant. There are many fears and feelings to be dealt with, especially during the first and last trimesters.

Dream research has much to tell us about the characteristic themes of pregnancy. Typical images of the first trimester show us struggling with ambivalence at being "invaded" by the pregnancy. We dream of strangers in our house, of being injured. The fetus often appears as a small animal or a semi-human creature. This dream of my own, with its aura of some weird alchemical rite, reveals the sense of strangeness a woman may feel about pregnancy:

> A teacher is leading a kind of experiment that precipitates something in a large vat of blue water. A cat appears in it; apparently it doesn't need to breathe. The top surface of the

water is thought to interface with a different dimension.

In pregnancy, we tend to dream of our own mother. She may represent our wish to be the dependent child instead of the responsible parent. In the not uncommon dreams where "Mother" is injured or even dead, she may be a stand-in for the dreamer, expressing the fears we face when preparing to surrender to the elemental power of childbirth.

The second trimester is often the easiest time of pregnancy. Sleep is less disturbed and dreams may be more pleasant. Still, dreams of injury to others are common. In this middle stage, we may envision ourselves caring for the baby, in dreams of nursing and other mothering skills.

In the third trimester, sleep is often broken and we easily remember many dreams. We dream of labor and delivery, though the "newborn" is usually pictured as at least six months old. We have nightmares of accidentally losing or forgetting the baby. One mother tells of frightful recurring dreams of a "gargoyle" that crawled out of her closet and onto the ceiling above her bed. Such images perhaps speak of our fear that the baby may be abnormal.

Once we have accepted the possibility of pre-birth communication, we can take a broader view of the dreamworld. While keeping the traditional psychological interpretations in mind, we can be open to other clues. If we also take into account the possibility of existence before conception or in previous lives, we find ourselves considering very different interpretations of some of our dreams.

Jean Fejes's experience is a good example of a dream whose meaning is open to divergent views:

> A week before I gave birth to Chris, I began to have a sort of panic attack whenever I drove over a small bridge near my home. I would have this irrational fear that I was going to drive off (going through the three-foot-high concrete side), and I would grip the wheel very tightly and really concentrate on staying on the road. A much longer bridge, over deeper water, had no effect on me.
>
> After several days of this, I had a dream. I was wearing a long, dark, hooded cloak, and I was standing on a wooden bridge holding a baby, which I dropped into the raging river below.
>
> Upon waking, I realized this was the cause of the strange experiences on the bridge, and it never again disturbed me to drive across.

Jean believes the dream was of an event in a past life. The fact that it resolved her anxiety, instead of distressing her as one might expect of an ordinary nightmare, adds credibility to her feeling that she had reached the source of her problem.

With the "normal" pregnant dreamworld as background, we are ready to survey the ways that dreams may connect us with our children before birth.

DREAMS PREPARE US

Through dream rehearsals, we can prepare ourselves for giving birth, and even practice some of the skills of caring for a baby. Does this involve communication with the child-to-be? Or is it a way of connecting with our own instinctive "know-how"?

In retrospect, one mother realized that her dreams had given her helpful information, but she had failed to use it when the time came:

> I had two dreams showing me birthing on hands and knees. I thought this odd and have always thought hands and knees a strange position to birth in. I was not in this position during the actual birth and there was some shoulder dystocia (which means in effect that the shoulders get stuck). I learned later that hands and knees position is helpful in cases of shoulder dystocia. My dreams had been advising me to use this position, but I hadn't realized their significance.

Kristina Bystrom felt that both she and her baby were preparing for breastfeeding through several "nursing dreams" in the weeks before birth. "When Arne arrived," she says, "he latched on within the first half hour, and nursed like a pro. I too was totally prepared and comfortable though I'd never breastfed before. I believe the dreams I had were shared with Arne."

Another woman overcame a lifelong aversion to breastfeeding through a series of dreams in mid-pregnancy. They changed her, she says, from fearing the thought of breastfeeding and doubting her ability to accomplish it, and left her with an overwhelmingly strong desire to nurse her baby.

Marion Nelson rehearsed her long labor in a dream three weeks in advance, and accurately envisioned her baby:

> I worked hard, harder than I'd ever worked before and hours passed. In the dreamworld time seemed slowed -- each moment that passed as I puffed and blew was stretched out. Eventually,

after many long strenuous hours I gave birth -- to a very large, very dark, almost Asian looking daughter. She had lots of black hair and was very calm and peaceful.

After this dream I was quite excited because I really wanted a daughter and I was sure that I knew the sex of this child -- somehow! And best of all the dream did come true. After many long hours I birthed a large (nine pounds), calm, dark haired baby who resembled an Inuit Indian. When she was taken to be weighed and washed she looked around the room and then began to suck her thumb. She stayed relaxed throughout.

DREAMS GIVE INFORMATION

Becci Wolfer's dream foretold details of her baby and accurately previewed a situation that developed during pregnancy:

I am a mother of four children; the first three were girls, the last a boy. With my fourth child, I had a dream at thirty-two weeks. I dreamed that the baby was in a breech position and my midwife couldn't turn him, so she had me go in to a birthing center for a sonogram and to have a doctor she knew try to turn the baby. In the dream, the sonogram showed a big boy.

Two days later I saw my midwife for a checkup. She thought there were twins and that they were breech. She had me go to the birthing center where the doctor turned the baby. The sonogram showed no twins but one big boy. Our son entered this world weighing ten pounds five ounces, and twenty-two and a half inches long.

Many people have dreams in pregnancy that turn out to be accurate glimpses of how the baby will look either at birth or (more commonly) some time later. Janette Patterson dreamed of her daughter's face when eight months pregnant and says, "When she was born, I recognized her immediately from my dream. She looked just like in the dream, especially the next day after the birth, when the puffiness of having been squeezed through the birth canal had subsided."

Elyse Karlin learned specific physical details about her son from dreams:

I did dream about my son twice before his birth and both times he looked exactly the way he did when he was born. The second dream was a week before the birth and I saw him lying in the birth canal waiting to be born. I knew his weight and length from my dream, and that he had a thick head of dark hair. When he was actually born my obstetrician said, "He's smaller than I anticipated." I said, "No, he's not, he's eight and a half pounds." My husband went down to the nursery to weigh him and came back and confirmed that I was right. "Is he twenty-one inches?" I asked next, and the answer was yes.

Another woman recalls:

I had a dream, very early in my pregnancy, in which I saw a little blond girl of about three or four, in a dress and pigtails. Upon waking, I knew I had seen the child who was now in my womb. When I was encouraged by my doctor to undergo the myriad of tests done to fetuses, I refused, knowing she was safe and perfect. Throughout my pregnancy, however, everyone assured me she was a boy, and towards the end I wasn't sure myself. Sure enough though, I birthed a beautiful, perfect, blond baby girl.

Lori Elmore was six months pregnant when she fell asleep one night "pondering what was growing inside of me":

As I dreamed, I envisioned a small dark-haired boy and heard a voice tell me that I would have a boy and to take good care of him. When I woke up, I knew in my heart that my dream was true. Three months later my first son was born with a head full of dark hair. I was not surprised when I looked at that face and saw that little boy in my dream.

In 1984 I became pregnant again. One evening as I lay in bed I felt a strange sensation. I fell asleep and once again had a dream that touched my very soul. I could see that beautiful face, tiny hands and once again that bushy mop of black hair. I knew and let it be known that the life inside of me was a beautiful dark boy. My second son was born at home six weeks premature. He suffered three bouts of respiratory failure, but I knew he would live. My dream gave me the strength to believe. He is now thirteen months old and full of energy.

Early in her pregnancy, Gina was hoping for a girl. But then she had a particularly vivid dream and felt convinced it was the baby communicating with her:

I dreamed I was on a plane and nine months pregnant and huge, then all of a sudden I was holding the baby and I thought, "That was easy, they said labor would hurt and it didn't." Then I put the baby to my left breast to feed him and as I did so he looked at me and I knew he was a boy.

I woke up the next morning and said to my husband, "We're having a boy." When I describe the dream it sounds so ordinary but it was so real and so vivid I can remember it clearly to this day.

Dreams that turn out to be accurate predictors of the baby's sex may have a different feel from other dreams. Gina later had a second dream of meeting her baby boy and says: "I know beyond a shadow of doubt that this was my son communicating with me. During my pregnancy I had many other dreams, sometimes of boys, sometimes of girls, and I knew they were just ordinary dreams. These two dreams were very different and special."

Julie Klekas concurs: "During my first and third pregnancies I had dreams about boys. They were different from ordinary baby dreams. I somehow knew they were predicting the future."

Patricia Chubb recalls:

While pregnant with my first baby, I was *sure* it was a girl. I had two dreams; in the first I was playing with a baby girl (there was no female imagery, only a strong sense of the baby's sex) and in the second I was calling to an older child by her chosen name. When she was born and the doctor announced it was a girl, I said I knew. There was never any doubt in my mind.

With my second pregnancy I did not have the same experience. I felt it might be a boy, but the feeling was not overwhelming as it was with my first, and I had no dreams or other indications. The baby turned out to be another girl. My doctor told me of a study which concluded that the mother's overwhelming feelings and consistently one-sex dreams were accurate predictors, while dreams of one sex followed by dreams of the other tended to cancel each other out.

No matter what our dreams and feelings are telling us in pregnancy, it's wise to keep an open heart to both possibilities. The most definite impressions of the baby's gender may turn out to be mistaken!

DREAMS GIVE A GLIMPSE OF THE CHILD'S PERSONALITY

Not everyone feels comfortable admitting that they have intuitions about their children-to-be. The dreamworld is a stage where we can safely envision what we may know about our children, including impressions of their personality. Says Stacey Mott:

> In my third trimester I had a dream which, while humorous, turned out to be quite prophetic regarding my daughter's personality.
> In the dream I was nursing my child, about a year old, who was wearing glasses. All of a sudden, she stopped nursing, looked at me, and said with perfect diction and a most serious expression on her face, "Mommy, how does the milk get in there?"
> Now the interesting things about this dream weren't really apparent at first. It was a very realistic nursing position, considering I'd never nursed a baby and rarely seen it done. She was a girl in the dream, but I was always sure she would be. (Coincidence? Who knows?) But as Emily grew I saw that the dream had been incredibly consistent with who she is. She is a very verbal child, always preferring interaction with people to toys as an infant. She was an early talker, and an avid nurser. She's also an early reader, and although her eyesight is just fine, I think that her reading ability is connected to the glasses in the dream. Most strikingly, Emily asks me the trickiest questions I've ever been asked by anyone, of any age. She wants to know how everything works, how all sorts of everyday things are made. Simply put, the child that looked up at me in my dream WAS Emily.

LEAPFROG DREAMS

An interesting feature of dreams in pregnancy is that they occasionally pass over the child who is already on the way and offer glimpses of future children. For example, Ginger had a dream during her second pregnancy that turned out to be an accurate portrayal of her third child, a strawberry blond girl with delayed speech, just as the dream prefigured.

Debbie Smollen was expecting her third child in January, 1980. She hoped to have a midwife-attended home birth, but her husband was strongly opposed, and concerned about their Rh incompatibility. He insisted that she see an obstetrician. Debbie was unhappy with her lack of options, and just before her first visit with the doctor she had a dream:

> I had made an appointment to see my obstetricians, however they would not accept me as their patient until I accepted that I had a miscarriage prior to the birth of my first child. I insisted that this pregnancy was my third -- but they insisted that it was my fourth and until I accepted it as my fourth they would not accept me as a patient. After much arguing, the doctor then recounted the details of my miscarriage and insisted that I remember: I was outside my husband's hardware store in a blue van -- I miscarried in the blue van.
>
> This dream stuck with me for five years. In 1980 my husband did own a hardware store but we didn't have a blue van. Strangely enough, four years later he bought a blue van for his business. On January 1, 1985, I found out I was pregnant for the fourth time. On January 29 my husband drove me to the emergency room in the blue van as I miscarried one of the twins I was carrying. As we drove past his store, I remembered the dream five years earlier.

Fiora had two dreams in her early weeks of pregnancy; the first foretold her daughter who was on the way, while the second is yet to be fulfilled:

> Before I knew I was pregnant, I had two birth dreams. In the first, I labored in a beautiful, wood-panelled house with my friends -- members of a New Age choir I belong to -- singing softly in the next room. The baby was a girl, and was very outgoing and assertive right from the start, looking everyone in the eye and obviously *seeing* them!
>
> In the second dream, I was just moving into my new home in the country when I went into labor. My husband was out looking the land over with some friends. The "baby" was a two year old boy, very quiet and mellow.
>
> The next week we moved into a beautiful, redwood panelled house and I found out I was pregnant. My husband and I are working towards living on land in the countryside, but that's a year or two away. I knew my baby was a girl, and the actual birth was much like what I saw in the first dream, including the part about my new daughter looking everyone in the eye, and being quite assertive! And I am fairly sure my second child will be a sweetly contemplative boy, born on our dream land.

DREAM MEETINGS

The most compelling dreams are those in which we feel that we truly meet and are met by the spirit of our child.

In her book *The Dream World of Pregnancy*, Eileen Stukane warns, "When you look back after childbirth, a dream about your baby may seem precognitive, but it is important to understand that visions of your newborn... are reflections of your attempt to sort through the possibilities ahead."

But there are dreams with a special quality that sets them apart. In them, we feel we are in touch with a presence, and we are left with an unforgettable sense of having met someone real.

Toward the end of her pregnancy, Gina dreamed of giving birth:

> I had the baby and somebody put him face down on my chest. He lifted his head and looked directly into my eyes and smiled. It wasn't like he was a newborn although physically he was, but like a real person. That sounds strange -- I mean it was like looking into an adult's eyes, wise and knowing; but he was looking at me with such love as if to say he was happy he was coming to be with me.

Martell Williams's dream connection with a little boy began long before conception and continued throughout pregnancy and after his birth:

> My son was born five months ago and the first contact that I remember happened three years ago when my husband and I first met and fell in love. It was during our first month together that I entered into my journal a dream where I saw our son Austin playing with his dad. My husband and I named him the first time we starry eyed new lovers talked of having children together.
>
> The dream was very vivid and the image of him as clear as a photograph. I wrote a physical description of him and knew what a beautifully special little soul he is. I fell so in love with this child that for two years all I could think about was getting pregnant and being able to hold him in my arms.
>
> After two years and finally a commitment to be married I became pregnant. Throughout my pregnancy I dreamed of him and he always looked the same. Same golden red hair and beautiful blue eyes. This physical description wouldn't be considered a "genetic given" considering my husband and I both have dark hair and eyes.

And in our dreams we'd fly together. We'd meet at the mouth of a river where it meets the ocean and we'd fly the stretch of the beach together playfully. These were the images and connections I'd have all during my pregnancy.

Now that he's here I get physical tangible evidence of what I felt about him all along. He sparkles magically like the sun on the ocean on a clear day. His spirit is as free as a happy gull flying along the beach. His hair is like spun gold, each strand holding rays of sunshine. And his violet blue eyes shine with the hope and purity of intent of all humanity. My son was to be a child like no other, and I knew years in advance. I've known forever. For nothing in my life has inspired me like the passion that has driven me to motherhood. And now the absolute perfection of my life with him here fills my heart and the infinity of our connection.

I still have dreams where we fly together only not as birds; just as we are. I know that when I'm having a flying dream where I'm holding him as we fly, that he's having the dream simultaneously on some level. I always go to him and talk very directly saying, "I just had a dream where we were flying together. It was fun, wasn't it?" Of course I always get a sweet sleepy eyed grin that could be saying, "Yes Mom, I remember, it felt great," or, "Good morning Mom, so nice to see you."

SHARED DREAMS

Pregnancy brings heightened awareness of the inner world and a more fluid boundary to the psyche, so perhaps it is not surprising that some couples experience shared dreams while expecting a baby. A mother recounts that several times she and her husband "would actually have the same dreams the same nights, although because of different psyches, not all elements were identical. This occurred only during our pregnancy, and not before or since."

A husband and wife shared a dream that settled the question of what to name the baby. The father recalls:

> One morning we woke up to discover we had both had a dream where our child was named Sef. We figured that this is her name and that's all there is to it. Upon investigation I found this name in Egyptian means: all things that ever were and ever will be.

DREAMS HELP US SHARE THE CHILD'S WORLD

The dreamworld can be a place where we nestle close to the child within, as if our sleeping mind is more attuned to the baby's consciousness. Says Candice White, "I would have conversations with her in my dreams at night. Mornings would come and the words would melt away and I'd be left with awareness, nuances, confidence."

A woman's dream in the fifth month of her first pregnancy was like a visit inside the womb:

> I had gone to sleep feeling very peaceful and comfortable with my pregnancy; almost in a meditation state. Upon waking, the clearest dream-vision was overpowering my memory. I was in my womb. I was seeing through my son's bright blue eyes -- his hands drifting through the pale fluid. Then I was seeing his face. Large blue eyes; almost translucent skin, ears, nose, eyelids. I began to doubt myself, but I knew this was my son.
>
> We never did sonograms or any other tests to determine sex, due date or health. We knew it was a strong boy growing inside me fully aware of my husband and our friends.

Pamela Millar, while pregnant with her daughter, dreamed of swimming with her inside the womb. "We looked at each other, contemplated each other, which was very satisfying for me," says Pamela: "I fell in love."

With dream imagery like this we can come close to sharing our child's world. At the same time we nurture ourselves by identifying with the baby. While pregnant, Bunny Chidester dreamed of being an infant in the womb. "I felt it could be a real memory of my own," she says, "but now I am wondering if it could have been a kind of tuning into my baby by *being* him. It was the most wonderful peace I've ever known."

In the dreamworld, lines between identities become blurred. The child we dream of may be *both* the unborn baby and an image of our own childhood self, perhaps a way of reclaiming its innocence and its capacity for happiness. Anita describes the recurring dreams of her first pregnancy:

> I always knew I'd have a baby girl. There was never any question in my mind. I didn't have a sonogram; I just knew. During my pregnancy, I'd dream of her, I'd see her running and laughing, a child playing in the sun. She looked just as I did as a child, the same brown hair and brown eyes. We looked identical.

Did the child's appearance correspond to the dreams? "Yes!" says Anita. "She has the exact same hair color and eyes as in pre-birth dreams! She looked exactly as I did as a little girl." But Anita suspects another meaning may underlie her dreams' emphasis on their similarity. "I really want our relationship to be better than what I had with my own mother," she says. "Maybe my dreaming that we look alike was my hope that we'd be closer."

DREAMS REASSURE US

When there is concern about the baby's health, a mother or father may dream of seeing the baby and receiving a reassuring message or impression.

Barbara Umberger was expecting her first child. Close friends had given birth to a baby with multiple anomalies, and Barbara began to worry about her baby's condition:

> One night I dreamed that my babe visited me. I reached in and took him out of me -- he was perfect and I saw a penis so I knew he was a he! I looked him over and then placed him in a large metal bucket like a wash tub, and pushed him under the water. To me that symbolized placing him in the amniotic sac. I then knew I was having a boy and that he was all right!

Roxi's dreams proved to be both reassuring and prophetic. They revealed her children's future appearance and prepared her for stressful events to come. Roxi says she has learned to "read" her dreams and trust their guidance:

> I come from a long line of "dreamers" and my daughter Rayann has the ability also. My dreams take me into the past as well as the future. If a dream returns while awake or sleeping and pesters me no matter how I try to distract myself, then I know it's time to act somehow. I have found that I can tell myself, "Okay, mind, what is it you want from me, show me," or I can say, "I need your help, give me a vision -- please." In other words I'm learning to work with my dreams.
> End of November 1981. Dream! Body told mind I was pregnant, they argued -- body won. Mind said, "No, can't be!" Body said, "Yes! Yes! You are!" I awoke feeling nauseated, flu-like. I ignored the dream as flu was going around. Two weeks later I had blood work done -- I was pregnant. This seemed to be

the beginning of my "dream awareness."

First trimester dream: I saw Rayann as an eight-month-old with rash, crying. At eight months old Rayann had to go on formula as I had to take radioactive material that would go through my breast milk. She broke out in a rash from formulas. As soon as possible I resumed breast milk and the rash disappeared. Rayann at eight months was exactly like the dream.

Following Rayann's birth, Roxi had three pregnancies that ended in miscarriages at about seven weeks. Curiously, she had no dreams with these pregnancies. She continues:

Winter solstice 1990: I dreamed of a white-blond haired baby boy with round head and face -- he *was* Augustus. Next morning I knew I was pregnant. I was very pleased as I had given up hopes of having another child. I was fearful of miscarriage though the dream gave me courage.

Twelve weeks: I was asking for a vision as I felt a great need for reassurance. While falling asleep one night I saw Gus's face in a bright flash. This lasted a fraction of a second. He appeared to be a two month old baby. That night I had a powerful dream. Words cannot give it the strength it deserves. I call it my Teton Vision.

I was taken back to summer of 1982 when I made a trip to Grand Teton National Park alone. This was a very brave thing to do as the women of my people (and my husband's) are not much for risk taking. I went to celebrate my grandparents' fiftieth wedding anniversary. In the dream I actually relived the moment when I first saw the Tetons with the sunrise all gold and pink -- indescribable! I've been to the Tetons probably thirty times before this and since but never this feeling of autonomy -- strength and courage came to me. It was great to get to see and feel this all over again! A voice told me (my mind talking to my body) that only I can travel this road of pregnancy alone and to take courage and power from this vision. Several other things happened during this trip where I had to make decisions and get tough, alone. Yes, this pregnancy was a journey only I could go. This vision was very encouraging and I hung onto it during tough times ahead.

At week sixteen, I dreamed that at approximately twenty weeks something negative was going to happen. At nineteen weeks I got out of bed that morning and blood fell between my legs. The problem was diagnosed as partial placenta previa and

I was put on strict bedrest. After zooming one hundred miles per hour, this great screeching halt was maddening! My mind worried and my body wanted to go... go... The glimpse of Gus and the Teton Vision helped a lot as I knew Gus would be all right.

Week twenty-two, I was buggy with the bedrest but had help organized, and quiet projects to do to occupy my restlessness a bit. I begged my mind for another vision and one night during a dream I saw a three year old white-blond haired boy. He walked up to Kevin and me and said, "I'm not retarded." (I have had to take thyroid and heart medications for the thyroid dysfunction which caused my miscarriages. We had feared a problem with Gus's health because of all my medications.)

The last month of pregnancy I was huge but able to be up and about. It was a very cloudy month; I dreamed that Augustus would be born on a night with a clear sky and a full moon. One night the sky was clear and the moon full -- Augustus was born on the fall equinox!

The power of Roxi's reassuring dreams is even more evident in light of her experience during labor with Gus:

Right before delivery my chest (heart) cramped real hard and hurt badly. I recall grabbing my chest and then, though I was aware of what was going on, I couldn't respond. I felt like I was falling down a long black tunnel. The nurse had summoned the doctor and other nurses and they were going to treat me for cardiac arrest. I stared at Kevin and he at me and I was actually able to take his strength into me and pull out of this tunnel. My mind sternly told my body to hang onto life, hang on -- *you* want to mother Augustus and Rayann, not someone else. Kevin later told me he was so frightened and felt me using his energy. This was the hardest thing I'd ever done mentally and physically and I've done a lot in my day!

My heart medications went to Gus and his heart rate dropped to sixty after delivery. Two neonatologists were there as this was anticipated. Gus was in Neonatal Intensive Care for four days -- very stressful but I knew he would be all right because I had seen him as a two-month-old and as a three-year-old. The first time I saw him after birth I cried with what? Relief?! Joy! Anyway, yes, it was Augustus, the white-blond haired baby of my winter solstice dream!

CHAPTER FIVE
VOICES AND VISIONS

My whole pregnancy was a time of learning to connect and communicate with my internal voices, including those of the children who will come through me.

-- *Fiora*

Images of our unborn children and messages that seem to come from them do not belong only to the world of dreams. Parents describe the same kinds of experiences happening while awake, though often in an altered state such as deep relaxation. They tell of perceiving clear pictures in the mind's eye, and words that seem to be spoken in the mind's ear.

Do these voices and visions come from the child? Or do we create them ourselves, perhaps building on impressions that we receive from the baby's physical presence, but adding our own words and pictures?

Kristine Kovach, who felt an inner voice during pregnancy, offers an idea of how such communication may work. She was left, she said, with the sensation "that this was knowledge that was part of my own mind or subconscious, and part of my child's mind or subconscious, which were somehow able to interact."

The inner voice is often described as something "felt/heard." It may be more a feeling than a voice, though for some people it is as if another person were actually speaking words into their ear. It always seems in some way very different from the "voice" of our own thinking, and what it conveys does not seem like our own thought. (None of this, of course, proves that it comes from another consciousness.)

In my own experience, to hear such an inner voice is extremely rare. But just a dozen days into a pregnancy that miscarried, I heard a voice calling at the edge of sleep: "Cressida!" What did it mean? I still don't know. But I wonder whether pregnancy lowers some threshold of perception and leaves us more open to "crosstalk" -- whether from an unrecognized part of our own mind, or messages we intercept as they pass by, like radio programs meant for other receivers.

Many of the "voice" experiences occur, as mine did, in the transitional state between sleeping and waking: while deeply relaxed as in meditation, or while falling asleep or waking up. A mother recalls the enigmatic utterance of an inner voice during one of her pregnancies:

> I was falling asleep after trying to contact the soul of the baby, and as I was drifting off, I felt as if I heard a deep growling voice coming from my throat -- which means I may have mumbled these words in my sleep, rather than hearing them spoken in a dream. It was like a man's voice, and I felt as if I were a man in a coffin, saying, "Louise... Louise, help me." I awoke with a start, and could not really make sense of the dream. Who was Louise, and why would some man want to call her?

Lucy Kennedy's experience was similar, but closer to a sense of real communication:

> All during my pregnancy with Duke, I meditated for a while early in the morning, every day. At least twice it seemed to me that I heard a voice speaking to me in my head -- a deep, resonant, male voice. I felt that it was the baby's spirit speaking to me, communicating with me although I couldn't consciously understand what it was "saying."

Some verbal communications are short and simple greetings. Deanna Finney treasures the memory of a day, at about five months pregnant, when her daughter spoke to her:

> I had always felt I would have a girl and on this day I felt/heard my daughter say, "Hi, Mom, it's me!" in her little girlish voice. It was as real as if she was standing next to me. I felt a sense of warmth flow over me at the same time and an incredible sense of familiarity -- like we had known each other for a very long time. I immediately stopped what I was doing and paid attention. I'll never forget that small moment in time and my daughter will hear about it when she is old enough to understand.

Deborah Prince felt a pre-conception message from her child-to-be, telling her that its name was "Shawn." She assumed that the baby would be a boy, but during the pregnancy, "one day while practicing deep relaxation, I asked if there was anything he wanted to tell me and I heard, loud and clear, 'Yes, I'm a girl!'"

Another woman describes a very similar experience: "I felt almost immediately that it was a girl. At the end of one or two months, I woke up at night and got a distinct message from the baby -- *I'm a boy*."

Isabelle Kessler was one month pregnant with her son when she had a startling experience:

> I was sitting in a sun filled room, feeling blissful with the contemplation of this child inside me. I was wondering what names I would choose and whether a boy or a girl. I heard/felt a voice (it was a knowledge) within me say, "My name is ABRAHAM, I'm a little male child, it takes nine months to make a body, then we'll meet."
>
> My first reaction was to look skyward and think, "Oh my God I've gone crazy." Then I realized that this wasn't the case. That this was communication with my child and that it was good. (The voice inside was such a powerful voice, it was a little frightening.)

Some parents even hold detailed conversations with their unborn children, asking questions and receiving answers. Linda feels that this kind of telepathic communication opened up during her first pregnancy because the unsettled conditions of her life at the time made her wonder "why this special soul chose us to be his parents." She writes:

> Last week, Philip celebrated his sixth birthday. Has it been so long? I'm trying to remember how all those fascinating communications occurred. Most of my major conversations took place like this. I would be alone in our bedroom and feel a presence (this in broad daylight), a soul, a spirit, whatever you may call it -- wishing to reincarnate. I would softly ask, "Who are you?" and the reply would come back to me in a nonverbal way and I would verbalize it.
>
> I started by asking, who are you? His answer was Philip Etienne.
> Do I know you from another life time?
> Yes.
> Do you know your father-to-be?
> Yes.
> Where do you know us from?
> From France.
> Were you and I ever related?

Brother.

Blood brother and sister?

No. Brotherhood.

(I am still investigating this brotherhood since there are many "white brotherhood" orders around and I know very little about it.)

We are at present financially unstable. And I am emotionally unstable. Can you bear with us and help me accept this situation?

I will help as much as I can. I love you both very much.

Do you plan to come as a male or female?

Male.

When do you think you'll join us in body?

February one four.

(We kept thinking the fourteenth of February though the doctor said February fourth was the due date. It turned out he was born on the fifth: one plus four equals five.)

CHANNELING THE CHILD?

Linda also describes an occasion when, instead of having a silent mental conversation with Philip, she spoke his words aloud. "A friend of mine (she's quite psychic) was visiting. She sat with me and addressed this spirit hovering around me and I became the medium who replied or verbalized the child's words."

Another instance of apparently "channeling" the unborn child is described by Adam Tritt, who claims to regularly channel various guides or spirits:

> Often we would get together with friends and I would go inside myself and speak to all their guides or let all their guides speak through me. Sometimes I get a knock inside my head, "I would like to speak too." Lee was six months pregnant and we did this. We spoke to several people and then I got a thought, "I want to speak too." It was from Sef (our daughter).
>
> She spoke to us and answered all our questions for forty-five minutes. She was scared to be born and would need lots of love. She went on to say the reason was that she was beaten to death early in her last life. She stated she did not want to live in the city, that she needed trees. Her voice and manner were very innocent, very pleading.
>
> "Are you promising me that you love me? You won't hit me,

please. I couldn't take that. Will I have trees, daddy? Will you love me?"

When we let go we were all silent. This was a most amazing thing... She was born in October 1985 and is wonderful.

Katryn Lavanture describes how her daughter was apparently channeled by a friend, during the pregnancy:

> The voice change, the feeling in the room and in myself were very profound. She had a sweet, soft voice, and spoke to me of how much she wanted to come, how she was preparing herself, and how much she loved the name Elyssia. I was so moved by the energy and feeling around and from her presence that I cried from my heart the whole time -- in joy, and feeling honored to have this experience of her in her purity, with no personality overlays yet.
>
> I had felt a female soul when I was pregnant with my second son, and was convinced it was a girl, but by the seventh month it became clear that she was not coming, and a boy soul had replaced her. She said this was true, and that she and he had to work out who was coming when. She gave in to him, as she needed more peace and stability in her life, and there was more urgency for him.

*   *   *

The experience of hearing from one's unborn child is almost always welcome and enjoyable. But it can be disturbing; it can feel somewhat like an "alien invasion." Vicky had such a reaction to perceiving an inner voice in her first pregnancy:

> For a two week period in about my fifth month of pregnancy I had daily "conversations" with him. I became quite uneasy with it so at that time I cut it off by shutting down my receptors.
>
> Most of the time the "speaking" happened "in my head." I remember being struck with the feeling that this was what I felt "they" described in science fiction movies when the alien was communicating telepathically. It was "deeper in my brain" than normal communication. I usually have to work "harder than normal" at verbal communication because I am an extremely visual person and often have to translate others' words into my own language of feeling before I can grasp their question and respond.

In this case, with my son, the conversing flowed very easily and naturally. There was no effort to it at all. I'd have to say that rather than a voice form it seemed to feel like *thoughts* but not from me. They were *in* me but not mine. It was also definitely words not pictures, which may seem strange since I just said I am much more visual than verbal.

At first, I didn't take the conversations seriously. I figured my mind was playing tricks on me, but I thought, "Let's just see where this goes since it's being so insistent." So when I could relax with it, the "entity" let me know there was nothing to worry about, that I'd do just fine, that it was a very old soul and would help to guide me in our mission of life. I remember thinking I was stuck in a Shirley Maclaine book. I don't dwell on stuff like this but it intrigues me. I didn't care which sex it was so I didn't ask, but I thought that I might as well ask if there was a name since I had been grappling with that, and it told me it was "Kelly." We named him Kellin and he goes by Kelly.

Soon after this was when I cut off the communications. The whole period ran about two weeks but that involved three to five talks a day. I didn't tell anyone about it while it was going on, though I did tell my best friend and my husband within days of shutting it off.

Since his birth, he and I have had a definite psychic connection. It usually shows itself in a telepathic form. He will make comments about the things I'm thinking about which have nothing to do with the present activity. Some of them appear to be beyond his possible scope of knowledge. This psychic connection still exists but is less noticeable to me now. We have another child, a girl two years old, so I'm much more distracted. I am currently pregnant with our third child and am feeling a similar tie (I never felt it with our daughter).

Vicky is more relaxed now about the possibility of contact with her unborn child. She says, "It's only the second month so I remain open to possibilities. I am definitely more comfortable with the thought that what happened with Kelly might recur and I am worlds more mature so less inhibited."

Kristine Kovach also became aware of an internal "voice" when she was in the second trimester of her first pregnancy:

The "voice" was not my own, yet not a stranger's. I wasn't afraid or surprised, and although the voice did not use words or sounds, I was made to know that it was the voice of my child who would be a girl and who would be named Ava.

I had thought of several names up to that point, though none of them very seriously and never the name Ava. I had had no tests indicating the sex of the baby and had never read about or given thought to the idea of true communication between mother and fetus.

At the time it felt so natural to speak to my child this way. I remember it feeling as though someone were "speaking" things into the *inside* of my ear or that I was receiving a message on a picture screen in whole sentences, not in a word at a time as we normally process information.

I was comforted several times during my pregnancy by this "voice" who "showed" me that I would have a good delivery and a healthy child. By the time Ava was born, weighing in at eight pounds after an easy labor, I felt certain that I already knew her quite well and this feeling has remained since.

THE MYSTERIOUS VOICE

Intrigued by descriptions of an inner voice, I have tried to gather more information about these experiences. Kristine provides additional details of her perceptions:

> The "voice" that I heard during my pregnancy with Ava came from a place where I have always heard a "voice." As a child I sometimes felt guided or comforted by the same sensations and I believe this sense has been with me as far back as I can remember.
>
> It can come at any time and often I realize that it has been "working at me" for some time before I acknowledge or understand it. It isn't unusual for me to hear this "voice" (or get these "feelings") while I am engrossed in some task that requires my full concentration. For example -- during my pregnancy I worked in a Center for deaf patients suffering from mental illness and retardation. I would often become aware of my inner voice while trying to take blood pressures or interpret Sign Language -- both of which involve using several senses to capacity at once. The only other time I noticed a frequent occurrence of this voice was right upon waking -- often from a short nap.
>
> You asked if the "voice" I receive is more on one side of my head or the other. I've thought about it before and it seems that the messages are given to me in their entirety from a place that

is distinctly central but toward the top of my head -- like right at the hair line. The image or impression is presented within my head and it feels as if it is "transmitted" (all of these words don't really describe things well) at an *angle* through my mind.

Like Kristine, Nancy Cohen is aware of hearing an inner voice at times other than during pregnancy:

> I often receive an inner voice (the voice of Holy Spirit? What is it?) that sometimes tells me to do things. In 1986 a voice inside me told me to take an outrageous trip to Russia. Which I did -- petrified -- and met my husband! And changed my life -- especially spiritually. There have been other less dramatic instances, but always it is a greater leap than I would normally dream of.

THE MIND'S EYE

Visionary ways of connecting with our unborn children include dreamlike reveries, imagery in the mind's eye and even detailed visions complete with symbolism and powerful emotions. Like the voice experiences, these often (but not always) occur at the edge of sleep or in similarly relaxed states.

Amy Oscar felt contact with each of her two children in pregnancy but they communicated in different ways. With Max, her first child, communication was in words,

> ...strings of thought which so differed from my own I automatically fell into conversation (rather than wondering whether they were my thoughts) and I never had a doubt that the baby was telling me things. And Max was what I call "boy energy." A completely unfamiliar vibration going inside of me. In a separate place, somehow, from the place where my own "feminine energy" lives. When Katie was conceived, I never once felt that foreign-ness, that strangeness. That's one of the ways I knew I would have a little girl.
>
> Katie also communicated with me in utero, telling me she was a girl and helping me choose her name. She told me plenty but her communication was subtle. She put pictures in my mind. That's as close as I can come to describing it. Where Max and I communicated with words, Katie spoke to me in images. I could see her fingers, her face. I got feelings from her -- love, patience,

peacefulness. But no words. When Max spoke it was my right ear but on the inside. Katie's impressions came (and still do!) from the left. (I never noticed that. Thanks for asking.)

Another woman envisioned her baby when she was a few months pregnant:

> One sunny morn I was very tired, but had an appointment to keep. When I rose I had a dizzy spell and collapsed back to the cushion. In my mind's eye I could see a black silhouette of the fetus within, and its umbilical cord coming up to my placenta in curls. The baby was curled in the fetal position, hands near or in its mouth. Its womb was the sun and light was radiating around it, and it did a somersault -- I saw it and felt it in my womb!

For one first-time mother, a vision of her baby in the seventh month of pregnancy created the emotional connection that had been missing before:

> I'm a fairly pragmatic person. My sister tells me I'm "grounded," that my feet are firmly planted in the soil, and it's true; I am a devout agnostic. I don't believe -- or disbelieve -- in the presence of a spiritual Other. I just don't know.
>
> One afternoon, I came home from a long, crazy day at work -- and, I remember, it was a snowy, miserable New England day so the commute home had to have been pretty rough. And when I got home, for some reason I became absolutely furious at my sister-in-law, who was staying with us then. I was completely livid.
>
> I ran upstairs to my bedroom, and slammed the door behind me. Today I am terribly ashamed to admit that I wasn't very self-aware; wasn't even remotely spiritually connected to the little life growing within me. I needed to vent the fury that was making me shake. So... I grabbed my Walkman, and popped a tape in -- the most raucous, wildest rock-n-roll I could find -- and I turned the volume WAY UP, and began to dance insanely around my bedroom, to get rid of this crazy energy.
>
> Well -- my son moved within me. He protested, strongly, against this horrible disturbance of his peaceful little place. And I remembered, "Oh, this is awful! What is it doing to my little person?!" and I ripped the headphones from my ears, and threw them down.
>
> And then I suddenly, gloriously, wonderfully, miraculously

became AWARE of this little guy. I had a sharp, clear vision in my mind's eye -- oh, it was so clear, a photographic vision -- of my infant baby's face, his tiny and perfect features, his lovely dark hair -- I knew, all of a sudden, *exactly* what my baby looked like, and that he was a little boy -- though I hadn't yet had the sonogram that would confirm what I now knew to be true. When he was born, when he came out of me, he looked like my vision, of course!

After I had this vision, or whatever it was, I felt terrible remorse for the temper tantrum I'd just had, for disturbing his peace, for my lack of intuitive connection with the little person growing inside me. I lay on my bed, with my hands on my belly, caressing him, comforting him, and weeping, over and over again, "Oh, I'm so sorry, so very sorry, so sorry..." And from that day, I felt a bond with him that hadn't been there before. He was *real*. And I loved him *fiercely*...

Diana Lorenz's vision announced the imminent birth of her first baby and included a glimpse of her second child:

I was asleep in my bed, the bed in which I had consciously conceived this child and in which I planned to give birth. I opened my eyes and stared straight up towards the ceiling. Above my head was a tunnel-like structure, consisting of a series of concentric hexagons made of dark timbers (similar to railroad ties). Alternating hexagons were rotated thirty degrees, giving me a twelve-sided perception of the tunnel (or tower, depending how you look at it).

At the very top of this tower was an opening, and peering down at me through this opening was a child's face. The face appeared to be that of a baby or very young child, not more than two years old, with fair skin, fair hair and round cheeks. I sensed that it was male, but it was too far away for me to see its features with any clarity. I could see a second, partially obstructed face *behind* the first one. I believe the second face was that of another child's spirit, waiting to be born to me.

I instinctively knew that I had seen the child I was to bring into this world. That night my labor began. It was a long, arduous travail, lasting three days start to finish, culminating in the birth of a healthy, robust home-birthed son.

The complex and unusual structure of the tunnel/tower in Diana's vision held several meanings for her. She explains:

First, it symbolized the birth canal that my child was soon to pass through, and second, it represented the passageway from God (Heaven) to the physical plane. Its hexagonal, spiralling shape symbolized both the carbon atom (the distinguishing feature between living and non-living matter), and the DNA molecule, which determines who we are.

Perhaps the stories that offer the most compelling evidence of contact with the child-to-be are those where the pregnancy is unplanned and no one is yet aware of it or watching for signs. This was the case with Claire Baiz, who had no idea that despite her precautions, conception had occurred:

I used to sit on my husband's front porch with his ugly mongrel dog and wonder if I would ever like a child as much as I liked this smelly, blotchy mutt. I was never the kind of girl who enjoyed Polly PeePee dolls or neighbors' babies (who in my opinion often smelled worse than this dog). I had minimal maternal instincts. I decided I was going to agonize over having children for an appropriate period before making a drastic, dramatic decision. At least I felt more confident at agonizing than parenting.

When Tom and I left for our belated honeymoon in Mexico, we had been married for seven months. I had scheduled our getaway to coincide with non-fertility; nevertheless, I wore a diaphragm with spermicide. But I think it was in Mazatlan that we must have conceived, though I didn't find out until several weeks later.

Back in Montana we settled into the remains of winter. I felt more tired than usual, as if I had some kind of flu. One afternoon in March I lay down for a nap on our huge old waterbed. I tossed despite my fatigue until I was in a strange state of consciousness that is neither awake nor asleep, but which bears the earmarks of both.

My eyes were open. The room was silent. I was aware of my body and fully within it, but I could not move. Paralysis extended to my voice -- I figured if I could only scream I would wake up, but no sound came from my effort. This state was perturbing, but not unfamiliar; often as a child I experienced this limbo. I tried to relax back into a sleep state, thinking that if I climbed back down and came up again I would take the right road to the conscious state.

Then I saw her. She was at the foot of the bed -- patient, not trying to catch my attention. She was perhaps three years old, simply dressed, with long dark hair and a quiet look on her face. No anxiety, no concern. She just watched me in my paralysis.

I was really curious about her. Was she real? Did she get in the front door without the dog barking? Was she lost? Was I having a vision? All these thoughts passed through me, but without feeling frantic about any of them. It was a real slow mental inquiry, as if I knew rapid thoughts might frighten her away.

She climbed gracefully on the footboard, as though the move was choreographed. She began to crawl toward me, one hand, then the other. Perhaps she grew smaller, or became translucent, I do not know. She reached my legs and kept moving until she faded to become part of my own body. She was inside me.

I do not want to say that I woke up, because that implies a dream state. It was not a dream. It was something outside my conscious understanding. When I got up I remember calling my husband on the telephone and telling him about the experience. I knew that what just happened *could* mean that I was pregnant, but my interpretation was not necessarily so literal. It could be that I was admitting some inner quality of myself, or having some other kind of recall. But inside, I hoped that if I was ever going to have a child, there would be some sign that I was making the right choice. To me this was the sign.

My period never came and late in the autumn Samantha was born. She is eight years old now, and has long dark hair and the body of a dancer. I knew her the moment she popped out. We both just smiled.

CHAPTER SIX
THEY SEEMED TO NAME THEMSELVES

The baby's name plays a part in many pre-birth connections. Choosing the name is an absorbing process -- a dialogue with our family history and with all the different images and possibilities that names bring to mind. This dialogue often leads into the experience of contact.

We may dream a name that is compelling, or a name enters our awareness so vividly that we feel the child is telling it to us. The name seems to be a medium or channel of communication, one of the most powerful ways of linking up with this unknown person coming into our life. Seeking the "right" name is really a way of asking, "Who are you?" And when the name comes "out of the blue" with a sweet insistence, we are left wondering: did I choose it? Did you choose it? Did we somehow decide together?

Many parents have a strong impression that their child communicates a name to them. Ann Wasserman says that her daughter "whispered her first name in my husband Larry's ear and her middle name (a name I never would have picked myself) in mine." Their family tradition is to choose names with initials of deceased family members, and in honor of an uncle they were looking for a "K" name. Larry recalls:

> I was driving in that semi-dazed state one often gets into when driving in the city. I was thinking about what to name the baby, trying to think of "K" names, and I suddenly heard, inside my head, "Katrina." I smiled and thought, "I like that."

Ann continues:

> We picked "M" for the middle initial, honoring three of our four

grandparents. A few weeks after we settled on Katrina, I heard "Margaret" in much the same way, while sitting quietly at the table after dinner. It's never been a name that I've liked, so I knew it wasn't my idea. But Katrina Margaret Atkin was just right. We never did get any clear direction on a boy's K.M. name, but then, we weren't going to need one.

When Leigh McCune was expecting her second baby, she regularly tried to contact the child during meditation. She learned in this way that her baby was a girl, and maintains that the baby chose her own name:

> Her father and I were having trouble deciding between two other names and I was frustrated because I felt the name to be very important for this child, so I asked her what her name was and Iris was the name I received. Iris was not a name that had occurred to either of us, but when I looked up its meaning and associations it became clear to me that this was the perfect name. It means rainbow; Iris was the Greek goddess of the rainbow and a messenger between the gods and humans.

Janette Patterson writes:

> Greg and I struggled with names for the baby (as we did with all our children) until the very end. During the last week of my pregnancy I sat in front of my list of baby names, and as I was reading off the names for a girl, the name Angelica slipped into my consciousness. It was as if it had come from within me, but not from me. I had not ever considered that particular name, but I immediately liked it. And even Greg liked it at once. The name Brooke just seemed to fit nicely with it -- and the name was born! We wanted to call her Brooke, since Angelica sounds like such a long name. When we told Kati (our little girl) about our decision on the girl's name she said: "Yes, Angelica is a good name."
> When Angelica was just born, I said: "Hi, Brooke," and Kati looked at the precious little baby and said: "Mom, her name is Angelica." It seemed like Angelica told me her name a while before her birth -- and I heard it, but wanted to fudge a bit, by adding another name and calling her by it. Kati was the one who was so connected with Angelica and was able to correct me by saying that the baby really wanted to be called Angelica. I was truly amazed (as I usually am when I allow myself to pause and observe my children). Needless to say, now Angelica is called by

her chosen name.

Mary Bohman is another woman who feels that the names of her two daughters were given to her. In one case the name was simultaneously received by a friend, as if to ensure there would be no mistake! Mary writes:

> At least a year before she was conceived, Jael's name was given into my mind one day, at the same time that one of my closest friends got it, and mentioned to me that this person named Jael was coming to be with her -- but would not be her baby but mine.
>
> My daughter's name is actually Maya Jael. Another friend was the one who said she wanted Maya for her other name. He is a medical doctor who is into hypnotherapy and does have a lot of intuitive abilities, and she has also had quite a bond with him.
>
> I was not aware that the name Jael was in the Bible, but a minister mentioned it to us after we had named her. We found it fairly significant and curious that she had chosen such a beautiful name.

Nancy Cohen asked a psychic friend for help in finding the right name for her daughter, but feels the name finally came from the baby herself. Did the friend's imagery provide a suggestion, or was she sensing what the baby was trying to convey? Nancy writes:

> A month before she was born the baby gave us her name: Gemma. While we feel strongly that the name came from her, I can't tell you how! In the eighth month -- still no name -- I asked my psychic friend, "Help!" All she could "see" was "a pile of precious jewels glistening in the sun." We had been toying with foreign or Sanskrit names, so my friend suggested maybe the name was "diamond" or "emerald" or "sapphire" in a foreign language. This led nowhere. Nothing sounded right. As with most things -- it comes when you stop pushing. Of course we later realized that Gemma means "precious jewel"!

Mary Halter Petersen feels that each of her four children came with a name, and she simply needed to attune herself to it:

> Jonah means peace, dove in Hebrew and I don't remember how I "chose" it. I feel rather that it was told to me. It just came into my consciousness during that pregnancy and immediately felt perfect, much as Hannah's name came to me and there was no

real choice about it. They were given perhaps by these people as their names, or the best expression of who they wanted to be, or were. Actually it was the same for Lukas and Aren. I felt attracted to the names by some sort of inner pressure, it's hard to describe.

I cannot help wondering whether the name Jonah held another message. The biblical Jonah is one who was sacrificed for the good of the others -- thrown overboard to calm the storm. Could the name Jonah have come from an awareness (on Mary's part or the baby's) that the pregnancy would not last? For this child was miscarried; his story is told in Chapter Nineteen.

The name can be a channel for information about the baby's gender. The day I received the phone call with the results of my amniocentesis, the caller assured me my baby was genetically normal, and then asked, "Do you want to know the baby's sex?"

"It's a girl, isn't it?" I quickly replied.

"How did you know?" she said, sounding surprised.

How did I know? I didn't, really -- but all through this second pregnancy I had been fascinated with girl's names and couldn't spare a thought to any other possibility. That was enough to give me a subtle sense of knowing.

Knowledge of the baby's gender may come linked with a dream of a name: "When I was four months along, I had a dream that the baby was a brown haired, blue eyed girl named Amanda. Amanda's now four months old..."

Juliann Mitchell and her husband had discussed baby names for years before her pregnancy, and when they talked about female names they had always favored either "Lauren" or "Megan." But Juliann awoke one morning to find that the question had been decided differently. She didn't recall having a dream, but she says:

> About four weeks before my scheduled sonogram I awoke one morning and told my husband that the child I was carrying was a little girl and that she should be called Mirabella. From that day on we called her Mirabella and began talking to her by name.
>
> My husband is the one who had a dream before the sonogram; in the dream he had put a "pink" bicycle in the shed in the back of our house for our little girl. The day of the sonogram I was told that yes indeed it was a little girl, but I already knew. Where her name came from we don't know. It is not an old family name, we had never heard the name before and know of no one with that name. Yet we never even thought of naming her anything

else. It was just a given.

As the pregnancy progressed, when we would say "Mirabella" she would kick in response.

That moment of finding the name can be lit up with a surge of energy or a flush of warmth that parents may feel is the child's answering approval. (When I finally thought of the "right" spelling of my daughter Roselyn's name, I saw it flash sparkling and silvery in the air.) Candice recalls:

> Throughout my pregnancy Dannika and I talked. We would try out names, none that she cared for until two weeks before her birth we discovered an ancient Celtic word meaning Morning Star, Dannika; suddenly I couldn't remember any of the names we had been considering. Dannika was born in the early morning shining like starlight.

Debra describes the feelings that came with the name -- and along with the name, a sudden certainty about the child's gender in each of her two pregnancies:

> I made dozens of lists of names for this unknown child and talked often with my husband Terry about names (which drove him crazy sometimes). When I was about eight months pregnant, and Terry and I had gone to bed and were almost asleep, he turned over to me and said, sleepily, "How about Melissa?"
>
> I immediately felt this warm exhilaration and I knew at that moment that there was a little girl named Melissa inside of me. I told Terry, "Yes! That is who it is! Our child is Melissa!" Melissa was not a name on any of my many lists, but I don't feel as if I named her. She named herself.
>
> Melissa was born about a month later. When she came out and was placed on my stomach, I felt as if I already knew her and said, "Hello, Melissa, I was expecting you!" She was very alert and looked at everyone. I have a picture of my mother holding her thirty minutes after she was born, and Melissa is holding my mom's finger and looking up in her eyes. She was expecting us too.
>
> A similar instance happened with my son. This time I was five months pregnant and was looking through a catalog of children's clothing. At the time, this catalog printed the names of the models underneath the children's pictures. I turned a page and all I could see was the name Wesley jumping up at me. I

couldn't see the models, the clothes -- only the name Wesley. Again I had that warm, exhilarating feeling and knew for certain that I was carrying a son named Wesley.

I don't feel as if I "talked" to my children in utero, but I had a deep sense of who they were, and when they were born I didn't have the feeling of meeting a new person, but someone I already knew. Should I ever have another child, I am not going to bother with names. I'll just let the child tell me!

Finding the name can be the key to making a connection before birth. A mother writes:

After six and a half months of a second pregnancy that was emotionally unsupported by my husband, he came to some acceptance. We had been for a walk having an emotional discussion about the impending birth. I had not come upon any name for the child that seemed to fit, though I felt she was a girl.

That very day, I had received a letter from a close sister who suggested the name Magdalene. I had thought of that name for our first child four years earlier but had forgotten it. I liked the name and suggested it to my husband. He immediately responded to it favorably. That had been his grandmother's name. Upon his obvious enthusiasm, I felt a warmth in my womb. It wasn't so much a describable sensation as a connection.

That night I dreamed I was massaging my abdomen. The baby reached up from within me and grabbed my little finger. I knew at that point the baby was indeed Magdalene and that we had a connection and relationship before birth. It was very powerful for me.

DREAMING THE NAME

A French mother describes how her children appeared in dreams to comment (not always favorably) on the names she had chosen for them:

My second child's name is Clarisse. One week before she was born, in August 1986, we chose her name. That night I heard a voice in my dream telling me, "You are right, my name is Clarisse and I have been with you since La-Chaise-Dieu." That was weird because my elder son Clement was born in 1983 and "La-Chaise-Dieu" meant since I sang at La-Chaise-Dieu which was in 1981.

My third child's name is Adeline. One week before she was born I dreamed I heard a voice telling me, "This is not my name. My name is A...a..." It was something like Agadangada or Amaranda, that was not French anyhow and impossible to remember!

If we can recall the name we dream, should we feel bound to call our child by it? I don't believe so! We can take it first as a symbolic message from ourselves or from the baby, and try to decipher it at that level.

While pregnant with my daughter, I dreamed she was called "Shulamith," perhaps in part because I have never known how to pronounce that name; dreams often seem to riffle through the mind's uncertainties and loose ends. I didn't choose to call her Shulamith, and have never regretted it. Yet I still think of it from time to time and wonder what message it holds from myself, or from her...

The name that is dreamed may stay with us and feel too imperative to be dismissed. It may turn out to be beautifully fitting. This was one mother's experience with her second child:

I had a dream that her birth occurred either in early morning or late evening because the light in the room was soft and diffused. In the dream, when she was born she looked at me and said, "My name is Eve." So, of course, when she was born -- in the early morning -- I named her Eve. The name Eve had no special significance for me before the dream. Now, there would be no other name for her. Eve means "giver of life." She is a warm, sympathetic child. As a baby she was patient and made lovely cooing and singing noises that I could never hope to copy or ever hope to hear again...

We can keep the name in mind and wait to see if it "fits" the baby. Kristine Kovach felt the name "Ava" suggested during her pregnancy (not by a dream in this case, but by an inner voice), but she postponed committing herself. She writes:

I have not known any Avas personally and as names go it was one of the few that I felt no previous connection to at all.

I liked the internal alliteration of Ava Kovach and although I kept my mind open even after being "given" this name, I was not surprised when she and I first saw each other that the name fit her. I was a little wary still -- afraid to totally surrender to the sensation of certainty, and I left myself the "out" of wanting to look at her and make sure this name was as right as it felt. The definition of the name pleased me, and my petite, resourceful and quick-moving daughter is truly "a thing like a bird" or "birdlike."

On the other hand, a Canadian mother's dream was so insistent that she felt compelled to follow its instructions when her baby turned out to be a third daughter:

> I had two girls whose birth weights were nine pounds and nine and a half pounds. While expecting my third, we all thought it was a boy because of the low position and different signs.
>
> Three days before the baby was born, just as I was waking up in the morning I was dreaming of a girl spinning around in circles on a skating rink, and I assumed it was the Olympics or something similar. Then as I was coming fully awake, I heard, "Natasha. You've got to call your baby Natasha."
>
> It was a strange dream since I cannot skate nor can my two girls. The name Natasha had no special significance to me. Actually I had never even heard of the name.
>
> When I got up to go to the bathroom I was thinking, How stupid! I'm not calling a boy Natasha, and besides I have ten-pound babies, I'm not going to be able to call it Natasha, it's going to be a big brute. I had actually forgotten the name by the time my seven pound eight ounce girl arrived, a shock to all. Luckily, I had told my mother and my husband about the dream.
>
> Of course we called her Natasha, no doubt about that.

Every name carries a multitude of meanings and associations that can lead us into intriguing speculations. Beyond our own personal symbolism, there are larger trends. Why does a name suddenly become popular? For example, one can't help noticing the frequency of variations of "Luke" in the stories presented in this book. Luke is related to "light" -- is this a group prayer for more light? And the name Devin, suddenly reappearing out of an obscure past, seems to bridge the sounds of "devil" and "divine." Could it be a sign that we are growing towards a less divisive consciousness?

Or do our name choices come from less exalted hopes and wishes? Occasionally we catch a glimpse of what's going on behind the scenes of our thinking and have to laugh at ourselves a little. I suspect, for example, that we're all a lot more susceptible to media messages than we'd like to admit.

At least, I discovered that I am. The experience I want to relate does not bear directly on communication with children-to-be, but it brought me an insight into the unreliable nature of mind and memory -- and the subconscious messages our name choices may carry.

When my husband and I were expecting our first child, I felt it would be a boy. We made lots of lists and studied many name books. We found the name "Devin" and liked the sound of it as well as its meanings (a poet, a teacher), but were quite sure we had never encountered it before. When our little boy was born, we contemplated him and his possible names for several days and settled on Devin.

A little while later I noticed an advertisement in an old magazine and remembered that I had seen that very page during the pregnancy, some time before I "first" found the name Devin. I recognized the photograph; it showed a handsome young man leaning against an expensive car, in mellow golden light against a background that looked like a wheat field -- the impression was of a wealthy young gentleman farmer.

Though I had no conscious memory of the words accompanying the scene, I certainly had absorbed the fact that this attractive image went with "Devin" -- the advertisement was for a new men's cologne by that name! My husband (who also recognized the picture) and I both had to admit that we must have liked the idea of such a life for our son.

It's interesting to consider what message we might be sending -- or receiving -- in our choice of names. What are we invoking with this name?   It may be a vehicle for risky information, for wishes we might not want to acknowledge openly -- as I might have denied I wanted material riches for my son.

Since that eye-opening experience, I tend to discount anyone's statement, including my own, that something is entirely new, never-heard-of-before. We take in such a huge amount of sensory information and "forget" so much of it, that the probability is on the side of having seen or heard the name in question, though we may have taken no conscious notice of it.

Still, who's to say that the undeniable feeling of "rightness" might not be the child chiming in with agreement? "Devin," after all, does seem a fitting name for my handsome son, as he tramps off in soccer shorts and wellingtons to irrigate the fields...

CHAPTER SEVEN
BODY LANGUAGE

Once babies are big enough so their movements can be felt, a new world of communication opens up. Curiously, it is often at this time that telepathic contact seems to taper off. As one mother puts it, the baby "seems to be settling in to being a fetus spiritually, too." But now there is a new language, comprising subtle touches that only the mother perceives, and strong kicks and rolls easily felt by fathers and other "outside observers."

What could be more intimate than the communications these mothers describe? Amy Oscar recalls "the time at eight or nine months pregnant when I sat crying one rainy afternoon at the window, sad and lonely, and from within little fingers began to stroke me and comfort me. The baby was patting and then stroking me from inside!"

Another woman writes:

> One day, I could feel him moving inside me, just random motions, happy motions. I stopped and put my hand on the top of my tummy. The movement stopped, he pressed his hand against the wall of his home and mirrored my stroking.

Parents and babies can be very creative as they invent ways of interacting with each other using the language of touch. The following stories describe some of the communication games that parents can play with a baby in the womb.

> Once I could feel movement on a regular basis, I began to use two fingertips to rub my belly in response. One finger would be right over the spot where I felt the movement and the other would be moved away slightly. My son would then kick where the second finger had rubbed, and I would repeat the rubbing process again, moving my fingers in circular patterns around my belly.
>
> We "played" this game frequently and each time it would last for about three minutes. During these experiences I always felt that the baby was seeking to contact me, to get to know me. After my sixth month he was too big to move in circles so we

couldn't play in that fashion any more.

During my last month of pregnancy he would leave a foot sticking at night under the left side of my ribs. I would rub the heel and then he would tuck it back in. Although this happened at various times during the day, it always occurred each night when I got into bed. It must have been his way of saying "Good Night."

Another woman recalls:

During the last month of my pregnancy, my husband and I got a lot of fun out of watching my belly-button turn "inside out." One night in bed, we were looking at it in wonder and mirth, and I pushed it back in, laughingly telling the baby to "give me my belly-button back!" At that, I felt a very strange pulling sensation in there, as though a tiny hand were pulling the place from the inside! Throughout the last month, every time I pushed my belly-button during an active, kicking period when she was obviously awake, my baby would "pull" from the inside.

THE DADDY BOND

While still in the womb, a baby can make a special connection with its father, by feeling his touch and hearing his voice. In *The Secret Life of the Unborn Child*, Thomas Verny writes:

A child hears his father's voice in utero, and there is solid evidence that hearing that voice makes a big emotional difference. In cases where a man talked to his child in utero using short soothing words, the newborn was able to pick out his father's voice in a room even in the first hour or two of life. More than pick it out, he responds to it emotionally. If he's crying, for instance, he'll stop. That familiar, soothing sound tells him he is safe.

Kristina Bystrom recalls how her husband spoke to their son all through her pregnancy:

He often repeated "I love you" in a musical tone, and "Hi, baby, how ya doing in there?" and "This is your dad..."

When Arne was born, he was put on my chest immediately (I squatted for the birth, so I actually held him to my chest while I delivered the placenta). After about two minutes, my husband, Carl, said, "How ya doin' baby, I love you" -- and Arne immediately turned his head and focused his eyes on Carl -- and stared. We were all amazed -- Carl was, of course, in heaven -- knowing his baby had heard him and that he recognized his voice and seemed so eager to finally see who was talking!

A woman writes of her impressions while pregnant with her first child, noting how the baby has a definite relationship with its father:

Baby knows Daddy's touch; if my husband lies beside me and comes in the slightest contact with my belly, Baby begins thumping at the point of contact to get his attention. My husband then turns and puts his hands on my belly and feels for little body parts and massages and talks to Baby. I can feel tiny hands feeling of Daddy's hands from inside me. The level of Baby's awareness is incredible. If anyone else tries to contact Baby, at first touch Baby turns away with indifference and disinterest.

The baby in the womb can play special games with its father. Amy Oscar writes:

My husband communicated with Max in utero. He would tap a rhythm on my swollen belly and Max would repeat it, kicking (we think) against Matthew's cheek. A few times, we think Max, hearing his father's voice, initiated a rhythm he remembered and I told Matthew and they played for a while.

Max clearly and definitely responded to these patterns: a series of taps. He repeated them accurately and with increasing levels of complexity. If a rhythmic pattern was too much for him, he did not respond. Then Matthew would use a simpler pattern which Max had responded to before and he would repeat it.

When I tried to initiate this game, I don't think he ever played it with me. It was a Daddy game.

Candice White recalls:

Dannika's Papa worked long hours so I would bring him lunch at different times every day. I wouldn't feel a stir from her all morning, no hiccuping, no kicking, nothing, but as soon as she heard his voice all hell would break loose. You could see her excitement, my belly would ripple and my dress would move with it.

Similar activity would occur at 3:30 A.M. in bed at night. That was when K.C. would arrive home from his night job. Five nights a week he would curl up with us in the wee hours and she would begin kicking him, beginning what became a ritualistic quality time if you will. K.C. would talk with her and they'd play games: he would tap on my stomach a certain number of times in varying places and she would follow. It is still busy around here after midnight.

INFLUENCING BABY'S POSITION

Many mothers report that their babies respond to requests for movements or position changes in the womb. For these women, the physical responses deepen their sense of a mental link with their baby.

Amy Oscar writes, "While Max grew inside of me he was very aware of what went on around us. From simple things like repeating rhythms tapped on my belly, to more subtle ones like responding to my requests for changes in position so I could be more comfortable." Her second child, Katie, responded especially well to "mind pictures." Amy would visualize what she wanted the baby to do -- "move, kick, get off my bladder -- I would imagine her body, then I would imagine it moving the way I needed it to move and she'd do it!"

Several women tell how they requested their baby to turn from breech or transverse positions to head-down, and apparently won the baby's cooperation. When a mother experiences her baby cooperating with the necessary change, it creates a heartening sense of connection. Each of the women in the following stories felt that the position change was part of a larger pattern of communication with her child. Kristina Bystrom writes:

> The midwife checked me at thirty-two weeks. Arne was breech, so she gently turned him. Within a week he had turned back -- I felt this occur -- first as he turned sideways, then all the way back to breech.
>
> That evening, I lay quietly on my bed, my bottom slightly elevated by pillows. I relaxed, breathed, and visualized my baby inside of me. I talked to him silently -- first about general things (I love you, how are you doing in there? warmth, etc.). Then I specifically asked him to turn head-down, while envisioning his movements and concentrating heavily on his head in my pelvis. I explained to him (again, silently) that this position would make

for an easy birth, and just kept visualizing. I lay there for forty-five minutes or so before getting up. Within two hours, I again felt him turn -- his entire body shifted, a *huge* movement.

I believe what made it effective was the fact that I communicated with my son virtually from the moment of conception, speaking to him both aloud and silently. I visualized him within me as well. Also, I remained receptive. It is all very exciting!

Cynthia had a vision of her baby as a little boy during her second trimester (that story will be told in Chapter Fourteen). Just before her due date, the midwife informed her that the baby was breech. Cynthia writes:

My midwife wouldn't deliver breech at home, so I had to get to work to ward off an impending caesarean. I did the exercises as prescribed, but felt nothing had changed. So, one afternoon I reached deep down inside, asking Bryce if we could talk.

Again he appeared, but this time he was in his pre-birth form. We "talked" for a while, and I explained that if he turned around, we'd be able to have this birth at home, where we would all be more comfortable. All at once I got a very strong sensation that he understood and would do his part. The next day I went to the midwife, and lo and behold Bryce was no longer breech!

An Israeli woman writes about her experience with her fifth child:

My daughter, Margalit, was born with G-d's grace, just two and a half weeks ago. I am well aware that babies may not necessarily become "engaged" until labor begins, but from early in the pregnancy I knew that Margalit's position was something to be concerned about. Most people including my doctor tried to reassure me that there was plenty of time for the baby to position properly. I, on the other hand felt that the baby was choosing to lie in the transverse position. As a matter of fact, when one night I felt her change to a head down position, I expressed my happiness with this fetus to my husband. The next day she was sideways again! I knew she had done it because I was pleased with the head down position.

I expressed my concern in my sixth or seventh month to a healer friend of mine. She communicated with the baby and found out that this baby wanted to do things *her* way. It was basically a power play, and my friend told me to use imagery and to send loving messages to the baby and sooner or later she'd come around. I tried but to no avail.

Finally, in my eighth month I went to another healer who has been helping me with medical problems. He sensed my tension and I told him of my obsession with the baby's position. It was all I could think about. He communicated with her and told me (without knowing what the previous healer had said), "This kid is having a power-play with you and he's very strong willed." He told me that I have to communicate two things to this child: 1) We are a team. What's good for him (he thought she was male) is good for me and vice versa. We are not at odds. 2) I must communicate that I am boss. My helplessness was feeding her and egging her on to continue in her obstinate way.

So I did as he said. I went home, practiced my autohypnosis to reach full relaxation and while "under," communicated these thoughts to my baby. At the same time I felt overwhelming love for her and this too was transferred to her. I felt her receive these messages. And within days, Margalit went head down and stayed there until she was born.

Just to express her individuality, though, she was born with her hand presenting before her shoulders. She still had to "show" me in the end.

COMMUNICATING WITH ENERGY?

Unusual feelings in various parts of the body are an aspect of pregnancy that is not often discussed. For example, one woman's earliest sign of pregnancy is a soft fluttering vibration in her throat. There are probably physical explanations for these sensations, but we might also speculate that mother and baby may have overlapping "energy bodies" that create new waves. Could some of these unfamiliar feelings actually come from the child within -- a communication in the medium of energy?

Holly Richardson describes a sensation that occurred in early pregnancy:

> I would get "prickles" down my back -- the same feeling as having someone stare at you. This happened on a frequent basis, sometimes two or three times a day, and I started telling my husband that the baby had come to visit!

At seven months pregnant, a woman in Germany describes

sensations that may be sciatica (symptoms of pressure on the sciatic nerves), but that she feels are coming from the baby, "as that is where they seem to originate:"

> I have experienced electric pulsations coursing through my body especially in my legs. They come when I lie down and shut off my own thoughts and am just present with the baby. They came strongly during a Shiatsu treatment which I had "given" to the baby as treatment for him. I simply try to lie still and endure as the baby expresses his balance and life. It's difficult however to endure these shock pulses especially when they come on strong. I don't believe they're simply a physical consequence of pregnancy. The pulsation and rhythm that occur remind me of polarity treatments that my husband and I exchange which are an expression of life energy in balance or balancing itself and flowing free.

Another woman describes a most unusual experience that occurred about eight times during the last trimester of her pregnancy with her son. Sandra recalls:

> When I was either waking up from a nap or particularly relaxed after exercise and deep breathing, I would hear him cooing and humming. At first I was startled because it was so loud and distinct. Then I came to treasure those times it happened. Although the recollection of exactly how it sounded is vague, the pleasure it gave me is what remains the sharpest memory.
> The first time it happened, I had been taking an afternoon nap. I woke up, startled by the distinct sound of humming, and lay there a few moments wondering if it had been a dream. It was more a "vocalizing" sound than a "musical" humming. Then it started again.
> I could just barely feel the vibration that humming causes when you do it yourself, but it wasn't being caused by me. I remember humming a little myself, just to make sure that it wasn't me, and I noted the big difference between the feeling of the sound I made and the feeling I had had when the baby was humming. It was like the vibration was very gentle all over, and not just in the throat as it feels when you do it yourself.
> I really can't say that it sounded like a voice coming from my womb. But it didn't sound like "music in my head" either. They were always just fleeting moments, maybe five or ten seconds at the most. Nobody was ever around to hear it with me.

The first time, I was startled and skeptical, but when it started happening again, I just "gave in" and enjoyed it and was convinced that it was my baby feeling happy and relaxed and just "sounding off."

The mystery of this experience is that the child in the womb almost certainly cannot make audible vocal sounds. Although unborn babies go through all the motions of crying, their cries can only produce sound if air is present to vibrate the vocal cords -- not a normal situation (though it happened in former times when physicians injected air into the uterus to make "air amniograms").

So we may ask, what was Sandra hearing? Could it be a variation of the "inner voice?" (Another woman observed that the voice she heard in pregnancy was "like a buzzing sound.") Or could it be one of the sounds described in the literature of yoga, such as the "Om" heard by advanced meditators? Could there be an undiscovered way that the baby can set up an audible vibration inside the womb?

According to obstetrician Dr. Marshall White, Jr., the most likely source of the mysterious sound is the placenta. The placenta hums. Its sound, caused by the turbulence of the blood flow, can be heard with a stethoscope. Recordings from within the womb reveal the hum of the placenta, and it is a deeply satisfying primal sound. It soothes the newborn baby to hear it again, and gives a thrill of pleasure to adults as well.

As Dr. White points out, some women are remarkably attuned to their bodies and their pregnancies, for example feeling the baby's movements long before the "official" time. And so perhaps Sandra, who recalls that she thoroughly enjoyed her pregnancy and found it beautiful, was able in moments of deep relaxation to commune with her baby by sharing his experience of hearing that inner sound.

THE COMMUNICATING KICK

> *Throughout my pregnancy I felt we communicated.*
> *Sometimes if I hadn't felt him kick or move for awhile, I*
> *would verbalize this and within a few seconds he would. He*
> *would put my mind at rest.*
>
> -- Barbara Umberger

The baby's kicking is often interpreted as a message that s/he is alive and well. A kick may be taken by the mother as a sign of pleasure; in other cases it seems to be a protest. Research in this area has produced information that sometimes supports and sometimes contradicts the parents' impressions.

One situation that is apt to produce strong kicking is the sound (or perhaps the feeling?) of parents' angry voices. It's hard to imagine the baby's reaction could indicate pleasure in this case. A woman describes her perception in pregnancy:

> I know that our child is unhappy when we argue. He kicks, but in a different way than usual. This has prompted my husband and me to reconcile each time. This was not so much for the sake of the child, but because the child's perception was accurate, and we needed to come back to our senses, my husband and I.

Many mothers feel that the baby kicks in purposeful response to their requests for reassurance. Perhaps the mother's anxiety triggers the kicking, by way of an adrenaline surge that soon reaches the baby's bloodstream, or through the sound of her quickened heartbeat that the baby hears immediately. Or perhaps the baby telepathically feels the mother's need and responds to it. Judy Goodale describes how reassuring a communicating kick can be:

> I was ill during the last trimester of my pregnancy with a condition called "cholestasis of pregnancy."* The cause is mystifying to me, but the effect is horribly clear: I itched, all over, day and night. The worst part was missing sleep, and the effect my exhaustion had on my state of mind. Also, my mother, with whom I was very close, died in my seventh month after a long illness. So my state of mind was delicate: I alternated between feeling miles away from reality to having hard-core panic attacks for no reason.
>
> I was very much in love with my baby, however. I "knew" he was a boy, and I enjoyed nothing more than talking to my stomach and feeling him move around inside of me. One day in about my eighth month, I was lying in the bathtub at my mother-in-law's house. It was a hot, still day, and I suddenly realized that I hadn't felt the baby move for quite some time. I couldn't remember whether I'd felt him the day before, either. I was so tired and it was so hot and I felt unaccountably lonely and sad. So I put my hand on my belly and asked the baby to move, which he did, unmistakably, at that exact moment. I felt a strong wave of well-being and confidence, and asked him to do it again, which he did, and did again.
>
> I realize that there are coincidences, but this felt completely

"right," somehow;   I wasn't surprised, but it felt sort of "other-worldly."

In the following story, we might question whether the sound that "pierced through" the mother was truly pleasurable to her child. But it is certain that the answering kick was greatly reassuring to the mother!

About eleven weeks into the pregnancy, I had a terribly disturbing nightmare, as many pregnant women do. I dreamed that for some reason my family had convinced me to have a sonogram (something I am strongly against). The picture showed that my uterus was enlarged, but there was no baby! I was devastated, and woke screaming and sobbing in terror! My wonderful husband comforted me as well as he could, but at eleven weeks, I couldn't feel any reassuring kicks from the baby (typically, that doesn't start until at least sixteen weeks).

That day, we went to a Tibetan fair in Berkeley. At one of the booths, a man played a giant Tibetan singing bowl made of quartz. The pure, clear sound of that bowl pierced right through me, and I immediately sat on the grass and closed my eyes, allowing the tones to fill my spirit and ground my emotions. I felt a sudden "coming together" (the only way I can describe it) of spirit and matter within me and then... my baby kicked! I felt it with my hand on my belly as well as inside. I felt as though my child had sent me a very strong message -- "Don't worry! I'm here, and I'm fine, and I LOVE this sound!"

The next week, at a prenatal visit, I told my midwife what happened. She was amazed that I felt the baby move so early, but her assistant wasn't. The assistant, a massage therapist and psychic healer, reminded me that I had an abortion five years before at eleven weeks, and suggested that my body held a "physical memory" of that, and my dream was a manifestation of fears generated by the abrupt ending of my previous pregnancy at that stage. She seemed to think the early sensation of fetal movement was a clear communication from the baby, too.

I didn't feel any more of my baby's movements until I was well into my fourth month -- the "normal" time for this to happen. I guess she was just dancing that day!

Once we are dealing with physical interactions and sensory information, we begin to get some feedback from the baby. We discover that we cannot be sure of automatically pleasing our babies with the sensory input we choose for them. As an example, I assumed that the music I played for my newborn would hold a special attraction for him later on -- but he has never really liked those lovely classical melodies. Nikki Lee had a similar disillusionment:

> My husband and I read aloud to Clelia almost every day in the last two trimesters. We read the book "Ferdinand the Bull." It was my idea. I was expecting a positive response from her once she got out. But there has been none. When last I asked, about two months ago, she said she didn't like that book. So much for pre-birth conditioning!

In his book, *Babies Remember Birth*, David Chamberlain recounts how a pregnant woman noticed her baby becoming more active when she sang loud, low notes. She interpreted this response as a sign of pleasure, but when the child was two years old, he spontaneously revealed many detailed memories of birth and before -- including a complaint that the loud, low notes had been painful to him!

Perhaps the lesson is that we need to be cautious when we attribute meaning to our baby's kicking communications. We may not be able to tell whether they indicate pleasure or irritation or something quite different. However, we can compare our baby's reactions during pregnancy and after birth. For example, a music teacher sees a continuity between her son's musical responses before and after birth:

> Towards the end of my second trimester, I noticed the baby kicking during lessons. At first I didn't make any connection, but after a few weeks, I realized that he only kicked when someone was playing Bach minuets on the piano. He didn't kick during any other pieces, except incidentally, I think. I would also sing and pat my belly in rhythm and he would kick back. After he was born, I noticed that my son reacted more vigorously to Bach minuets than any other music.

Psychologists who study the musical preferences of unborn babies identify a favorable reaction by a steadied heart rate and *decreased* kicking. Of course, for the pregnant woman, a strong kick is much more noticeable than a quieting response. Perhaps by combining the findings of research and our own impressions, we can recognize our babies' likes and dislikes more accurately.

According to research cited in *The Secret Life of the Unborn Child*, musical preferences before birth are quite predictable:

> Vivaldi is one of the unborn child's favorite composers; Mozart

is another. Whenever one of their soaring compositions was put on a phonograph, reports Dr. Clements, fetal heart rates invariably steadied and kicking declined. The music of Brahms and Beethoven, and all forms of rock, on the other hand, drove most fetuses to distraction. They kicked violently when records of these composers were played to their pregnant mothers.

The researcher seems to assume that "violent kicking" always indicates displeasure, as though any strong stimulus must be unwelcome. But having seen babies reveling in their bouts of fierce kicking and arm-waving, I wonder whether the assumption is warranted in every case.

Babies may be more individual in their tastes than the research suggests. The mother who feels that her baby "likes classical and rock but protests against country music" may be interpreting the signs correctly after all. It seems that we need to develop more sensitivity to the physical signals we receive from babies in the womb -- and the evidence that we can misread them should help to keep us open-minded.

CHAPTER EIGHT
THE ESSENCE OF HER PERSONALITY

> *When I was nine months pregnant, I saw her standing in front of me reaching out her arms to hug me. I didn't have a sense of her being necessarily a girl, but I really felt the essence of her personality.*
>
> *--Susie Helme*

In many subtle and surprising ways we may sense something of what our children will be like. Impressions often come in a flash, a sense of "just knowing," or what many call intuition. No doubt some of these ideas are lucky guesses or wishful thinking, but some may well involve communication with our unborn children. Or might they reflect a knowledge that we ourselves possess in the wider ranges of our awareness?

We may actually know more about our children than we realize. During her pregnancy, Janette Patterson painted a picture of a baby in the womb and gave it as a present to the midwife who was caring for her. "When Kelson was born," says Janette, "I could recognize him from the picture I had painted. Of course, you might say that the unborn fetus looks kind of generic, but the features of my painted baby really resembled Kelson's features. It became clear to me that I had painted a picture of him, while I was still pregnant with him."

Long before the birth, parents often gather impressions of their child's personality. The baby's activity in the womb generates some of these ideas ("I could tell my children's personalities by how they moved and kicked, how 'present' they felt --"), but the source of our impressions is often more intangible.

Says one mother, "It's difficult to describe our communication. It's as though her thoughts and feelings were blending with my own; I didn't hear them, I felt them."

Susan Sitler began to sense the differing personalities of her two sons in the characteristic way that each seemed to communicate with her in the womb. She writes that her contacts with both boys during her pregnancies were by way of dreams,

> but also more commonly via images, "messages," sensing, feelings, talking. I'm not sure what word to use... telecommunication? It's hard to pinpoint.
>
> I do know that I was told they were boys and knew their hair color. They also communicated differently with me. Luke's messages came to me strongly, vividly and quickly, which corresponds to his present way of interacting with life. Daniel's messages were softer, gently rich and vivid. So far (if you can tell from a four-month-old), Daniel appears to be a person who soaks in life and gently relishes it. It would fit that my communications with him had been softer.

"I don't think I ever had a true sense of the baby's sex," says Denise Boggs. "Some traits I did however recognize:"

> A good sense of humor, strong willed and very sensitive to the world. This last trait became very evident to me during a workshop on therapeutic touch. The entire weekend the energy of the participants was very high, and the baby was right in there too. During one exercise called "Making the heart connection," where two people try to connect through their heart centers, my partner found that it was impossible to make the connection with only me. She had to also make the connection with the baby. She said it was like the baby was saying "me too," so we had a triangle connection.

For those of us who have never sensed any pre-birth impressions of our children's traits, it is difficult to imagine how this might feel. Louise Richardson compares the feeling to a sensation she had known in earlier years, when walking home after dark through a poorly lit and isolated neighborhood:

> A few times, I had a feeling that someone was nearby and that I was in danger. It was a strange tingling feeling in my bones that had no logic and no sounds to support it. Whenever I had this feeling I ran home as fast as I could.
>
> The feeling I had with my daughter about her personality was a similar kind of feeling "in my bones." The facets of her personality that I picked up were emotional traits and I picked them up on an emotional level within me. It was as if her

personality would try to come into my body and my emotions, but since we are two individuals, it couldn't quite be done.

I somehow knew she was a girl. Throughout my pregnancy, I kept getting vibes about what she would be like. I only had these feelings with her when I was relaxed with no interruptions, usually when I went to bed. I used to lie there and rub my belly, even when it wasn't very big yet, and just massage it and enjoy the feeling of a baby inside me. This was the only time of day I could pay much attention to my pregnancy and actually feel it, after tending an active toddler all day.

I learned that my daughter is very determined and headstrong when she has her mind set on something. I know all curious babies are like this but she seems to be more so than any baby I've ever seen. She doesn't give up easily when she is deterred. When I sensed her personality prenatally, I felt she would be someone who would get her way by using her charm, good looks and smiles with an ulterior motive. This is becoming very obvious as she develops.

At the time of conception, Mary Halter Petersen sensed a strong and loving person nearby. From later experiences in the pregnancy, she says she "came to identify this feeling/person with the being of our son." She writes:

All throughout the pregnancy I'd feel this same adult male figure as a very strong, determined, intense personality. Though at first during the pregnancy I dreamed only of girl babies, by the seventh month I could only imagine holding a boy baby and began to feel that this intense male figure was somehow our son. We never had any other boy's names chosen other than Luke or Lukas, which seemed to be the only fittingly "strong" name.

Now eight and a half years old, Lukas is definitely a strong-willed, intense, determined personality. He screamed quite a bit as a baby and has ever since been very vocal with what he wants and how he wants it. He once told us that he was here to help people understand things, perhaps much like that Jesus type personality I kept envisioning with his pregnancy. He has always been an intense person, expressing acute particularities and great frustration when things don't work out accordingly. I feel now that his personality is very much in keeping with those early pre-birth feelings and images I had.

Some mothers tell of having specific thoughts or emotions that they perceive as belonging to the baby. One woman even felt that certain dreams she experienced in pregnancy were not really her own but the baby's, "as though brought about by some ability of the child to go into my psyche and conjure up images."

A mother describes occasions when she felt she was sensing her baby's feelings:

> It wasn't guessing on my part, because I wasn't thinking about her at the time; it was a sudden sort of thought that came into my head that I was sure was *her* thought, not mine. She was a really active baby throughout the pregnancy; I felt like I had a gymnast inside doing tumbling tricks. A couple of times I swear I knew that she had her head upside down and was trying to right herself and was getting a little miffed with herself.

Says Sally Calvin, "I never knew anyone else had this happen, but for me it was so real and undeniable":

> I suddenly felt taken over by another being. Because it sure wasn't me standing in the doorway looking side to side and up and down as if it were the first time ever doing so. As I walked around the house I felt as if the baby's personality or thoughts and feelings were coming through me. I had a smile on my face but it was the baby's smile of being happy to be alive. Euphoria! I'm so happy we shared that together. Now I know fetuses do have happy thoughts. This was in the twenty-seventh week of gestation; the child is great and well now but was born at twenty-eight weeks.

Rosalie Denenfeld is a psychotherapist whose Master's Thesis focused on pre-birth attachment. As part of her research she invited a group of women, pregnant for the first time, to participate in a series of meetings. Together they explored and shared their discoveries about the relationship between themselves and their unborn children.

One woman, Barbara Wolf, reported, "Every once in a while, I have a sense of a feeling that I don't know where it is coming from. And then I realize that I am not the one having the feeling." The first occasion was during a summer thunderstorm.

Barbara describes how the bedroom in her hilltop house has big windows and feels very open to the weather, which she enjoys. "When there's storms," she says, "it seems like it comes right into the room." She loves hearing thunder and watching the lightning flash. But one night during a storm she woke feeling intensely afraid. She got up and walked around the house, puzzled at the fear, since she knew she personally was not afraid of storms. "And all of a sudden, I realized that I wasn't the one who was afraid; it was the baby who was afraid. So I talked to it, I told it that it was a storm and that it was the noise that was probably disturbing but it was okay. The fear went away."

MOOD AS MESSAGE

In pregnancy, when we share the same physical space with another being, perhaps our spirits and personalities overlap and blend as well. Thus there may be a kind of communication through altered awareness, unfamiliar moods, changes in ourselves that later we look back on and wonder: was that my baby's consciousness mixing with mine?

Mary Halter Peterson's impressions of her second child were associated with changes she noticed in herself, almost as though the baby's personality were affecting her own:

> From the very beginning of her pregnancy I "knew" she was a girl and I never called her anything but Hannah. The feelings I had about her were always gentle, mild and with an emotional quality about them. I chose many pinks and laces as I sewed clothes for her, making little clothes that to me were pretty as well as practical. I was never one to want to lean heavily to cultural dressing patterns, for instance I never chose clothing that said things like "little slugger," "champ" or "little princess" on them, nor wanted to have primarily "pink for girls and blue for boys."
>
> However with Hannah I continuously found myself attracted to the pinks and "pretty." These kinds of feelings were my main pre-birth contact with Hannah. Now six years old, her proclaimed favorite colors are "pink, purple and red." She loves "pretty" things and is very observant of women's dress, sometimes more than I wish. I have never worn makeup or high-heeled shoes, or much jewelry, yet she watches these in other women and comments.
>
> She is a very sensitive person and has required almost opposite parenting styles to Lukas. She cries easily with little provocation. Her personality seems to fit the impressions and feelings I experienced during the pregnancy with her. She is a very "motherly" kind of person, in touch emotionally and in tune with relationship needs.

Another woman describes a similar feeling that her consciousness was infused with the personality of her child, bringing some surprising and welcome changes:

> My second pregnancy evolved as an altered state of consciousness, started off slowly, gradually grew and grew. I felt a tremendous sense of spiritual well-being during pregnancy, although I experienced to a heightened degree the travail of pregnancy with a toddler to mind. Sexually, I was quite alive, awakened to new experiences, broadened -- enlightened to a surprising degree, pleasant nonetheless. This experience continued right up until weaning last month; gradually I have felt a shift now that I've ovulated again, baby now ten months old. Many times during pregnancy I sensed that baby enjoyed lovemaking along with us in a very healthy, pure way. Almost as though "she" (didn't know then, but guessed) directed, orchestrated us to lovemaking!
>
> Now that she is weaned I can see the whole of my consciousness was altered by her presence in my body, from pregnancy to birth to nursing, her personality, her soul enveloped me, accompanied me. This feeling has now changed more into the gift she has given me through my experience of "her." I wrote in my very sketchy journal halfway through my pregnancy, "Getting to know how loving and gentle you are, my little friend," and this characterizes my impression of my second daughter, a gentle, loving little friend, companion, who came to stay and brought me her gifts of sensuality and well being.

These stories make me wonder whether we may all be sharing one another's moods and feelings more often than we realize. Perhaps we are always blending together to some extent, and never more so than during pregnancy.

An American woman living in Greece experienced an unusual mood change while pregnant with her first child. Only much later did she realize that it may have been a subtle and wonderful kind of communication:

> I hoped for, even expected, some kind of psychic contact with my child. I am a bit intuitive and can often sense the feelings of those around me; I do receive dream messages and impressions that later are proven correct. So it seemed natural to expect a psychic connection with my child before birth. I looked forward to it.
>
> Throughout pregnancy, I waited, often sitting or lying quietly

with my arms and hands cradling my belly. I felt fine, at peace, receptive. No message, nothing. There did not seem to be *anything* coming from this child (except physical movement, of course).

As for myself, I was *very* happy, healthy and whole. I had lots of every kind of energy (more than usual), a tremendous sense of optimism, and absolutely no fear whatsoever (although I was in a foreign country, far from family and friends and would give birth there, in "foreign" hands).

I felt -- an over-riding sense -- *complete*, as if nothing in the world outside of myself and this baby had any significance.

After the birth, and in the years that followed, I wondered about the experience and thought very much about pregnancy. I did not become pregnant again; I did have a wonderful bond with this very special child (who has good psychic powers of her own). I wondered how we could be so connected in life-after-birth and not have felt any contact before. And often I missed -- longed for -- the wonderful feelings of pregnancy. That *wholeness*.

Recently it occurred to me. Perhaps the "message" I had expected *was* actually received. The wonderful feelings of wholeness, content, not needing anything outside of myself/and the baby -- this unit of closeness -- the great optimism and total lack of fear -- perhaps this was my baby's experience as well.

It is very easy now, remembering the wonderful way I felt, to project that, to see it as the baby's sensual experience. And it makes sense, too, that the "message" from the child is a physical/emotional one, without words.

It's good to be reminded that contacts with our unborn children do not have to be in the form of voices or visions or dramatic dreams. Even something as subtle as an attraction to a new color may be the connecting link.

The hungers we feel while pregnant are not just for foods that the body may need; there are cravings for emotional and spiritual nourishment as well. We can pay attention to these cravings, with the possibility in mind that they may be a connection with our child. For instance, while pregnant with my son I felt intense "hunger" for cool white thoughts of snow and mountain peaks, and (oddly enough) for isolated communities of women only. I wonder whether such uncharacteristic desires could be symbolic images of the child's nature -- or his memories filtering into our mind -- or perhaps even our own memories of lives we have shared with him.

A mother may be able to tune in to her baby's nature through the "flavor" of her consciousness during pregnancy. Often a special quality is felt, such as love or strength or peace, as though it is imprinted on the mother's psyche by the child's presence.

Thanks to my nervous nature and too-busy mind, I seldom feel the quality of peace, though I often wish for it. My strongest experiences of peace have been connected with my pregnancies. One of these came on the third day of a miscarriage, when towards evening a gentle rain began to fall and suddenly my distress and confusion gave way to a soothing peacefulness.

Then there was an unforgettable experience a few nights before Roselyn was born. Sitting up in bed, gazing at the nearly-full moon, I felt the deepest peace, and along with it a sense of great beauty. What I've learned since then about pre-birth communion has me wondering whether Roselyn was touching me that night with qualities she was bringing with her.

In an earlier chapter I related that during the pregnancy I had dreamed her name was Shulamith. While working with the material of this chapter, I came across a book of names that listed Shulamith and gave its meaning. And a shiver ran down my back when I read it -- for Shulamith means peace.

CHAPTER NINE
A PRESENCE

The sense of presence, while it might seem a simple self-evident thing, is really quite mysterious. In the first place, it can describe at least two differing experiences, and probably many more.

There is the pervading presence that fills our whole field, enveloping us. Parents sometimes feel such a presence in the days after their baby's birth, filling the house with "something," an almost tangible substance.

And there is the more boundaried presence that we sense as a being, with various degrees of definition such as size, location and even personality. Throughout the cycle of pre-conception to birth, this second kind of presence is typical. Though some encounters begin with a pervading "thereness," they usually come quickly into focus as a being.

Let's take a closer look at these perceptions. How do we become aware of a presence? Do we even feel the presence of a person in the same room with us? Not necessarily -- we tend to rely on other senses. But most people have felt, for example, the uncanny sensation that someone is staring at them. This feeling is akin to what people describe in their encounters with a "disembodied" presence.

The sense of presence is near neighbor to several other senses. It can be closest to a touch, or it can blend into an image or a sound. It can be an enveloping atmosphere electric with meaning. It can be frightening, or reassuring and warm. It can be soft and rustling like wings.

The sense of presence can bring with it an intense feeling of familiarity -- a feeling of "I know you! You are someone I know well and yet I had forgotten you..." It may convey a quality of wisdom, or sweetness, or great love.

Like the sensation of deja vu, which is thought to be associated with small electrical "accidents" in the brain, the sense of presence can be produced by the brain as hallucination. What this means is that even when we feel most certainly that we are meeting another consciousness, we are wise to question our experience and bear in mind that we are capable of creating it literally out of nothing.

Which is all very well to say -- but our encounter with a presence may be so soul-satisfying that it becomes difficult to question. To feel that one is in touch with a consciousness, another being, is a thrilling part of many pre-birth contacts.

BEFORE CONCEPTION

Many, if not most, of the contacts before conception are experiences of a presence. Often the presence has a quality, such as feminine, loving, joyous, warm, playful, soothing. It may be "almost visible," as in Lani Rosenberger's description: "It's like seeing something out of the corner of your eye, but before you can turn your head or focus, it's gone!" It may resolve into communicated words or feelings or even a distinct impression of personality.

Sometimes there is a "knowing" that this is contact with a child coming to be conceived. In other cases there is simply the sense of a presence without a clear feeling of who it might be, and later we come to identify it (rightly or wrongly) with the child. My own encounters were of this kind.

A few months before conceiving my daughter, I noticed something odd that occasionally happened as I relaxed before falling asleep. It was a sudden delight, a sense of having just caught sight of the dearest person in the world to me. "But when I think of everyone I love," I wrote in some puzzlement, "it doesn't match anyone I know."

Later, exactly one month before her conception, I recorded an "extraordinary dream experience:"

> There was one bizarre dream I can't even remember, then a gap, then I feel an "angelic presence." What it comes down to is perceiving the presence of another being. I felt an intense desire for this "presence" and it seemed as though I was trying to merge into it in a sexual way -- but I woke up realizing that this desire was only partly sexual and partly beyond sexual. Somehow I knew it was "too late" to satisfy it on the level of sex. It was like a desire for another being that I felt in my whole mid-body. This presence that was just there in front of me and around me was like a missing half of myself...

IN PREGNANCY

From the evidence of the stories, the sense of a presence is more common before conception than during pregnancy. In fact, as we have seen, it sometimes disappears when conception occurs. But what may be more significant is that it is virtually the same experience whether it is felt before or after conception, or even following miscarriage or a baby's death.

Would we expect a presence felt in pregnancy to be centered in the womb? Only rarely is it described this way. Nikki Lee recalls "little bursts of sunlight warmth from within," and Clare Adams feels an "energy" in her womb different from her own. More frequently, people speak of sensing a presence near them -- beside, above, or just "around," as in Lucy Kennedy's recollection:

> Throughout the pregnancy, from the moment of conception (if not a little before!), I felt the vitality of Duke's energy in the air around me, as it were. I wasn't surprised when I saw that our baby was a boy!

Vivien Beirne explains in detail what the sense of a presence was like for her:

> I can best describe the feeling that I had for a few months (at least) before conception, and then after it, as the same awareness one has of another person standing in the same room -- only not being able to see the person physically, or hear with the ears what is being communicated.
>
> And although the body was developing within mine, my communication was directed more toward the presence I felt near me than to my womb for many months -- as if the ego didn't quite enter the body directly until close to the end. Even at the end, I communicated to this presence *both* within and around me. It didn't feel like the soul of the baby could fit into the little body.
>
> This is similar to the sense I now have, when considering my almost six month old baby; I sense that he's been around a lot longer than that. He also seems bigger than his little body can hold.

It is not easy for people to give exact descriptions of how it feels to experience a presence. Carole, a writer, explains something of the paradoxical nature of her own encounter. Part of the difficulty, she says, is that it felt "so strange and so natural at the same time."

Carole was using an IUD which had just thwarted a beginning pregnancy. A few nights later, she was visited by "a presence like a tiny ball of light which expanded and made itself felt as a soul." She writes:

I was completely conscious and present, and experienced the being as another being in communication with me. I do not know if I was awake or asleep; I may have been out of body; I was certainly in some altered state. I remember as it began to happen being aware of lying on my back in the bed and not being able to move.

As a visual phenomenon, it started as a "pop" of light in a dark room, and I kind of tuned to it I guess you could say. I was fully present as myself and gradually became aware of who the other being was. I experienced the being bouncing around like a tiny sparkling light in the dark -- like Tinkerbell from "Peter Pan." I also heard (or felt) words communicated and just talked with her/him and it seemed like I was looking at a person.

I think I'm trying to describe at least two levels of experience going on simultaneously here, both beyond the ordinary, but I'm not sure that they are different, just different ways of perceiving or explaining one experience. I didn't see a person exactly, but it would be easy to give the experience those dimensions (i.e. describe the person) because the sense of who and what the being was became very clear. It is like there is a pattern of energy that this being is and that translated to my daughter in this life. But even then I had a sense of knowing the being.

The "light" (being) was clearly outside of myself, yet the experience of communicating was different from talking to someone. It was more like dream communication or telepathy. It's almost as if I moved into an envelope of some sort so that we were parallel and communicated through a higher body/dimension than my usual physical dwelling. At the same time it was exactly like standing around talking with someone except that I wasn't using my physical apparatus at all, and it was perfectly natural and comfortable to communicate that way.

Carole remarks that it feels insufficient to recount the experience as a sequence of events -- first one thing happening and then another -- since it bore a sense of timelessness or of an expanded present.

The sense of presence can also be a physical sensation. In Chapter Seven, Holly Richardson described the "prickles" down her back that she interpreted as the presence of the baby she was carrying. She adds:

I savored every visit and sometimes told the baby "Hi" and that we loved him (or her) and were excited to have him or her in our home. These visits pretty much tapered off after I could feel her moving. When she was born, it soon became obvious that she had come into this world with some pretty severe handicaps. It was some time later, before I was completely through my grieving, that I read again about her visits in my journal. I realized that she had come to comfort me! She knew that her physical body would have many problems, and I feel that she wanted to convey her love for me, as well as her readiness to come. She is now four years old and remains severely handicapped, but is truly a joy to have around.

Holly felt the same prickles at the beginning of a pregnancy that miscarried. Eventually, they became her way of recognizing the spiritual presence of a child wanting to come to her -- either through conception or by adoption. (Her remarkable story continues in Chapter Thirteen.)

THAT LOVING PRESENCE

How does it feel when a "spirit child" visits? A thread that runs through so many stories is the love that is experienced with these contacts.

"A great feeling of love washed over me as if pouring over my head... the sensation of great all-encompassing love was overwhelming." Expressions like this recur throughout stories of pre-conception and pregnancy as well. People speak of being cuddled, hugged, soothed and surrounded by love. They mention feelings of warmth and familiarity. One mother describes the presence as feeling "like an old friend had hugged me." Another says:

> I remember feeling my "companion" with me when walking, driving, working, listening to music, reading, sharing time with my husband and other friends and family -- even before I could physically feel him in my abdomen. I could never feel lonely... It felt like I was reunited with a friend, a friend who is easygoing and joyful.

Laura Ziemba describes her sensations while pregnant:

> There are times when I will be just sitting down or not necessarily thinking about the baby but just this wave of love will come over me and it is just like the being is hugging and nurturing me. It's so special.

Lucy Kennedy recalls similar impressions, that intensified during the last, "extra" week of her pregnancy:

> Throughout the pregnancy, I felt love and caring for me flowing to me from my baby. Danny was a week "late" in being born, and I believe that he needed that extra time inside to complete this bonding process with me before we entered into the distractions of bodies and personalities. Here's what I wrote in my diary three days before Danny's birth: "I've been feeling a new sense of bonding with this baby during our extra time together. I feel very strongly, yet gently, how this baby loves me and loves being with me..."

Many people believe that we are born into a particular family in order to learn lessons that we need. But in the stories collected here, a stronger impression is that we come for love... to love. I can think of no better way to end this section than with four stories that illustrate the experience of that loving presence.

The first story is from the journal of a man whose wife was eight months pregnant with their first child. His experience came during a "rebirthing session," a breathing technique that is intended to bring emotional release and clarity:

> I'm home now from a most amazing rebirth. I drove there thinking about my family history -- fears and anger. But my rebirth was all about love!
>
> Our baby, or "spirit" baby was with me, on my chest during the rebirth. I was crying so much. So much love for this beautiful being. I cried and cried. It was so beautiful.
>
> I loved my baby. I felt so honored and grateful to have him/her with me.
>
> The big message from the baby is that *I am love.* I have heard this message before but never felt it like I did today. I felt myself totally and fully *as love.* I just kept crying. It felt so wonderful. The baby said s/he was coming to bring this love to us. And then I thought, "Well OK, this love stuff is great. Now I'll keep breathing and get to some old messy family stuff." But the baby said, No -- love is the only answer. Just be loving. Just keep loving.
>
> Another message was that the baby was so happy to be coming to be with us. To play with Nancy and me and have fun and heal our inner child. Later the message came, "I am here to heal your whole family." I even got an image of my mom and dad (who are divorced) hugging. Yes, I kept crying. Happy tears.

The last message I got from the baby was that I have to remember to "let go." At that moment I was actually clasping my hands tightly over my chest -- I had to physically let go!

The next story is from a mother of two, who wanted a third child. "At times the yearning was so strong that it actually hurt," she says...

I was sitting with my two sons Matthew age six and Daniel age three. We were kind of laughing and being silly. My husband was in the next room working. It was the strangest feeling. It was as if someone was watching us. I could even sense the direction it was coming from in the room. I was filled with a very strong love feeling. It filled my entire self. No one else seemed to feel or notice anything. It was a beautiful moment -- I knew it was not coming from me. I knew it was someone else, and I knew it was a gentle and strong love that someone felt, but I didn't know who.

It was truly unique for me and something that is hard to describe to someone who has not experienced it as well. My husband laughs at me while I am writing -- but I know it happened. I just can't explain what it was. It was a lovely experience. I remember feeling sad when it was over and wishing "she" or "it" would come back.

I'm not sure if I was pregnant at the time (and didn't know it) or if I became pregnant shortly after. My husband and I were blessed with a beautiful baby girl. She is who I was yearning for so badly and she is my dream come true. I always felt there was someone missing in our family until she was born.

A loving presence can also be met in a dream. "One night, at the beginning of my eighth month, I had the most wonderful dream," says Janette Patterson. She has no doubt that the presence she encountered was the baby girl soon to be born:

In the dream I was pregnant, sitting on a chair, very relaxed and still, as if I were waiting for something. Indeed, I was waiting, waiting for my first child. While I was sitting there, gently embracing my beautifully rounded belly, the little baby inside me started to emerge from my womb. It was a painless, very gradual process. I was in awe and filled with joy and curiosity as I patiently watched this birth. The baby simply unfolded herself in my lap and I embraced her tenderly and lovingly, letting her rest on my lap. I bent over her lovely face to be closer to her, to study her and get to know her. We were both quiet and looked at each other. She was pretty with soft features, pale smooth skin and dark sparkling eyes. We just gazed at each other for a long time and felt the love between us and the knowledge that we belonged together. I was happy and proud to have such a lovely child. I was content to just be with her and embrace her. What a precious moment.

I wanted to greet her, tell her how much I loved and appreciated her, so I said, "Hi, baby," very softly and lovingly with a big smile. She smiled back at me and very peacefully responded, "Hi." In the dream this was the most natural, wonderful experience. There was nothing else to be said. We were so close and knew intuitively that we loved each other very much...

My little girl let me know in my dream that she was peaceful and happy and we could feel the love between us. All I had to do was be open and receptive to the little person inside of me -- and listen.

In the final story, a waking vision accompanies the experience of a loving presence.

"In Touch With Love Itself"

I was one month pregnant with my second child. My four year old daughter, Catherine, and I were folding laundry in the family room. Oddly enough, Catherine, who hadn't needed an afternoon nap in perhaps a year, goes to the couch and immediately falls asleep! "Some unexpected, precious time to myself," I think.

Suddenly, I feel a heaviness in the room, a *presence*. It becomes almost palpable, a never-before-experienced feeling of "someone" being there with me. I can laugh at the situation; am I losing my mind or what?! It lingers, heavy. I look around, finally saying out loud, "Who's there?" I continue asking and looking, laughing a little at what I must look like. Finally, a feeling; a feeling that I am in touch with something very GOOD. LOVE ITSELF.

I suddenly see an image directly in front of me of a young, fair-haired, fair-skinned man. I know he is the spirit of the child within me. I feel such a sense of love, "karmic destiny," of HISTORY between us, but yet a sense that I haven't been with him for a very long time. A someone I have deep, deep love for and a profound connection with. I now know that we are reunited as mother and son. I feel such GRATITUDE. With tears running down my face, I say out loud, "Thank God we are together again, you and I! We're back together and my love for you runs as deep as deep comes! Welcome. Welcome back."

I quickly get up and go to another room to find paper and pen to write down what occurred. I am still emotionally overcome. When I finish writing, I pause a moment and breathe deeply. Suddenly Catherine calls my name. She's awake! I am struck by the coincidence of her brief, unexpected nap and my "visitation."

Much of what I have written today is quoted from what I wrote that afternoon in 1988. I went on to have a fair-haired, very fair-skinned boy. He's sixteen months old now and we're very close!

PART II
THE COOPERATIVE BOND

At first, as I gathered accounts of pre-birth communication, I found myself arguing with every story. Playing devil's advocate, I probed for signs of self-deception on the part of each person claiming to have felt a contact.

But my focus shifted as I began to see a pattern emerging from all these varied experiences -- a pattern so consistent and so exciting that it can change our concept of the parent-and-child connection.

These contacts and communications reveal a relationship whose essence is cooperation. There is considerable evidence of the child's helpful intent, and of a mutual process of adjustment that involves both the parents and the baby. As one mother put it, it almost seems that "the spirit and the parents are all in psychic cahoots."

In the following chapters, experiences are shared that illustrate this cooperative bond of prospective parent and child. Here are stories of people reaching out to invite a soul into their family, stories of children apparently persuading a reluctant parent to accept them, and stories that suggest the importance of an agreement on all sides. Further experiences related in this section explore the cooperative bond in adoption and other non-biological families. Finally, there are stories that afford speculation about the powers of the soul.

Accounts of pre-birth contact seem to imply a different relationship with our children than what we once supposed. They suggest that the coming child is not the fragile, totally vulnerable "blank slate" we may have pictured, but a strong, self-determined entity with pre-existing personality and intentions. If this is true, some of our traditional attitudes about parenting may need to be aired out, checked for wear and possibly discarded.

CHAPTER TEN
INVITATIONS

Where does the parent-and-child connection begin? Who takes the first steps in this dance?

Though some people become parents without really planning it, for many of us the transition to parenthood begins when we first consider having a child. Even before taking physical form in our lives, a baby begins to change us.

We look with newly critical eyes at the world we've created, to see whether it can support and nourish a child. We sort out old fears and prejudices about having children. We question our readiness to be responsible on so many levels, especially when anticipating our first baby. Some people consult oracles for guidance; some pray or devise special rituals to invite a child into the family.

The time of preparing for conception (or adoption) can be a period of intensified effort to know ourselves better and to remove inner obstacles. This work is perhaps the beginning of our contribution to the cooperative bond -- part of a joint creative enterprise that may begin well before the pregnancy.

As we try to create a welcoming environment in our lives and within ourselves, we may sense the first connections with our future children. One mother describes it this way: "There was a long 'pre-conception bonding time' before my second child. I spent a long time planning her, preparing for her, and felt I was getting a sense of who she would be."

In this chapter we will explore the many ways of preparing ourselves and inviting a child into our lives. We begin with one woman's account of how her inner work dovetailed with her sense of approaching parenthood.

A Message of Pure Love: Brenda's Story

The spirit of the being I'm carrying (until early July) and I made contact before conception. It was a very powerful experience.

I guess it all began with yoga class, although the visions I'd had on the acupuncture table and the experiences I'd had while pursuing my Native American heritage certainly set the stage and made me more open to such possibilities.

Before beginning yoga with Donna, I had a dream. I dreamed that I was going to a Moon Lodge in the woods bordering on our property. (A Moon Lodge is a retreat for women during their "moon time" or menstruation. Such a retreat was common among most Native American tribes.) I was a newcomer to the lodge. When I arrived, only one other woman was there. I didn't know her, though she somehow seemed familiar. The lodge itself was a small cabin -- one room. In it was a massage table, among other things. The woman greeted me, offered me tea. Then I lay on the table, and she began massaging me. She eventually massaged my pelvic area which, though it initially made me uncomfortable, I allowed.

The next evening, my friend Julie called. A slot in Donna's yoga class had opened up. I could take it if I chose. It was a small class, only four people, and only a few miles from my house. When Julie asked me about the yoga class, I realized that the woman in my dream had been Donna, whom I didn't know, but whom I had seen in the Co-op and around. When I told Julie about my dream, she was astonished and told me that Donna had just told her that she'd dreamt about me the very same night that I had dreamt about her.

Donna later told me about her dream. She was standing by a small waterfall which was running over a smooth, slanted stone, like a slide. People were coming up to her out of a crowd, and she was helping them down the slide. Somehow she knew that this was some sort of rite of initiation. Then she saw me in the crowd. We greeted each other with recognition and embraced, which she thought strange upon awakening, as we really didn't know one another. Then she helped me down the slide.

Our dreams, though using different images and metaphors, were essentially about the same thing. In both dreams, she is the teacher, I the initiate. In my dream, the root chakra, located in the pelvic area, was the focus. In her dream, the water slide is a symbol of sexuality which is governed by the root chakra. As it turns out, at the very first yoga session I attended as in many later sessions, we did a lot of work with the root chakra through our yoga postures. Through this I learned to relax more, to rid myself of some of the inhibitions and tensions that had built up over the years. An interesting aside is that Donna is also a Shiatsu masseuse, which I didn't know when I dreamed that she was massaging me.

Our yoga classes progressed for several months: winter through spring into summer. Gary and I had decided the previous summer to try to conceive near the end of the summer of 1992. The coming of this child was on my mind a lot.

In August, I missed a period. I felt sure that I was pregnant. I began feeling that the child was near me. I would be driving in my car when a ray of light would enter my car and I would feel a presence, loving, male and somehow familiar. I talked to him, explained how I felt about him coming into this life as my child, and I felt like we were communicating, that he was listening and observing intently.

The message I received was one of pure love. There really seemed to be a spirit present. He (it?) was there to check me out, but also to acknowledge all the conscious work that I had been doing on myself over the last couple of years. As I communed with my "Bright Star," as I had begun calling this spirit to myself, I was being told that I was ready. The breaking of old patterns, the reconnection with a personal spirituality was paying off. I had not been found lacking. My breasts swelled; my face glowed.

Around this time I had scheduled a private session with Donna who wanted to do some Shiatsu on me. It was an incredible experience. While she was working on me, I continually felt the presence of my "Bright Star," as well as experiencing many other visions and sensations. Wind seemed to be coursing all around and through me, though we were in an enclosed room. At one point I lost my sense of physical mass and couldn't distinguish where my body ended and the floor or air began. Images of dragonflies on the wind appeared. Then I felt like a dragonfly, even feeling my wings.

As I came back to myself, the presence was still there, bright and loving as always. I felt it in my uterine area, yet it was also definitely still of the spirit world. Communing with this being was like communicating between worlds. I refer to this being sometimes as "it," sometimes as "he," because that's the sense I got, that as a spirit it had no gender, but that it was appearing to me, for some reason, as a male.

As the session ended, Donna said, "A lot was going on with you!" I agreed. Then she said, "I really sensed strongly the presence of a being. Are you pregnant?" Then we shared the experiences we had had during the massage and discovered that our impressions of this gentle, ancient being were very similar.

I can't exactly remember when the communications with "Bright Star" ceased, but they did, and in September I had a very heavy period with one extremely heavy clot, most likely an early miscarriage.

We conceived officially in October. During this pregnancy, I haven't quite felt the same definitive connection with a developed being, but I do feel that the baby I now sense is the same being who visited in August. I don't know why he came, left and returned, but I believe that that is what happened.

After the birth of her child, Brenda wrote, "Patric is a loving, gentle soul. Yes, he is that wondrous being -- I'm sure of it."

SEEKING GUIDANCE

Should I have a child? Is this the right time?

Some of us find help with these decisions by consulting oracles such as the Tarot and the I Ching, or we may turn to counselors and psychics for another perspective on the situation. Miriam writes:

> The last few months, we have been asking for guidance regarding enlarging our family. I asked the I Ching about the upcoming fertile cycle and the answer I received said, in part: "Life begets life and evolves itself in an ordered and divine fashion. The attraction between mates, with an underlying interest toward social unity and, perhaps, progeny is the emphasis here." We shall see what unfolds. I am praying that only a soul truly interested in joining us make the journey because I don't want to yank someone in off a cloud. If no one else wishes to join us, we're fine.

Uncertain of our decision, we may wish for a sign of divine approval and an indication that the time is right. Inner experiences may not be enough; we look for confirmation in reflections from outside ourselves. Shortly before conceiving her daughter, Kathryn Mayton wrote about the process she was going through to clarify her thinking and confirm her intuitive feelings:

> I have decided to have a baby. Yesterday, during my meditation, I felt the energy of my baby girl. She came to me in a soft golden glow. I could sense her presence on the left side of my body and the glow was "seen" in my mind's eye also on the left side. When I meditate, I allow my consciousness to just sort of sink into my body and focus on my third eye in the center of my forehead. All is black there and occasionally I "see" various muted colors. At the time I felt the energy, I asked if this was the energy of my baby and I felt or sensed (instead of heard) the answer was yes. All day I had been feeling very aroused sexually and knew that I was indeed very fertile.
>
> I have been asking Father/Mother/God for a sign; and for me, a sign would have to be very dramatic and forceful for me to get it. Some sort of sign that I could know without doubt that God's will is for me to have a baby. My sign wasn't very dramatic and what's more, I have to trust myself that I even felt it. Before doing my meditation, I was consulting my Book of Runes. The Book of Runes is an oracle that addresses the hidden fears and motivations that may shape the future by their unseen presence. The issue I raised was the timeliness of having a baby now.
>
> My interpretations of the Runes I drew:
>
> (1) I am told to listen to what I am telling myself in my meditation -- listen to my inner Self. I am definitely in tune with my own rhythms. And this period of not working has been very beneficial for that. I am definitely revaluing and realigning, as there are also unseen powers at work here.
>
> (2) Again, mention of the moon and intuitiveness I need to cultivate. The completion of beginnings signified that I must complete what I began a few years back when I became pregnant and then aborted that pregnancy. I believe that before I was born, the Powers That Be and the essence of the energy that I am, all got together and decided what sort of lessons I needed to learn in this lifetime. My family all had lessons to learn with me and I with them so we all agreed to come together. The wonderful part of all this is that nothing is pre-destined. I had a choice in every situation -- to interact or not. Based on that belief, my first child wanted the experience of life in human form for just twelve short weeks. When I remember my state of mind during that pregnancy, I am glad I didn't have the baby. I felt so unhappy with myself, and I believe that abortion helped me to realize that I had to shift my perception of myself and indeed of

life itself. Consequently, I now have the strength to achieve completion. I need not become pregnant right now, but I did need to resolve indecision about it.

(3) The joyful opportunity regarding ill-timed action is that yesterday an action may have been ill-timed, but today it could be right on the mark. That's the beauty of knowing that every moment is new. Matters of trust and confidence are at issue -- trust and confidence in my decisions and in myself.

Not only did the Runes and the meditation happen in one day, but I went to see the trance medium who channels an energy called Aronk. He is amazingly correct in his predictions and seems to know things about me that no one else could. I have asked him before about having a child and he was the one who told me that a female child energy was around me and that I could become pregnant if I wanted to and if I did, it would be a time of completion for me. So, I asked him again (almost wishing he would say Do it! so I could give myself permission), and he said the same thing, basically, that I have had some close calls in dodging seed.

I told Aronk that I notice in myself a reluctance to bring another life in to share this lifestyle and my husband with me and it coincides with a reluctance I feel to let others into my life. I am so content by myself. What he said is that I hate restrictions. I'm a rebel. This is true. One of the biggest considerations I have is the restrictions a child would impose. No more picking up and going when I feel like it. Not so, Mr. Aronk said. Take your child with you and find a job where you can take your child to be with you. We assume that is not an option for us and then don't ask. The thought of that brought me so much joy.

Then, as if all of this wasn't enough for one day, when John came home in the middle of my meditation, I shared with him all of my revelations, though I was not then clear about my decision. He said he thought it would be exciting to have a child. He wants to teach her to sail, to allow her to stand watch when she's old enough to know that we trust her. He said that all he ever wanted was his mother to trust him and he would give his child that trust. He thinks he would be a wonderful father. I asked him if he would participate 100% in the care of our child and he said that is the only way he would do it. He said he is not resisting it anymore. Oh, I cried. Heartily. It was as if I released him from being the resistance or reason I couldn't make my decision to have a baby. Now it seems he is willing to participate in the decision as well.

It took me a long time to fall asleep last night and when I did, guess what I dreamed about? I am thinking, thinking, thinking, but with a peace I've not experienced before. I am also trusting, trusting, trusting, that I will know when it is time. What I know is that I have asked Life for what I want and everything I ask for I receive, as I have asked...

WE MAY TELL OURSELVES WITH SYMBOLS

Even without Tarot cards, runes or the I Ching, we may find symbols and oracles in our own dreams, telling us when we are ready to conceive. We notice synchronistic happenings -- suddenly there are babies and pregnant women everywhere we go. Or we feel a sudden attraction to baby images and symbols of fertility, conception and birth.

Katryn Lavanture, for example, found herself drawn to the baby section of a bookstore, and to a card with the image of a fetus surrounded by dolphins. (Dolphins are becoming a symbol of birth, perhaps because we recognize that the word "dolphin" literally means "womb." But there's more to the connection, as we'll see later.) Not long afterwards, Katryn unexpectedly became pregnant.

Joanna's first husband was opposed to having children and induced her to abort the pregnancies that occurred in spite of contraception. Over the years, Joanna developed an awareness of the dream symbols that spoke to her of impending conception. She writes:

> Just before the conception of one of the babies who never got to be born, I had a very vivid dream. There was a bird perched on the rim of a shallow bowl -- I think there is a Pompeiian wall painting that resembles this dream! The bird was vomiting something red into the bowl. Somehow, in the dream, I could taste it, and it was sweet and delicious -- like berries. I could not make sense of this peculiar dream until one of my friends reminded me that birds feed their young by regurgitating berries or whatever they are carrying home for dinner. So this was really a dream about something nurturing, and it contained an extremely feminine symbol of a bowl, cup, or something else receptive, a symbol that recurred in subsequent pregnancies.
>
> The significance of this dream was not clear to me until I realized I was pregnant. Then, looking back on the dream, which occurred about a week before ovulation, I was able to interpret it as a hint from my subconscious that there was a soul hovering around, wanting to incarnate.

I eventually did get married to a partner of my own spiritual persuasion, and started trying to conceive in earnest. I was thirty-four by then, and had been told by my doctor that I had a few fibroids in my uterus which could interfere with pregnancy, so naturally I was distressed that here was my big chance to get pregnant for real, and it might not happen. For two months my periods came as usual and I was very sad. Finally I had an intense dream that was very vivid in a sensual way.

I was in a building that looked like a medieval castle, only it was scaled down, cozy and charming. Outside it was pouring rain and lightning, but inside was a warm, quiet, pleasant gathering of gentlefolk, slowly circulating and chatting amongst themselves. Everything had a rosy glow. I stood by a tall, handsome young man with light brown hair and glasses, who wore a grey suit. We stood close together, face to face, chatting over a cup of pink wine -- we both held the silver chalice and looked deeply into its depths and I was aware of how rosy and glowing it was.

Soon after that I became pregnant. My son may be the man in the dream -- he has that coloring. Or maybe it was my husband. Or maybe it was the angel Gabriel. There were symbols of water in the dream -- the thunderstorm and the silver cup -- similar to the one with the bird and the bowl.

When Alek was eight months old, I accidentally became pregnant with twin girls, whom I miscarried at four months. I did not recall a dream, although I did have pregnancy on my mind in a general sort of way. But after finding myself pregnant, I suddenly recalled that this time, it was my husband who had the warning dream!

He woke up one morning from an unusually vivid dream in the form of a sword-and-sorcery animated feature. The plot involved the hero's efforts to protect the Queen, and included a weapon, which was a magic cup into which a person would speak to make something appear. There was lots of violent action in the dream, and as the enemies were about to overwhelm the castle, my husband (the hero) spoke the words "Wolf! Wolf!" into the magic cup, and a giant animated wolf appeared over the horizon and routed the enemies.

It was interesting that we had another castle dream with a cup symbol in it. But the Wolf is a symbol of Hecate, the hag, and is also the word the irresponsible shepherd boy cried once too often in Aesop's fable -- because the pregnancy did not continue past the fifth month.

Joanna observes that once she became aware of the nature of the cup symbol, she watched for it anxiously, and she feels her vigilance interfered with receptivity:

> I would wonder each night before I went to bed if I would have a "cup dream." My body was terribly messed up following the miscarriage; I wanted a second baby, and was panicking that I would not be able to conceive or carry another one. I was trying to force a pregnancy to happen by anxiously sifting through my dreams every morning to see if there was anything I could construe as a "cup dream." I think I scared the "cup dreams" off by my harsh and controlling attitude, because these seem to be a gift to the still and quietly receptive soul.

Symbols of conception and pregnancy can be varied and individual. Joanna suggests that by learning to read our personal symbolism, we can be more aware of those times when pregnancy is likely to occur. My own dreams once turned a "cup" into a clearly negative answer to my wondering whether I might be pregnant: "a bowl shaped like a big pregnant belly, turned upside down with its rim stuck in the ground, and I can't dig it out to use it!"

PRAYER

In whatever way we choose to prepare for parenthood, our values and priorities are revealed. They become clearer to us, especially when we express them in prayer. Vivien Beirne describes the prayerful attitude that she and her husband maintained while inviting a child to join them:

> I have been open to the idea of little egos being with us for a while before conception (the "cherub" images on Valentines), especially since I had a friend many years back who saw children, specific children, around her when she was dating a certain man.
> My personal spiritual philosophy includes the belief that angels are the ambassadors of the divine, and know the past relationships and future needs of each ego, and help to match each ego with the parents, family and community that it needs based on the laws of cause and effect.
> Since I came to believe this, about ten years ago, I have been sending "requests" for guidance concerning my creative potential (via becoming a mother) in thought and sometimes in my

journals as written prayers. I often wanted to hear my answer like a booming voice, but more often the answers to my prayers take the form of changes in some area of my life or in my own thoughts and attitudes. Sometimes the answers come within seconds, sometimes months. I like to write my concerns down because this gets them out of my often anxious thought patterns, and also because I can then go back and read about all the insurmountable problems that I could see no solutions for, and then see how solutions come. This is how my faith has grown (yet I still tend to get amnesia if a new problem occurs).

I wanted to dedicate my creative function to God, and asked that if I could perform the service of being a mother, could I please be in a healthy and healing relationship with a man first (which was a big request considering a slew of dysfunctional relationships before this). I think that part of the answer to this prayer was an inner healing of many negative attitudes and patterns, in preparation for this kind of partnership.

My husband, Mark-Paul, and I were married last February and were looking forward to starting a family within the next five years or so. We worked extensively with a friend versed in astrology to find a day and date for our wedding that would enable us to carry out our highest ambitions through our marriage, and I think it was during this soul-searching process that I really began to sense (or imagine?) an energy or presence with us in our planning.

From the time that we were married, we stopped using birth control and prayed quite fervently for the privilege of having another join our relationship if it be God's will. As I know of many couples who tried to conceive for a long time before actually being able to, I had convinced myself that it probably would take a couple of years at least for us too -- especially since we didn't conceive on the first try!

After our wedding we went to Kauai, and continued to invite an ego down into our life. I started to really sense someone keeping us company, and we talked a lot about the future as we went on hikes, my husband and I.

Back in Chicago, we went to a couples' workshop in March, and at the end of the weekend, everyone had a chance to stand up and receive a blessing from the group. We felt so rich and full. Later that month we conceived, and looking back, I could *feel* this ego had been with us at our wedding, on our honeymoon, at the workshop, and in so many daily things.

Vicki Morrison, while taking part in a research project in which pregnant women met to share their experiences, described the "spiritual interview" she practiced when inviting a child into her life:

> Before we conceived the baby and we knew we wanted to, I did a certain little exercise with myself. I would ask God to listen to my prayers... I always start my prayers with "I am one with you, you are my life right now," speaking of my Maker, that I imagined. And then I would say, "I want to have a baby and I am inviting any entity that wants to manifest itself physically to please come and see what I have to offer, to please come and look at my life, see my house and my husband and me, in the next few weeks or months. And if you think you would like to live with us, I would like you to be my child." I just imagined that it would be perfect because it was like an interviewing on the spiritual level. That was what I did and then we conceived a baby and I hope that it is right for all concerned.

Charlotte was secretly longing for a third child, but her husband was opposed to the idea. She expressed her dilemma in prayer, and consciously tried to make contact with a soul who might wish to join the family:

> I spoke to the Creator and any being ready to incarnate, explaining the situation and saying that I was open to it if there was a soul who wanted to come, who could benefit from us as parents and we from him/her. I spoke mentally as if there were a being listening to me, that is I "imagined" conversations as if I were talking to a friend. I did this on a regular basis (usually just before sleep), not purposely but because it was on my mind a lot.
>
> Despite the birth control measures, which had always worked previously over a period of fifteen years, I was surprised to find myself pregnant about three or four months later! I had a feeling that if this being was coming because of being invited, it would be a boy -- because we didn't particularly want a boy even though we had two girls, and I felt there was much we (especially my husband) needed to learn in having a male child.
>
> The pregnancy was quite stressful in that I didn't have much support from my husband, but I never regretted it and drew much strength from the knowledge that this child was "meant to be."
>
> We have many family birthdays in July, the month the baby was due, including my husband's. A friend of mine said that it

would really be the coup de grace if the baby was born on my husband's birthday, after all the denial he was going through. Well, what do you know, we missed all those other birthdays and three quarters of my husband's.

That evening we went out to dinner and my water broke in the restaurant. We hurried home, I called the midwife, she arrived fifteen minutes later, we filled the birth tub, and the baby was born a half hour later. It was a very spiritual birth -- outside under the stars, at night, in the water, by candlelight, with the two older girls looking on -- and on my husband's birthday at that!

This baby has been a real blessing. He is five months old now and has been the happiest and most self-assured baby. His father is absolutely crazy about him and we all look forward to what life has to offer and teach us with this little gift of God.

How specific can we be in our prayer for a child? Can we actually influence the one who comes to us? Susan Stout and her husband were quite explicit in the prayers they made before conceiving their son:

We put forth to the Universe exactly what we wanted in the soul who was to join us. We made a list of all the qualities we wanted in a child, such as someone with whom we could share our spiritual path, yet someone who could also teach us; a gentle, sensitive, aware, kind soul with a sense of humor.

We borrowed from Native American ritual for our ceremony. We saged the room and prayed to each of the Sacred Directions. Then we called upon the Great Spirit and the Universe to hear our prayers and then we put forth what we wanted.

Upon the baby's conception, we had no doubt we had the special soul we desired to complement all of our lives. Both my husband and I felt very clearly the baby was a boy and his name was Joshua. We felt he had been waiting a while to be conceived. I have to say that Joshua so far seems to be everything we wanted!

How do these matchups work? When we "put forth to the universe" an image of the child we want, do we attract the souls that fit the description? Or are we paired by some higher logic with the one we need, to broaden our vision and correct our imbalances?

Or is the "match" developed during pregnancy and after birth, by the child's somehow sensing our desires and adapting to fit them?

One mother noted how closely the birth of her daughter resembled her dream of it while pregnant, even to the personality the baby manifested. She asks, "Did I program this out of the 'suggestion' of my dream? Maybe, but who suggested it? And how did my daughter manage to comply? Certainly, some communication took place."

I too wonder about the interplay of perception and "programming." When we feel impressions of the child to come, are we perceiving a pattern that already exists -- or are we creating one? Perhaps we are actually cooperating with the soul of our child in designing a pattern of personality. And if so, how do the genetic givens (that include even such traits as shyness and sociability) fit into the picture?

To speculate further, I wonder whether disembodied beings have a personality at all, or -- supposing they have lived multiple times -- whether they can choose from a palette of all the personalities they have used. Perhaps when we express our wishes, the child-soul is able to assume some of the qualities we hope for. Or perhaps the child's own wisdom directs it to take on the "colors" that balance the family spectrum.

If a child can feel our wishes and prayers, and adapt to fit them, then parents could focus on desired qualities even during the pregnancy. This mother's practice, which at first seemed strange to me, could make sense after all:

> I practiced positive affirmations about the child during my pregnancy, and for Havala it was that she would be a very evolved soul, bright and loved by all. During my pregnancy with Noah my affirmations were for this child to be the one who cared for me in old age, athletic, bright, well loved and loving to others.

INFERTILITY

Sometimes just deciding to have a child is not enough, and our invitations go unanswered for months and years. Infertility can be both an emotional and a physical ordeal. We go through an intense and seemingly endless preparation, a time of heightened attentiveness to signals of conception and pregnancy. It can be like a prayerful state of mind even if we are not specifically praying, as we wait and hope. Amy Oscar observes:

> I think that people who have experienced infertility have a heightened sense of how life initiates itself. The questions: "Is anyone out there?" "What makes a child who s/he is?" "Who decides to conceive: parent or child?" and many more rumble

around in the thoughts. Questions of personal worthiness, of being judged by an unborn child, and so much more. It makes you consider more the meanings and comings and goings of life; it's hard to take life for granted.

Amy speaks from personal experience. She relates:

I was two or three years into infertility testing and in a moment of despair walking down the hall of my apartment in the afternoon, I very clearly felt a touch on my shoulder and *perhaps* a breath on my neck. I knew with certainty that it was my *son.*

I told my husband about the touch experience. We both were alternately in awe and disbelief. We told ourselves it was wishful thinking and went on with our lives, but for me that moment represented the promise that I could and would become pregnant and in many ways kept me going.

A year later, we were about to give up and begin In Vitro procedures. I looked up and said out loud, right in the doctor's office, "If you are going to come in, this is the time." Max was conceived within days and we never had to do In Vitro Fertilization.*

While wishing and hoping for a baby, we engaged psychics, healers, a telemetrist and of course scores of doctors. A few months before Max's conception, I consulted a psychic who told me how to conceive and told me I would have a boy and then a girl (which I did), and many other things which have proved true.

At the time, I worked for a company offering courses in Creative Visualization-based ideas. So I was very good at getting in touch with my dreams and visions for the future and visualizing them. I had a few ways of approaching this, but one worked especially well. I would write a complete description of the vision and then draw or collage a picture of it as fully realized.

About six months to a year before conceiving Max I did this in a workbook. I cut out a picture of a little boy in snow pants and pasted it down. Around him I drew a snowy scene and my hand holding his. After Max's first birthday, Matthew and I got some pictures developed and I was stunned to find a picture which almost perfectly matched that earlier visualization.

And finally, I had two index cards. On one I wrote a description of a little boy. He would be gentle, thoughtful, quiet but sunny. He would love to read. He would be an inventor and he'd look like me. There were other things, but these stand out.

Max is all of this and is a carbon copy of me. On Katie's card
-- or the girl card -- was a bright, sunny outgoing child. She
would be beautiful -- blond with green-blue eyes. She is. She
would look just like her daddy. She does.

Coincidence? I don't know.

Dealing with infertility can bring us to make changes in our way of
life as we try to correct physical problems. For Barbara Umberger these
changes were vital, but the key to conception was found only when she
let go of her obsession with becoming pregnant. Or was she finally able
to relax because she somehow knew that her child was soon to come?
She writes:

At age thirty-one, I had wished for a child for years but due to
having problems with my periods -- having none! -- I was
diagnosed by the medical world as being unable to bear a child.
Intuitively I felt it would be possible; yet my partner through the
years had no desire for a baby and this, added to the physical
obstacle, presented me with confusion.

I sought out aid using chiropractic, herbs, massage,
reflexology... no periods. I finally resorted to taking medicine for
several months. The periods came! After four years of being
without them, I felt connected and whole again. The doctor said
I had quite a bit of endometriosis and that I probably wasn't
ovulating and so the chances of my bearing a child were next to
nil.

In October of 1988 my partner and I married. I became very
involved in eating macrobiotically and I stopped my medication.
My periods continued and were hardly uncomfortable at all. I
was thrilled -- I grew more and more interested in macrobiotics
and applying and seeing its principles work in my life.

I began going to a Shiatsu therapist and in one session I told
her that I wanted to work on releasing my preoccupation with
having a baby. I felt I needed to let it be -- give it up to the
universe. During that session I talked with my spirit child and
told him that he could come to me whenever he was ready -- I
was ready and I loved him. It felt very deep and beautiful.

That month I conceived my baby. In fact I dreamed the night
I conceived that I was pregnant -- I know because I was keeping
a dream journal at the time. I didn't know at a conscious level
that I was pregnant for about three and a half weeks. I had a
routine urinalysis done and was told. Imagine my incredible
surprise. Here I'd used no birth control for over ten years!

Fertility can be problematic for the older couple as well, especially for a woman who is debating whether to attempt a pregnancy as her fertile years draw to a close and the risks increase. A mother mused: "Since my second son was born I have sometimes dreamed of a daughter. I am forty-three years old, however, and I do not know if my husband and I will have another child. Perhaps someday I will just *know...*"

A year later, she delved more deeply into her feelings about the possibility of pregnancy, wondering whether her own doubts would discourage any prospective children from approaching her:

> I just turned forty-four, and although we've off and on over the last year or so tried hit-and-miss conception, we have not conceived. The hardest thing for me is to admit (if we are successful) that we actively tried to conceive.
>
> I keep assuming that I will just "know" when I should conceive -- I am charting, so I do know physiologically -- but spiritually things just haven't seemed right. When my second son, Liam, was conceived, it was just the right thing to do. Everything felt right, and in fact I had actually had a day, perhaps a couple of months before conception, when I just knew I'd have another child and the child would be physically okay. Liam was born when I was thirty-nine.
>
> For years now I've been very aware of when ovulation occurs -- but not of any spirituality involved. It's as if I'm more in the "physical plane" rather than the spiritual. In the past I was more attuned to beings who were around me. Now, perhaps, I'm an unknown risk (physically, that is) and perhaps no being is looking at me as a mother.
>
> Or is this all just my projected fear? I'm not worried that I'm too old, but that the eggs I have are. On a "spiritual level" I can see that my projecting this ambiguity is not helping my cause. Who would want a mother so unsure of her ability to give birth to a healthy body?

Ellen and Jeff Stanclift experienced infertility in earlier years. By the time she was twenty-five, Ellen had already been advised by one specialist to give up and accept the fact that she was "barren." She underwent four years of treatment and suffered two miscarriages. Ellen describes the obsessive sadness and longing of that time:

> The anguish I felt was so heart-wrenching that I found my work difficult at times. As a teacher, I encountered so many children

who needed love, and felt that although I could do my best to help them in the classroom, what they truly needed was love at home. I began to question the fairness of our situation and became very depressed. The fertility drug only made my anxiety worse! The two pregnancies that I lost made me sink deeper into a well of sadness.

During the time most of this was happening, Jeff and I were living in Germany. When we made the decision for Jeff to give up his commission of Captain in the Army and to move back to New England, we both felt liberated and happy. We had been back in Maine for about three months when I had an overwhelming feeling that I would be pregnant that month. There was no mistaking it... I was certain. Now, I had hoped for this many times, but this was an altogether new feeling. I wish I could describe the calmness that I felt. When my period was one day late, as it had been before, I didn't have any of the nervous fear of getting it the next day. In the past, I waited for my period like an executioner coming to take me to the gallows, but this time, I *knew* that I had received an acquittal from my infertility! When I did the home pregnancy test, as I had done in the past, I didn't wait for the "minus" sign, but rather knew that the "plus" sign would appear.

I always pictured myself with a little girl, and my husband and I had selected the name, Anna. Well, when I was about eighteen weeks pregnant, and beginning to feel the baby really move inside me, I had a dream of a darling dark haired little boy toddling around our yard with our labrador retriever, Hershey. Since I had an image of having a daughter in my mind, this came as a real surprise. I told my mother about it, and she said, "Well, I'll bet you're having a little boy!"

When Joshua arrived, I felt I had known him always. It was as if he'd always been a part of me, and the years of infertility just melted away. I wish there was a way of conveying how much this whole experience has meant to me and has changed my life. Joshua is now a three month old delight. He and I are quite a team! Joshua's a remarkable child, and we love him very, very much.

CHAPTER ELEVEN
PERSUASION: "I WANT TO BE WITH YOU"

Just as we may invite a child to come into our family, children waiting to be born may request permission to enter. There seems to be a two-way process of inviting one another and coming into agreement. Much of it perhaps happens "in the dark," outside our conscious mind. But sometimes we become aware of a knocking at the door...

This is one of the patterns we discover in stories of pre-birth contact: someone is persuading, asking to be conceived or carried, overcoming the resistance of the person who might become its mother or father.

The persuasion can be very gentle. Some people describe a feeling of being "courted" with patient politeness. One mother felt she was given ample time to decide without being pressured, and upon her decision not to become pregnant, the being simply withdrew. Another woman says:

> Philip really wanted to come into this world but was very gentle and noble. He did not say anything to persuade me into anything I didn't want to do and gave me absolute freedom of choice.

Joyce and Barry Vissell's third child, Anjel, died in the womb at six months. The story of the spiritual connection created through her short physical stay is beautifully told in the Vissells' book, *Risk To Be Healed*. Here, Joyce describes the patient, persistent way Anjel seemed to deal with their resistance to conceiving her:

> Our family, Barry and I, Rami, age ten, and Mira, age four and a half, packed up our old camper and set off for the mountains. Never had we needed a vacation more. On the third day of our camping trip I was sitting alone when I felt the distinct presence

of someone beside me. I knew this sensation well, for the same experience had happened to me shortly before we conceived both Rami and Mira. At first I felt in awe of the greatness of this being beside me, whom I could not see with physical eyes but could feel within my heart. "Maybe this is a helper," I thought, and then the message came:

"I am your third child and am ready to be conceived."

It was the last thing I wanted to hear at this time in my life.

"No!" I stammered, "I don't want to get pregnant. I don't want anything different right now. I just want to rest."

I felt this being smiling at me, loving me fully and offering the gift of its presence in my life...

"You can conceive me in three weeks. Your family is now ready for my presence in your lives."

"No!" harshly echoed through my being.

Where was that "no" coming from in me? For the first time in my life I was feeling strong resistance to having another child. My rational mind argued that we were both forty years old, too old to be having more children (though I knew this wasn't true). Rami and Mira were finally old enough to go with us on great adventures or else stay at Grandma and Grandpa's house while we did necessary air travel. Barry and I had felt long ago that our family was complete, and had gotten rid of all the baby things.

I felt this great being stretch out its hands in blessing and in love, seemingly amused by my obvious struggle.

The next three weeks were extremely confusing. We left our peaceful camping spot and flew east to my home town of Buffalo for several talks and workshops. Each morning upon awakening I felt the loving presence of our third child. Each morning I would then sit in meditation and watch my crazy mind resist. The more I resisted, the more love I felt poured upon me...

For some people, the feeling of being sought as a possible parent has an urgent, insistent quality. "When my wife Lee and I were just living together," says Adam Tritt, "we started feeling the pressure of a female child":

We both wanted a child badly, and always during sex we would feel a very impatient energy. We felt her saying, "Please have me!" Unable to support a wife and child at that time, we did not have her.

Then Lee had a dream. In a clear plastic bubble was a little girl, who looked just like our daughter Sef does now. When Lee asked her what she was doing, the girl said, "I am waiting in the waiting womb."

January 18, 1984 we got legally married. That night -- six hours later -- we conceived Sef. We knew this without a doubt and we knew it was a girl even though my family history has only one girl in thirty children.

Not long after intercourse (almost immediately) we felt the feeling of the impatient child completely disappear. For the last two months it had been strong, constant and almost pleading. Suddenly it was gone.

Kim Ilowit had definite reasons to resist a third pregnancy. A heart condition resulting from rheumatic fever makes pregnancy particularly hazardous and stressful for her. At twenty-five, before starting her family, she had sought the advice of her cardiologist, who performed a cardiac catheterization and determined that it would be safe for her to have children, but that she should do so before her thirties. Kim writes:

It took several months before I got pregnant and then at thirteen weeks I miscarried. I became pregnant shortly afterwards and again miscarried at about five weeks. It was very emotionally draining and my husband and I in consultation with my obstetrician decided to wait awhile before trying again.

Meanwhile we went to India and decided not to have children at all. That phase lasted about two years, at which time I reconnected with my lifelong extremely strong desire to have children.

Again it took me several months before I became pregnant. I woke up one morning with an absolute conviction that this was the day I would conceive a child. Amusingly enough, my husband Gordy and I had had an argument the night before and he didn't want to hear anything about conceiving babies. I felt half desperate as though the mere act of sex with anyone would have to do if need be to give this soul passage into my body. Anyway we made up, my son was conceived and born nine months later. I had a somewhat difficult pregnancy because of my heart condition and took digitalis from about the fifth month on due to shortness of breath and rapid pulse. Neither my obstetrician nor my cardiologist felt I should have another child.

After three years we explored the possibility of another pregnancy with a high-risk obstetrician, at the advice of my cardiologist who admitted he saw me only as a "heart," not a "whole person." This physician, a woman, was very open and after much research and testing encouraged us to go ahead.

Again I had a very strong feeling for the day of conception. I was sick that day and felt there was no way I could make love feeling as I did, but by evening as soon as our son fell asleep I was suddenly well. We had another son nine months later. I was now thirty-four and my second pregnancy had been much more difficult and sometimes quite frightening because I had a lot of trouble breathing and was truthfully scared at times that I would die and leave my other son motherless. Though I don't think my pregnancy was ever life-threatening, I could do nothing for four and a half months, took medication and was strongly told not to get pregnant again. My births were fine; they both took place in a birthing room and had no complications -- my particular condition eases in the final months as the stress on the heart levels off and the body adjusts to the level it needs to work at.

When my second son was two and a half, I was quite clear that though I would love to have a larger family, I would definitely not become pregnant again. In December of that year I told a friend that I was absolutely done, and the difficulty and fear I experienced in pregnancy were quite vivid in my mind.

Later that month I had a vague impression of a presence in our bedroom one night and told Gordy I felt it was a soul who wanted to be in our family. He jokingly responded that he/she would have to find another place. (My pregnancies are also very hard on my husband as he needs to take over everything in the household as well as working full-time as a teacher for emotionally disturbed adolescents.)

Three weeks later in January I had a powerful dream. In the dream my friend and I were pregnant together (she really was pregnant at the time). After a time our babies were born and people came to see them. She pointed to a blue eyed baby boy (which she did have later), and I would sadly point to my two-and-a-half year old son and say "two souls in one body." (Meanwhile my son had for quite awhile talked about his "sister who lives in the car.") The scene switched in the dream and I was in a room with Gordy, and I was crying and saying how much I wanted another baby. He said it's okay, we can have one.

When I woke up I felt euphoric but didn't remember the dream. Instead I had this overwhelming desire to go to India to see our spiritual teacher. Later in the day the memory of the dream suddenly flooded over me. But I didn't think much of it except that the desire to have another baby in the dream was one and the same with the desire I felt to go to India.

Three nights later I was awakened by a very strong presence in our room. I described it as "light, joy and female." I woke my husband up and told him we needed to make love as this soul was there and wanted to be in our family. He told me to go back to sleep and reminded me that we couldn't go through another pregnancy. We talked for about five minutes, me quite urgently as I had no doubt that this needed to happen. I told Gordy that if I didn't get pregnant that night (which was not the usual time in my menstrual cycle that I previously had conceived), I would never think about having more children; that I would understand this whole situation as an illusion.

So we made love and we did conceive our third child that night. A daughter was born the following October, quite full of light and joy. Yes, my pregnancy was difficult but the most difficult months physically were the summer months and my husband was off from teaching and able to take over. And I was so much more at ease during this pregnancy, being so sure that she was meant to be a part of our family.

The feeling that someone is asking to be born can develop into a dialogue with this unknown being. It can start us on the process of change and preparation as we come into agreement. Nancy Cohen traces this process that began with the unexpected approach of such a "someone":

I never was one to want a "family" and never had any plans to have "a bunch of kids" or "two" or "five." So when I started getting a persistent "feeling" that a baby wanted to come through -- I really balked! It wasn't in my plans! How could a baby choose me?

During the summer of 1990 I had an overwhelming desire to cut my hair all off, throw away my clothes, and go on a cleansing diet. I felt that 1) I was getting ready for a big change of how I saw myself (hair); 2) I was going to get all new clothes -- oddly, not office clothes! and 3) my body needed to get ready for a change. That fall, I felt the need to sell our house. The sense that a baby was coming was stronger. Many of my fears of mothering, parenting, etc. came up to be looked at.

The baby's presence in the months preceding conception was so strong that I often just felt guided to sit quietly and receive. We were also doing a lot of yoga and pranayam (yogic breathing exercises).

One of the strongest communications I experienced at that

time was while sitting in meditation. A great feeling of love washed over me as if pouring over my head. It was the spirit of our unborn child and the sensation of great all-encompassing love was overwhelming.

In meditation I also got a message to stop contraception in December, but that I would not conceive right away. Shortly after this my husband and I had an intense desire to return to an ashram in New England where we had both had deep spiritual renewal. We could barely scrape the money together to stay three or four days at the ashram -- and the weather was treacherous -- but we *had* to go.

We received another type of communication during a workshop at the ashram called something like "Contacting your higher self through writing." We thought of questions we'd like to ask our higher self -- then we got up, exercised a bit, walked around, and sat back down and got quiet. We were told to write down whatever came through. Part of what I got was this:

"Yes, a child of light is choosing you. You are *her* mother. Be grateful. You are loved. You are precious in the sight of God."

On another occasion I used the same technique with intent to contact my unborn child: "Fear not. I come to love you only. Wipe away your tears. Time has come to put aside the past and begin anew. Rejoice. An occasion to rejoice. My light will light your way as well as his."

Two weeks later we conceived -- I was very aware of the tremendous shift -- and a peculiar peacefulness descended on us.

The touch of a soul inviting us to welcome her can be very gentle, playful and light. Alicia Russell-Smith tells of an encounter that occurred while she and her husband were making love:

As we were making love in good, concentrated tantric fashion, I lost the trance because of a distraction of physical touch -- a small child's fingers pulling on mine. And I heard toddler level giggles of playfulness which neither Jim nor I was making, unless of course we were making a body to go with the soul who made them.

Alicia did not conceive in that cycle. At her next period, she says, she felt "a grief process that was partly in me and partly out of me," as if perhaps someone else was disappointed. She speaks of her ongoing conflicting urges to have another child (her son is nine years old) versus the desire to "be my own Mom," and nurture her creativity in writing.

And she still feels there may be a child connected with her, still waiting to see if she's going to "fish or cut bait" before moving on to another possible home. But there have been no further contacts like that playful touch.

UNPLANNED CONCEPTIONS

An agreement between parent and child may be reached after conception instead of before it. When facing an unexpected, unwanted pregnancy, one may go through a process much like the soul-searching that often paves the way to a planned conception. In this stressful situation, an experience of contact can have a powerful influence on the decision for or against bearing the child. A woman writes:

> When I discovered I was pregnant -- unmarried, at the point of graduation from college -- I was very confused, unsure as to what the pregnancy would mean for me. I had no friends at the time who had children and no models. After I was sure I was indeed pregnant I made an appointment to have an abortion in one week. During that week I tried to explore my feelings, tried to project into my future, should this baby be born to me now, or not? Needless to say the week proceeded intensely, tearfully, frightfully and soul-searchingly.
>
> After talking and talking with friends, it occurred to me that the answer wasn't going to come in talks with friends, but must come from some inner source. So the day before the scheduled abortion, I went into my room, closed the door and sat down to meditate.
>
> My meditation was a deep yearning, asking, opening for some sign, some answer that would guide my actions: abortion or birth? When I closed my eyes, it was a sunny spring afternoon. At some point (I had no concept of the passing of time the way you don't in a crisis), I heard a voice within myself, but at the same time all around me. *"I want to be with you."*
>
> At that moment, a feeling of peace fell over me and I began smiling and opened my eyes. Just hearing this voice, which was, in an image in my head, the child within, made me feel calm and the confusion melted away. It was dark and night-time when I got up. The next morning I cancelled the appointment. The child is now eight years old.

Linda, a Japanese-American woman who became engaged while in the United States, was thrown into turmoil by an unplanned conception:

> As much as my fiance and I were overjoyed to find out my unexpected pregnancy, I was confused and terribly saddened to think I would not be able to go back home nor take up the job offer I had (at this time my fiance was also out of a job). Also the prospect of putting my family to shame by being pregnant before marriage (Japan is still very traditional) made us consider abortion.
>
> I must have spent weeks crying, unable to make up my mind. We weighed and analyzed both situations, abortion versus having the baby. I got all the medical information on abortion and even made an appointment at the clinic to terminate my pregnancy.
>
> But one night my son came to me in my dream in the form of a boy four or five years old, begging me to keep him. His exact words were, "Mommy, I'll be a good boy, please keep me. I won't cause you any trouble."
>
> Still not convinced, on the appointed morning I went with my husband to the clinic, with my eyes all red from crying. We paid at the reception and as I stood in front of the receptionist, cold and numb, trying to hold back my tears, the receptionist turned to me and said, "Take this money back and go see our counselor. You're not fully sure about this and I don't want you to go through with it."
>
> That was the turning point; we never went back. A week later my husband woke up one morning and told me he had an unusual dream (at this point I had not told him of my dream). His dream had the same boy, even dressed in an identical outfit -- like an aristocratic English boy of Victorian days! And his dream was of this boy saying "My mommy."

In due course the child was born, a calm and happy baby boy. Says Linda, "We feel as though we've known him forever. There is a tremendous feeling of love, respect and friendship towards him. I never thought motherhood could be such an intense experience of total love and joy."

"I am a single parent," says Sue Jo, "and my experience with my child in utero was very powerful." When she found herself unexpectedly pregnant, the baby's father was opposed to the idea of having a child and strongly favored abortion. Sue Jo writes:

After an initial panic, I realized I wanted this baby very much and couldn't think of anything else I would even want to do. After several weeks of deliberation, meditation and a few visions of seeing myself in a warm climate with a small boy, I decided to go to the Light Institute* in New Mexico to get more in touch with my highest truth.   I didn't want to take on such an enormous responsibility as single parenting without really checking out, as much as possible, what my inner self was saying.

I landed in Santa Fe without much money and was taken care of by strangers, given rides to the Light Institute, and received a session with someone there (even though they were booked up for six months).

In the session I went inside the womb and "saw" him curled up, and saw his eyes developing. I had an ecstatic sense around his being there and loads of pink "heart" light glowing around him and me. I had a deep sense of love and connectedness and "rightness" and desire to do anything I possibly could to support his life. I heard the name Isaac and knew he was indeed a male child.

As I write this, the words naturally don't describe the intensity of the experience, but it was the "go ahead" for me to take on this adventure single handedly. I returned to my home in San Diego and had an underwater birth with a lot of support. I felt really supported by God/universe/whatever -- a real sense of being in the "groove." There's been so much good luck and healing around the birth of Isaac.

It's fun telling the story. It was one of those incredibly empowering experiences that helped me choose a courageous and difficult path, a path of heart despite the financial and emotional impossibility of my situation at the time.

Rachel was faced with an unplanned pregnancy when she and her husband already had four boys. They considered abortion, but felt they would want to go through with the pregnancy if only they knew the baby was a girl. Rachel suggested they should pray for a sign:

We did pray together and kept the thought-expectation for guidance in our minds. Two days later I received a letter from my older sister. In this letter she said she dreamed I had a baby girl with lots of brown hair.

This was truly miraculous. We hadn't told anyone that I was even pregnant (I was only a few weeks along). And my sister has never written me about a dream before. This was the sign we had been waiting for. We still didn't know the baby was a girl until she was born -- a big girl with lots of brown hair -- more hair than any of my others!

ACCEPTANCE

In so many pre-birth experiences there is a pattern of smoothing the way, untangling the knots -- actually dealing with obstacles to the parent-and-child bond.   One common obstacle is the very strong preference that some potential parents have for a baby of a particular gender.   A connection before birth can open our hearts to the other possibility.

Where there is fear that we may have a child of the unwanted gender, our fear may be dispelled through dreams or reveries that put us in touch with the baby's lovable reality.   Whether these dreams and images are communications from the child or from our own inner wisdom, acceptance is one of the most obvious benefits of a pre-birth connection.

The process of coming to acceptance can unfold before conception, as Karin Liedtke describes:

> While I had wanted to conceive, be pregnant and raise a child, it had always been a girl I envisioned.   A few months before I became pregnant, my husband and I discussed planning to try to conceive a child in a year or so.   He asked what I would do if I had a boy.   I realized I was not completely opened to the idea. I then started to have dreams: three, about a month apart, in which I had a boy child.   He was newborn to age six.   In each dream I loved my son very much and upon awakening felt there was no reason not to feel joyful about having a boy.   It did not matter at all.
>
> A month after the last dream, I conceived, a year ahead of schedule.   I knew it was a boy.   Rob felt it was a boy too.   I'm delighted with him; I adore him.   It seemed I had to be more open and realize I would love whomever I bore -- then this Being came to us.   Now it seems utterly silly that I ever had the reservations to begin with!

Another woman tells how envisioning her future child persuaded her that she could love a boy:

> With our first pregnancy, my husband John and I were most anxious to have a girl.   Intellectually, I thought it best to be open

to both, but I didn't realize till she was born how much I longed for a girl. On reflection, I think it may have been fear of having a boy that was an emotional block in the long, almost home birth labor that brought her to us. As we began to think about having a second child we talked, dreamed and worked our way through this fear.

In my yoga class, six to eight weeks before we conceived our second child, I experienced a whole sequence of feelings, intuitions and images. In a relaxed, semi-meditative state I had a kind of "dream." In this "dream," I first suddenly, absolutely believed that I was pregnant. My feelings were: oh no, this is too soon, we want better timing, John will be upset; and then, oh no, what if it's a boy. We need to come to terms with that... Then I saw in my mind's eye a little boy in our living room, a gentle, impy boy, with dancing brown eyes like my husband's. In my heart I felt, oh, I want *that* boy. He's right for us. And then I was filled with joy that I was pregnant. (I wasn't, but in the "dream" I believed I was.) I was so happy and excited.

After a few minutes, my feelings deflated. But what about when he's an adolescent? (John and I had fears of a huge, uncooperative son taking over our quiet household.) I then saw, leaning against the door frame between our kitchen and living room, a not too big fourteen year old boy with those same dancing brown eyes. He was just about to tease me about something... Then I was again bursting with happiness.

After class I told John and he said, "That's a good sign, a preparation, but you're not pregnant." I knew I wasn't and my period came on time. After this experience I intuitively was certain that our next child would have brown eyes and be like John in some ways. Later that summer, I went to visit our midwife and John and I began to feel ready to begin "trying."

And I did have a baby boy, his eyes are brown, like John's in shape, and he has the same impy look in them that I saw in my "dream."

If we haven't resolved a conflict about gender before conceiving a child, we may find ourselves being persuaded during the pregnancy. Nancy Mendez started her pregnancy dreading the possibility that she could have a daughter. She explains:

I didn't have a good relationship with my own mother till I was eighteen or nineteen years old. I was a "daddy's girl," born between two brothers. Dad adored every move I made and was more critical of the boys. To "correct" the situation, my mother admits to being harsh on me "just to balance things out."

A lot of conflicts were explained away as "sibling" and "female rivalry" as I was growing up. That seemed to be the reason for everything. I was certainly not a "sugar and spice" sort of girl and actually had more guy friends than women as I got older. "Girly-ness" was something I avoided.

When I became pregnant, I thought I just couldn't mother a daughter.

Would my husband love her more than me?

Would I play the "heavy," as my mother did?

How could I do right all the things my mother did wrong? I had no good role models. In my husband's family, the women are passionate about nail polish and perfume, ruffles and bows. What if my child actually liked *pink*? I never did those sort of things!

I began to have vivid, detailed dreams. In all the dreams, the babies were girls. They were embarrassingly easy to analyze and I would awake horrified that I could have such thoughts even subconsciously. But I could see I was working issues out. Some were funny, others frantic, but I became more confident of being a good mother and more open to a daughter with each dream.

At five months, I dreamed that I wasn't married, but my husband was some sort of show-biz partner and we were on tour. He came to me and excitedly told me about a wonderful girl he'd met in this new town and how he just knew I'd be nuts about her. I thought he was so dear to be finding new friends for me. But then I saw him having dinner with her parents. She obviously adored him, and they approved greatly. At first, I was crushed that I didn't know he was in love, didn't realize what was happening, wasn't invited along. But because I loved and trusted him, I mellowed and realized we would all be together. "What is your name?" I asked. "Well, I think they'll call me Madeleine," she answered. Madeleine was one name we'd considered.

After that, I couldn't think of my stomach as anyone else but Madeleine. We never even picked a boy's name. When she kicked, I cooed to Maddie. It just seemed to fit. At birth, as soon as the cord was pushed aside so I could see my baby's sex, I shouted, "It's a Madeleine," not "It's a girl."

I know the dreams prepared me for this child. I am more relaxed about mothering than I thought I could be. Although she is the apple of her father's eye, I can joke about it, not be threatened as my mother was with me. I can't wait to build her a dollhouse, buy party shoes with bows, share girl talk. She has tons of personality, and I feel that it is possible that she started "straightening me out" early so I would be ready for her.

OVERCOMING THE FEAR OF LOSS

Parents who have suffered the loss of a child during pregnancy or soon after birth may be reluctant to face the emotional risk of another pregnancy. Here are two couples who overcame their fear with what appears to be the help of gentle persuasion from the child-to-be.

Claire C.'s story of the birth and death of her daughter Andrea was told in my book *In The Newborn Year*. This loss left her unsure of her willingness to have any more children. She writes:

> Throughout my pregnancy with my first child, Erika, I had felt a strong sense of her presence. It was entirely different with Andrea. It was like no one was there. It was strange, and uncomforting. It was only during labor, in fact as I started pushing, that I felt that strong "Oh, she's arrived!" feeling -- and a few minutes later she was born. And then she died.
>
> So, the next pregnancy -- I was *afraid* to get pregnant. I still had a lot of grief -- I wasn't sure I ever wanted to have another child.
>
> I can't remember how I knew, but I came to know that I had a choice: I could either have no more children, or I could commit to having two more, first a girl, then a boy, who wanted to be together. And I wanted to have them both -- I felt that internal agreement, and my husband was willing, for one at least. But then the fear came in -- and I put it all aside.
>
> One night I had a very intense dream. I dreamed I was pregnant and in labor, pushing, and then the baby was born. I was afraid in the dream to look at the baby. I was afraid that her eyes would be closed, that she would be dead, as Andrea was. But after a moment I looked at her, and these dark brown eyes were looking intently into mine. She was very much alive, very strong personality, dark hair. So the next day I kept thinking about this dream, and all the fear came rushing back -- I thought, "Oh no, I don't want to get pregnant!" and I went to the drugstore and bought some condoms! Two days later I brought out the condoms -- and my husband said "I don't want to use these," so we didn't, and that night I conceived.
>
> There was strong presence throughout the pregnancy -- I felt

sure I'd have a girl. I did some therapy and grief work during pregnancy and felt good by the time of delivery. It was a wonderful home birth, and when she was born, she opened her eyes and looked at me, with those beautiful intent brown eyes of hers! And her hair was dark, and now at seven years of age she continues to show the depth of her strength -- she's always been deeply centered within herself, strong of will and powerful, yet also flexible and sweet-tempered. Lara is her name.

Two and a half years later, our son Luke was born. No unusual experiences with him -- just the strong certainty that I was carrying a boy, and the steady sense of his presence.

Luke and Lara have a strong connection and love for each other. They have very different personalities and interests, and many friends, yet they seek each other out and spend many hours together. They fight, too, but it always works out -- they have an understanding of each other.

Patricia is another woman for whom the loss of one child became an obstacle to risking another pregnancy. She and her husband had been devastated when their baby girl died in the womb at thirty-two weeks. Fearing a second loss, they nearly decided that they would never have children -- but after several months, something unexpected occurred that led at last to a change of heart. Patricia writes:

I met another child in my dreams. His name was Luka, and he said he would wait for us to welcome him into our lives.

The rest of that year, and into the next, I tried to handle the anger and intense sorrow that I felt. I verbalized many times all the reasons why not to have children, as if to convince myself. After all, the world wasn't a nice place for children; we were too old; without children, we could retire early and tour the world. And of course, the real reason was that we were too afraid to endure another loss, if one should occur.

Then Luka appeared again during a night dream. He basically said the same thing: that he was waiting for us to welcome him into our lives.

Why was this happening? How could I get this out of my mind?

That autumn, I started to realize how depressed I really was. I was functioning in the outside world, but it was apparent in therapy that this sadness had a grip on me. I even thought about whether life was worth continuing. I had had so many losses in my life, and this was about all I could endure.

Then, the vision to end all visions happened. I'll never forget it. I was taking a shower, alone, on a sunny Saturday afternoon. I heard this... voice. (There was no visual.) I can't say the voice was loud or startled me, or anything like that. But it spoke in no uncertain terms to me, and then vanished. He said that I was perfectly ripe to accept him into our lives, and that this was our last chance because he had to move on.

I opened up like a lotus to the notion of having this child come into our lives. I felt a cloud lift. But I stood in the shower in slight disbelief. I didn't know what to do, but I felt lightness, love, hope, and happiness. I told my husband Peter (as I had always done when I got these visions), and asked him if he would be interested in reconsidering our baby decision. When Peter said he wanted this baby, too, I can't tell you how elated I felt. Maybe I've never felt such joy. We made love once, and the rest, they say, is history. Luka was conceived that day. He stopped appearing in dreams, and was born to us August 21, 1992.

We found it hard to believe this story, even during the pregnancy. But I knew it was a boy, and the amniocentesis proved it. And he developed normally throughout the pregnancy with no complications. And to our amazement, we didn't spend the whole pregnancy in complete fear of another loss. It just seemed like everything was going to be okay, and right. In the end, it turned out to be a horribly long labor (thirty-nine hours), but Luka kept strong for the duration, and when he came out, we knew it was he. He lay there on the warming table, looking up at Peter and the lights, gripping Peter's fingers with great strength. And as his name suggests, he loves light to this day. He has the kind of eyes that look as though they are intensely studying everything. I can't wait to see what he chooses to do in life.

Patricia reflects on the experiences that persuaded her to have Luka:

I'm not sure how much credibility to assign to these visions. Are they really from souls in limbo between lives, or are they our way of healing ourselves or convincing ourselves to take the right path? But whatever they are, they are at least interesting, and certainly something to pay some attention to. We're glad that we did. So much pain has been lifted from us in the process.

CHAPTER TWELVE
PILGRIM SOULS AND POSSIBLE CHILDREN

When a child seems to be knocking at the door of our life, sometimes our answer is no. For one reason or another, the door remains closed.

In several stories, where we find intimations of a soul looking for a home, there are obstacles that prevent an agreement to come together as parent and child. In these stories too, though they seem to be about missed connections, we can see much evidence of the cooperative intention at work.

The premonition of a child to come is not always a happy one. Sarah was alarmed by the sense that a fourth child wished to join her family:

> At the end of the day when I pray, I mentally review the previous day, plan for the next day, and review my life in general. Sometimes I would find myself communicating somehow with this child, knowing deep down in my psyche that my family was not complete. I was very frightened because of my previous experiences of severe postpartum depression, and because my husband did not want any more children. I told this child of my fears and was adamant about my husband's desire not to have any more children -- I told her that her father's heart would have to be changed.

Ultimately Sarah bore this fourth child (who turned out to be a son) and found that many problems were eased in the process. But the dread she felt at the child's approach brings up a question. If we believe we have been chosen by a child who wants to be born, must we comply? Do we surrender our own power to choose?

We may believe that the child-spirit views the situation from another perspective and perceives things that we can't see. And while we can certainly say "No thank you" to a soul inviting itself into our family, perhaps we will be missing -- or just postponing -- an experience that we need. A mother of three writes:

> I know there is at least one more boy to come and have even seen

him in my house once. I have constantly been searching for one
more child when we go places and often do a head count and still
look around feeling as if I have lost someone. I don't know his
name yet but though I am still procrastinating getting pregnant
again I am pretty resigned that I will do it, because I don't want
to get to the other side and meet this person who will tell me that
I just didn't want him to come. And each one of our children is
so unique and fun that I keep telling myself that it will be worth
it in the long run. But I will be forty-three this year so it will
have to be soon.

In her book *Born To Live*, Dr. Gladys McGarey tells of a mother of
four who found herself being "courted" by a persistent entity:

> The family had decided that four was enough, but, several years
> after the fourth arrived, the mother was taking a shower and she
> saw a blue light appear in the top corner of the shower.
> Instinctively, she knew what the blue light meant. Another
> entity was wanting to make its appearance.
> "Go away," she said, "You know I don't need any more kids!"
> A month later, the blue light came back. Again the same
> dialogue. And again it happened. And again.
> Finally, the reluctant mother gave in to the persistence of
> whatever the blue light meant, and she became pregnant. Child
> number five arrived, a boy, and her family was larger. And more
> complicated, of course, but more enjoyable.
> Two years passed by. The mother of five had not ceased to
> take showers. And the blue light came on once again. This time,
> she didn't have the energy to fight it any longer. It was almost as
> if she was getting a message from these two souls, as the blue
> light came on, that said, "Look, this is the place where I'm
> supposed to be. You are the people I am needing to live with,
> and this is the right time. So please get ready for me, cause I'm
> coming..."

These stories raise the question of whether we do well to go along
reluctantly with the feeling of being chosen. My personal bias is that
the choice should be mutually pleasing. The freedom to decline a soul's
invitation may be a very important part of the cooperative process
between possible parents and possible children.

The following stories of "pilgrim souls" suggest that the pairing of
child to parent may not be absolute, and that there may be many other
doors available for anyone needing to be born. While this does not

imply that our connections are random, it suggests that we need not feel bound by an impression that a child wishes to be born into our family. We may not be their only opportunity.

SAYING NO

A mother of one recalls:

> A very strong series of dream images came to me in the mid years (my child was four, five, six at the time) -- images of a little boy, a curly-haired toddler -- *my* child -- in my arms, playing in my bed, being in my life. But I chose not to have another child, despite his appeal! And now, at forty-seven, I think it's unlikely.
>
> Was this a child I "could have had" (he had a distinct appearance and personality; it was one child appearing again and again) or was it a lesson -- of what one must sacrifice, say, for the greater good of the family one already has? I don't know.

A mother of two children was repeatedly "visited" by a very specific child soul. The visits compelled her to make a clear decision on the direction her life would take. She writes:

> I guess if you are in your forties and still fertile, you are bound to have strong feelings about getting pregnant, one way or another! As for me, I fall on the "NO WAY!" side. About six months after my second child was born, I became aware of another female being who wanted to be born to us. She would always appear off to my upper right consciousness and even though I love babies and nurturing, I knew having another baby would be very hard for me. I sent those messages to her with love whenever she appeared.
>
> I can't remember when she stopped visiting me; perhaps four to six months later. I wanted to get back into my music and I have been able to do that now. I feel so vitalized, so excited about what I am doing now that a baby would be quite an adjustment for me. As you can probably tell, much thought has gone into this, and a lot of emotions. I really love children.
>
> I feel that she hung around a respectable amount of time, giving me time to really think about my priorities yet not pressuring me in any way; I believe she stopped appearing when I made a firm commitment to pursue my music again.

Susan Sitler had a powerful vision of four children before starting her family; yet after giving birth to two sons who seem to match two of the children in her vision, she isn't sure she wants to have any more:

> One year before I was married I was working on biofeedback and meditation quite regularly. During a deep state of relaxation and meditation, I saw a very clear vision of myself with four children. The eldest, a boy, had golden colored hair, one child had red hair and two had dark hair. I was told in the vision that I would have a golden haired boy as my first born. I was also told that he was a very special "old soul" and to take great care of him. The other children appeared as wonderful, loving souls waiting to be with the first and myself.
>
> About a week after learning that I was pregnant, I had a "flash," a "communication" that this was the golden haired child of my vision. My husband Tim and I both felt all along that he was going to be a boy. Luke was born in May 1987, a strawberry blond whose hair turns the color of spun gold from the summer's sun. He is indeed a dynamic little boy and I believe is the boy of my initial vision.

Susan's second child was a dark-haired son, Daniel. She writes:

> As Daniel is getting older, we think often about whether or not we will give birth to another child. With thoughts of the family budget, the world population growth, and the fact that our midwife is gone, looming as major deterrents, I still feel the "presence" of a little one "waiting in the wings." A little boy, a little blond boy. This is a big decision for us in many ways (not to mention that I don't look forward to vomiting for four months again).

A year later, Susan adds:

> You may have wondered what happened to my little guy hanging around. Well, the feelings were strong all summer. While on vacation I had a strong sense that I could conceive if I wanted. I had a heated debate whether even to talk with my husband about going ahead and trying (never would I without our joint agreement). Somehow I felt I had to work it out with myself first, and decided no. Since that time, his presence is less. My little blond boy is still there but kind of in the background. He's a daily thought but not a daily presence.

I have questions as to what "happens" to these little guys who seem to have such a strong spirit, when you say "No" to their birth?

The following stories provide a possible answer to Susan's question about what becomes of potential children when we refuse their request for birth into our family. Perhaps we need to think in terms of a wider family -- a community of compatible souls. The first story is from a woman who lives, literally, in a community whose members share spiritual values. She writes:

In the first few years of being married, after almost ten years of being single, there was some question in my mind about whether we should have a baby. Our lives were very well-established in other directions, but there was a lingering desire that would come up from time to time.

Gradually, it became clear that it really wasn't what God wanted for our lives, so the question of what "I wanted" didn't seem so important. And pretty quickly after that I became very happy in the thought of not having children.

Some time around the time that the whole question got settled in my heart and mind, I became aware that someone was hovering around me quite often, hoping that she could be born to us.

One day, as I was walking through the woods on my usual morning "commute," the presence became much stronger than usual and it was almost as if I could see her -- for it was clearly now a she. I felt that I caught a glimpse of what she would look like if she were born to us. It would be an exaggeration to say it was a vision of any kind. It was more like a clear picture in my mind.

She looked, as you might expect, like a combination of David and me, although she resembled his sisters more than my side of the family. David's face is quite handsome -- or at least striking -- as a male -- but is not your ideal of feminine beauty at all. So she wasn't pretty, or even cute in the usual sense. But she was very interesting looking. She had lots of character in her face, and dynamic greenish eyes, a largish nose, dark curly hair. Very mischievous and looking very strong willed.

I spoke to her definitely, telling her that I could see she would be great fun to be with and that it would no doubt be a joy to be her mother. But it really wasn't in the plan for us to have any children at all. So I suggested to her that there were many other fine families around the community that she could join. And if there was any particular reason she wanted to know David and me we would still be able to be part of her life.

Shortly after this, I didn't feel her around any more.

Recently, it occurred to me that a certain girl in our community may be the same soul. Not because I have any particular affinity with her (in fact I have had little contact with her), but because she resembles the girl I saw in my mind and also because the personality she is apparently exhibiting -- which is quite forceful and unusual -- reminds me of the child that I met in my mind. That child is only five so it remains to be seen if our lives connect in any way at all.

When her mother had a horoscope done for her, the astrologer, wanting to help the mother understand the personality and nature of her child, said that the child had a nature very similar to mine! But that is the only connection I can refer to.

When a child is conceived but then rejected, can she take refuge in another more welcoming womb? A mother relates an experience involving her current pregnancy. It is a story which she says she doesn't share with many people, but she adds, "I believe that I have learned over the years to trust both my dreams and my intuition when it comes to my babies." She writes:

Three weeks before I conceived, my sister-in-law had to have an abortion and asked me to come along for support. This was very difficult for me, since my personal belief is that when a little soul chooses your womb, it really was meant to be so.

But anyway, during the whole procedure of the abortion, I felt such a strong connection to that little baby and was so grief-stricken that it had to leave. The next possible time I could conceive, I did. Although I was literally shocked on one level, because this was such an inconvenient time, on a different spiritual level I knew that this little soul, who had to leave my sister-in-law's body, decided to find another receptive womb, because he/she really needed to be born. This realization feels so true, although I have nothing to prove this, but intuitively this explanation fits. My husband agrees and we both feel very accepting and loving towards this little being who had such a rough start.

Could a child leave and return again to the same mother? A story from Gladys McGarey's book *Born To Live* suggests that it is possible.

Gladys McGarey is a physician who has studied and applied the teachings of Edgar Cayce and other alternative healing methods. She has practiced medicine for several decades, in addition to being a mother of six children. One of her patients shared a very private experience with Dr. McGarey:

> This mother had a four year old daughter, Dorothy, whom she would take out to lunch occasionally. They were talking about this thing and that, and the child would shift from one subject to another, when Dorothy suddenly said, "The last time I was a little girl, I had a different mommy!" And she started talking in a different language. Mother quickly retrieved a pencil from her purse and copied down what her daughter had said as nearly as she could understand it. (In the meantime, she has lost the precious piece of paper.)
>
> The magic moment seemed over, but then Dorothy continued, "But that wasn't the last time. Last time when I was four inches long and in your tummy, Daddy wasn't ready to marry you yet, so I went away. But then, I came back." Her eyes lost that faraway look, and she was chatting again about four-year-old matters.
>
> Mother was silent. No one but her husband, the doctor and she knew this, but she *had* become pregnant about two years before she and her husband were ready to get married. When she was four months pregnant, she decided to have an abortion. She was ready to have the child, but her husband-to-be was not.

POTENTIAL CHILDREN

There are "potential children" that seem to belong with certain relationships, and to fade from our lives when those relationships end. I remember "Faith," the little girl I imagined (sensed?) around me, as my engagement to her potential father was failing. At the time, I wrote wistfully of her charm:

> It's my faith that sustains me
> but Faith is our daughter
> yours and mine
> she has brown eyes
> she skips along beside me in the sunshine
> holding my hand
> and says, never mind never mind...

And there is the child Lynn felt herself losing when her marriage ended:

> It was the day I gave my first husband the choice of staying with me or leaving. After looking me long in the eyes and knowing we had to make a decision he walked out of the house for good.
>
> I was plunged into a major maelstrom of many feelings -- would I ever see him -- how could I live without half of myself -- panic at being my sole support -- sorrow -- despair and vast grieving for a solace lost -- a partner lost -- and our future children -- lost. I specifically felt die an unborn little girl whose name was Sara -- dark, petite, bright -- never to be.

Could these "children" be images of the hidden parts of ourselves that we had hoped to set free, to express in this relationship? Or are they actually child spirits who were waiting to see whether we would become their parents? Perhaps we lose them because, with our partner gone, we no longer look like parenthood prospects. Or perhaps their connection is more to the other half of the broken couple.

In contrast to the potential children that fade away when couples break up, there are others who seem to wait patiently for years, and who may even play a part in bringing their parents together. Says Amy Cohen, "I think that I have known for quite some time about my two boys, William and Edward." She describes an occasion of feeling their presence:

> After work I went for a walk down by the beach. It was the first nice night after weeks of rain and although you could not see the sun, the sky was bright. I walked about a mile and climbed up a life guard stand that was up a hillside, overlooking the water.
>
> I just sat there thinking and watching the waves which were almost an illuminated blue because of the light in the sky. I looked up at the sky and I could feel, sense and see my boys. William and Edward were kind of floating in the sky off in the distance, holding hands.
>
> I do not know how much time went by, it seemed like a long time. They talked to me and called me mommy and told me how wonderful I am and how much they love me. They said they are so happy and they love each other and are watching out for me. They said they are getting my man, their dad, and that I must be patient and have faith.
>
> It was so beautiful, I was so happy to be with them. They are so loving and gentle. As I was experiencing this, the sky lit up.

It was bright red, bright pink and bright blue right before my eyes. The clouds were a smoky grey and it was all so brilliant. I truly felt a sense of peace within myself. I asked them when we would be together and they said soon, reminding me to be patient and have faith. There was a smile in my heart all the way home.

I have especially felt my boys' presence in the past six months, particularly after I broke up with someone I had been involved with for a year and a half. When questioning myself on whether the breakup was for the best I strongly felt my boys, in particular the older one, William, spiritually telling me that he was not the one, that they did not want him for their father. At night in bed, crying sometimes, I could feel William. As if he were there with me, stroking my forehead and hair, comforting me. Those sweet little hands on me, telling me everything was going to be okay. I have also been driving in my car and I look over to the passenger seat and feel William with me, smiling and laughing and cheering me.

On a lighter side, I guess I tune into them as a dad meter. When I am unsure about a guy I like, it is like turning within and having other voices besides my own inner guidance to help me trust what is right and what is not.

I am very happy to have these experiences. They do not scare me. They make me feel good and confident not to worry or get discouraged because I know my greater good is waiting for me.

Midwife Lani Rosenberger's story offers further evidence that a soul may be so committed to a certain parent that it will go to great lengths to reach its destination. However, for the birth mother in the story, this child was like a pilgrim soul just passing through her on his way to his chosen mother. This is a story that challenges my personal assumptions about motherhood and reminds me that there are dimensions of cooperation I know nothing about.

Lani's Story

I was thirty-eight years old, and my husband and I had been married nineteen years. Our son was fifteen, and we'd been trying for years to conceive another child, and had also been trying to adopt. Over a period of five years, five adoptions fell through! Although we rejoiced for the mother and child who would stay together, it was, nevertheless, like five stillbirths: the clothes had been gathered, the car seat bought, all preparations made, when, suddenly, a week or two before the expected arrival, no baby! It was devastating!

For about the past five years, I'd been aware of the spirit of a child sitting on my right shoulder. If I turned quickly, I could see it there; and I could feel its weight -- only a fraction of an ounce, but definitely detectable. Others saw it, too; and although I desperately longed for a daughter, everyone agreed that it was definitely male. No one could figure out why he was lingering so long without coming through me, but we all knew that he was not ready yet.

One day, while having a massage, I had a vision. I was in a clearing in a woods, with slanting, dappled sunlight falling on an outcropping of rocks. A trio of children appeared: a boy of about seven, a girl about three and a tiny baby. It was immediately understood that these were my children. They were dressed for Easter and carrying Easter baskets. The boy was dark haired with pale skin, and was dressed in a white shirt, breeches and knee socks. The girl, a blond, wore a white dress and carried a pink bunny. The baby, also a blond girl, floated on a cloud a few feet off the ground. She carried a rattle. ·

I asked them what they wanted or needed of me. The boy's face clouded over and he told me to leave him alone, to stop calling him. He seemed angry and defiant. The girl said she needed only my energy and my enthusiasm. She indicated that she and the baby could come through me as soon as I let go of the boy. The baby indicated that she needed nothing. I then asked each of them for a gift. The boy gave me a four-leaf clover and a rock. The girl gave me -- I thought -- her bunny, but when I looked back, she still had it, and I had a brightly colored egg (pysanka). The baby gave me her rattle.

As I withdrew, the boy hugged me, but without looking at me, as though he really wanted to, but couldn't let me know. The girl melted into my arms like sunshine. The baby beamed at me, blessing me with a beatific smile. As they were leaving, the boy ran back to give me a big hug, then ran off. The vision faded.

Soon after this, the spirit on my shoulder disappeared. I woke up one morning and he was gone. I no longer felt him on my shoulder; my friends could no longer see him. I grieved for my loss, and resigned myself to the thought that I would never see him again. I had to accept that he had become tired of hanging around my barren body, and had gone to await birth through another.

It was nearly a year later that I met a woman, six months pregnant, who asked my husband and me to be father and mother to her child. Three months later, my husband, son and I attended the home birth of her baby boy, whom we adopted. Talking with my new son's birth mother, she told me that she had felt this child's spirit around her for about six months before he was conceived. That placed his presence around her at the same time as I had first felt his absence. She also told me that she had known from the moment of his conception that she could not keep him, but was carrying a child for another.

The story of how we met -- brought together to share this child, her giving him his heritage and me giving him his future -- is a fantastic and mystical journey. It began several years ago, when my midwife friends suggested one day that what I needed was a fertility ritual! Sure, I said, why not?

And so they carefully researched and put together a beautiful ceremony. It was magical and moving, and touched us all very deeply. We decided to begin meeting each Solstice and Equinox for ritual, and so we did. All this began with the fertility ritual in August, 1984.

As the midwives began meeting to celebrate each changing season, we began to incorporate more and more of the feminine into our rituals, until we realized that we had truly turned to the Goddess. At this point, we began studying the Old Religion of the Ancient Ones in earnest.

Just before my ritual, a dear friend and midwife was preparing to move out of the country for a while, and she asked if I would be guardian of a sculpture she had of a breastfeeding woman which she called Luna. It seemed that whoever had Luna in her house got pregnant. I readily agreed. But she left town before I could pick up Luna, leaving Luna in the care of a mutual friend until I could pick her up. The friend called me and said, good-naturedly, "You'd better come get this thing -- I already have five kids and I sure don't want to get pregnant!" We agreed that she could bring Luna to me at the fertility ritual -- but by that time, she was already pregnant!

A year passed, and in June of 1985, I left Christianity for good (I'd been weaning from it for many years) and became (or, more accurately, rededicated myself as) a child of the Goddess. After ten years of unanswered prayers for a child, I began to pray to Her. Our Summer Solstice ritual that year fully embraced our newly-found Old Religion. I only gave myself a month (from June 1) to ask Her for a child; if it didn't happen by then, I would give up. I'd been ready to give up anyway -- ten years of disappointment at the first drop of menstrual blood each month were taking their toll; I needed to get on with my life. But with my newfound spiritual path, I felt I had to give the Goddess a chance, or I wouldn't feel that I had truly tried my best.

Our Summer Solstice ritual was held on the beach. We danced and sang, crowned ourselves, chanted, built a fire ring around ourselves, meditated and prayed. Five days later, a truly extraordinary string of events began.

First, Luna's owner was back in the country and paid a visit. Suspecting that she wanted Luna back, I got her from her place of honor in our bedroom and placed her on the hearth. It turned out that I was right, my friend did want her back. She wished to conceive again. (She had a boy the following Spring.)

I said that perhaps Luna only worked if she was received directly from her owner. After all, the woman who had directly received her had, indeed, conceived. Perhaps I needed to return her, then borrow her again -- directly -- at a later date. (In retrospect, it all happened as it was meant: I received Luna indirectly from my midwife friend, just as I would indirectly receive my son from her!)

She asked if I was still trying to adopt, and I said yes, that I was still waiting for a child to come to me, and that I preferred that it be born at home. She told me about a woman she was presently caring for: she had caught two of this woman's children at home; this would be her fourth child and she was placing it for adoption. Unfortunately for me, she already had adoptive parents. I thanked my friend for thinking of me, and said that my time would come. I strapped Luna into the carseat for her ride home, and waved a fond farewell.

When my friend arrived home that night, there was an emergency call on her answering machine: the adoptive parents had backed out *that day*! She called me and said, "If you want it, the baby is yours."

I was stunned! It took several days just for the news to truly sink in! Then we talked to the biological parents, and all was arranged. We flew the mother down to meet us, and when she stepped into our house, she announced, "I've been here before, there's a room at the back with a big fireplace and a rocking chair!" It turns out that she had shared a house with our mutual friend when they both lived in this town, and she had come with this friend (the midwife) one day to visit me. She'd sat in my rocker while her two young children played in my yard!

In September she called to say that she was in early labor, and we flew to her city. (I should mention that she, our mutual friend the midwife, and all the ladies at her birth are all daughters of the Goddess.)   When we walked through her front door, our twenty-minute-old son was in her arms.   Our older son (age sixteen) cut the cord, and I took Caleb to my breast to nurse. We sang, prayed, gave thanks and exchanged gifts. And then we left and flew home with our son.   It was five days before the Autumnal Equinox.

My son is five now. He tells me tales of choosing me for his mother from his pre-birth home on a moon of Jupiter. He points out Jupiter in the night sky and says, "There is where I was before I was your boy." He drew me a picture one day of a fetus (not a baby) in a round, red circle in the sky, with a star nearby, and a woman under an apple tree, waving. He said that the picture showed him "on a moon of Jupiter" where he lived before he was born, and the lady under the tree was me, waiting for him to be born.

He strongly resembles his older brother (his birth mother's older boy), only lighter; and his older brother is the image of my vision. As for the girls, I don't know when I'll see them on this Earthly plane. Perhaps they will be my grandchildren. We'll just have to wait and see.

BY CHOICE OR BY CHANCE?

At this point the skeptic in us demands, "Does everybody choose? And why would anyone choose to be born to a heroin addict, or in a war zone?" Good questions!

Do we agree to our roles as parent and child?   Are these connections a matter of chance? Are they assigned by a higher power? The questions make sense if (and only if) we exist as conscious individuals before conception.   But having taken that as a working premise, let us ask the questions.

Do we choose our children? Do they choose us? There are clues to be found in these stories, as well as from other sources.

Parents who have experienced contact before birth often have definite views on the nature of our bond. One mother, who had a vision of her child as a young man radiating great love, writes:

> Up until the time of this experience, I held a vague, intellectual notion of children choosing their parents and environment prior to birth. After the experience, it became not a notion from the intellect, but a certainty from a place deep inside of me that there

exists a profound connection between ourselves and the people we choose to spend our lives with. It is a sacred connection that serves a purpose in our spiritual evolution. I cannot emphasize enough the profundity, the depth, the sacredness of these relationships we choose in life. Yes, my beliefs did change. Beyond the shadow of a doubt, our children come to us from a place of choice and with a plan in their pocket.

Beverly Hayes, an adoptive mother, felt she made contact with her child while it was still unborn. She describes her sense of the parent-child bond:

I believe that there are souls or "baby beings" that want to be born through you or come to your family to be raised by you. They choose which parents they want to come to. I also feel parents choose their children based on what lessons they need to learn in this lifetime. My ideas changed from this experience only in that I always thought I would be completely connected to my baby if I were pregnant. It never occurred to me that this could happen with an adopted child.

Many parents express the belief that children come into families where they will learn the lessons they need. And yet -- the feelings conveyed in communications from children-to-be are often more playful and light-hearted than we might expect from beings about to enter another level of "lessons." There's often a sense of willingness, even eagerness, from these newcomers that seems more in keeping with some degree of choice than with compulsion.

I suspect that most parents who believe our children come to us as pre-existing souls would not like to think mere chance might govern our connections. Concern that the link should be meaningful, not random, is especially evident in the stories of adoption. Each adoptive parent cites reasons to believe that their child is meant to be with them. The possibility of a "mistake" can be stressful.

For example, while Kathy McNeil was waiting to adopt a baby from Korea, her dreams and emotions seemed to connect her with the child before he was found. Excerpts from her journal reveal the intensity of the process, and her deep concern that the child offered by the adoption agency be the one she felt "pulling" on her:

July 6 -- We get a referral from Korea at last. A two-year-old. He's adorable and we accept the referral. Bruce and I had a moment of panic. Are we sure this is the right baby. But it must always feel like this when the reality hits home.

July 27 -- The adoption service calls to say that the little boy we accepted has a brother who has just come into care and the two children must be placed together. Bruce and I agonize over the needs of two children and decide that we cannot do it. This was not the right match we feel and we ask them to continue the search for another single referral. Please God, find my Niko soon. I keep telling myself you really are coming. I have to persevere through all this to get my special son.

August 3 -- THE CALL 10 A.M. My baby is one year old. I can't believe it. This must be the right baby, he's a year old just like my dreams. I told our caseworker three months ago that I keep dreaming of a baby who's about a year old. I'm scared they're going to send me a three-year-old and I'm not going to think it's the right kid. This baby's birthday was probably in late July or August back when we started the whole adoption. It's because you were born my Niko.

Oh, I know this time it's right, even if you're not cute. I just feel peaceful. The papers say you were abandoned early this year and are in an orphanage. Why are you in an orphanage? They are supposed to keep babies under two in a foster home. (It turned out for the little history we have that Niko was abandoned in March and taken to Seoul City Baby Hospital. He came to the orphanage June 27th. So all those months of panic, was he eating, was he being held, were because he wasn't. Many children died in that hospital. According to our director, the cribs are lined back to back and despite dedication there are too little resources and not enough staff.)

August 25 -- I always knew I had one more baby coming, just not through my body. Giving birth is hard and painful but quickly forgotten when you hold that most precious child in your arms. Adoption is the same. I didn't throw up for nine months but just cried, agonized and felt pulled by this relentless caller that I couldn't go find. God, I have felt such peace since we heard about you, even before the picture came I finally felt we got it right, the search has ended.

Leaving aside the parents' stories and impressions for now, where else can we look for evidence of choice or chance in our connections?

Hypnotic regression to apparent memories of womb-life should be a rich source of information. Helen Wambach, Joel Whitton and Michael Gabriel* are among the therapists who claim to have elicited memories of conscious existence even before conception. Popular books about their work can of course present only a fraction of their material -- but in the histories they relate, memories of choosing one's parents are conspicuously absent. (In fact, a study of Dr. Whitton's work presents some fait-accompli matchups of the "Oh No, Not You Again!" variety -- making me wonder why the pre-birth contacts I have gathered are so uniformly pleasant.) But this is a new field of experience and research; as more people explore their deepest memories through hypnosis and other techniques, we may gain many more clues concerning our existence before conception.

There are other, older ways of exploring the mysteries beyond birth and death, and we can find alternative views in traditional teachings. Probably no people on earth have accumulated more lore (or perhaps data) about the state between lives than the Tibetan lamas. In their view,* we are swept to our next birth almost like straws in the wind; choice is possible only to a limited degree and only with great mindful concentration beyond the capacity of most people.

Another source of clues is in the reports of children who seem to recall previous lives. Sometimes they describe memories of their existence between lives. What has brought them into relationship with their current parents? In his book, *Children Who Remember Previous Lives*, Dr. Ian Stevenson summarizes the evident connections between the child and the new family in hundreds of cases he has studied. According to Dr. Stevenson's findings, there seem to be three main streams that carry a soul into a certain family.

There may be a strong emotional bond from a previous life. A good example of this is the case (presented in Dr. Stevenson's book) of two daughters of an English family who were killed in an accident and, the following year, apparently returned to the same parents as twin sisters.

There are cases where the relationship is more casual but still involves some positive association, such as a more distant family tie, or even a friendly business connection.

Most surprising is the evidence that in many cases the only apparent link is geographical. The place of birth and the place of death appear to be powerful ties for a soul awaiting conception. For example, a Thai child seemed to recall a previous life which had ended in his being murdered. He stated that he had "stayed on a tree" near the murder site for seven years, until one rainy day he saw his new father-to-be and accompanied him home on a bus. No other connection could be found between the child's previous life and his present family.

One truly fascinating possibility that emerges from the cross-cultural stories in Dr. Stevenson's files is that the afterlife -- which we may like to imagine as being more free, more unconditioned than this life -- is still shaped by societal customs. And thus, to the extent that we have choice in our return, we perhaps return according to our culture's expectations.

✳　　　✳　　　✳

In stories of communication before birth, what evidence can we find that we have any choice in our pairing as parent and child? Many people describe the sense that they have been courted for some time by someone wishing to be born to them. Some meetings convey the message that the child has chosen and waited for this particular family.

Celestia Jasper recalls a conversation with her little boy Frank James:

> When our second son Ivan was about eight months old I was having a difficult time with him. I couldn't seem to comfort or nourish him. I said, "I don't think I'm the right mother for Ivan -- I can't do anything right for him." Frank James, who was four at the time, said, "But Mom, you are. Ivan looked down and picked you out to be his mom."

Some stories present the amazing possibility that parents may also, sometimes, choose their children. Isadora Paymer writes:

> Grandma Lazarus raised me for the first three and a half years of my life, after my mother died. We were very close and attuned. When my father remarried and I moved out of her house I was bereft. She died when I was eight.
>
> In my pregnancy with my daughter Nora, at six weeks I heard my late father Sylvan's voice. He said, "You have a healthy baby girl. Do you want to keep it?" I said, "Yes, I want to keep it. Not a screamer like Nicky?" The voice said, "No, not a screamer," and laughed. I said, "Yes, I want to keep her."
>
> Two weeks later, I heard my father's voice again. He said, "Which of your dead relatives do you want the baby to be?" I said, "Sylvan." He said, "Female." I said, "Grandma Lazarus." Then I suddenly smelled her perfume, which I had not smelled in thirty years. I understood that the baby's body would be the container for the soul of my late grandmother. The voice said, "This will make up for your early losses." (Most of my family died in my childhood.)
>
> Several months later, when I was ill and regretting the pregnancy, I heard the voice say, "Do you realize what a privilege it is to be able to pick the person that you get?"

Susan Bassett relates that she went to see a channeler when she was about two months pregnant with her daughter:

> She put me in a trance and I asked for the spirits that wanted me to be their mother to appear. I was busy "interviewing" each of them when the door of my room (on a metaphysical level) was thrown open and in came this energetic, bubbling, extroverted towheaded child who jumped into my lap with "Mommy, mommy." It was a done deal. We spent some time talking over agreements about how we wanted our relationship to be -- hers and mine -- and I just knew I was going to be the mother of this wonderful child.

A striking detail in both stories is that the mother's choosing was done when the fetus was already six to eight weeks into its development. This leads us to the intriguing question of just when a soul becomes associated with its body. We will explore this question later; here I will only mention that Dr. Stevenson's research supports the possibility that the timing is variable and may be well after conception.

How special is the connection between parent and child? Is it important and intentional, or do waiting souls simply enter whatever womb is available?

If we take all the stories here at face value we'd have to say there's evidence on both sides. There are parents who emphasize a strong sense that "this child is meant to be in our family -- has waited a long time for me..." But we've also seen evidence that children may wait for a while and then go elsewhere.

Perhaps both situations exist -- necessary and fateful combinations, as well as more casual arrangements. It may be humbling to admit the possibility that at least some of our children could equally well have been born to someone else. Ali recalls a startling conversation with her little boy:

> When Brett was between three and four years old, he was very angry with me one day. He said, "I hate you, Mommy. You weren't even my first choice for a Mommy."
>
> I somehow managed to stay centered and asked, "Who was your first choice?"
>
> "It was a woman from the Philippines but she was already taken."

CHAPTER THIRTEEN
BEYOND BIOLOGY: THE ADOPTION BOND

Suppose that mothers and fathers reach out in spirit to find the person who will be their child, and children choose the family to which they will belong. If these possibilities are real, then giving birth to a child and adopting a child may be very much the same kind of cooperative process.

In his autobiography, John Denver tells a remarkable story of connecting with his future child. Unable to have his own children, he offered a frequent "invitation" prayer while going through the adoption process: "Whoever you are, wherever you are, I don't know what you have to go through to get here and be with us, but we love you very much and can't wait to be with you." And then, he had a dream.

In the dream, three people in white robes came to him and placed a baby boy in his arms: "a dark-faced boy with round eyes and a little bit of an overbite -- and as I was holding him, he looked up, grabbed my thumb, and smiled." Eleven days later, the child who would become John Denver's son was born. The adoptive parents went to meet him when he was two months old. John recalls:

> We had just been told that the young woman who was bringing Zak had been delayed, and were trying to keep from feeling disappointed, when the door at the far end of the hall opened and the woman appeared after all, with our child. Without a word, she came running down the hall and handed the baby to me. He had round eyes, and this little bit of overbite, and when I held him he smiled and grabbed my thumb. Zak was the child in my dream -- exactly the same child.

These stories of adoption and other non-biological bonds all share a sense that the connection and the agreement were made in another dimension. The chain of events that brings *this* child to us, of all possible children, often seems "orchestrated in perfect detail."

One father writes of his adopted son:

> I came to feel I was filling a void in his life, almost as if he were saying to me, "Where were you the first five months of my life?"

I felt as if he had a special need for a father, and he seemed to love me from right off the bat before I had earned it. This experience strengthened my commitment to my child and the idea that we were meant to be together. Parenthood has little to do with biology and much more to do with the spiritual relationship which exists between a parent and child.

The parallels between adopting and giving birth are central to Holly Richardson's story. Over the years she has experienced numerous pregnancies, including miscarriages, and adopted several children. The "tingles" she describes are her way of sensing the presence of a child, both during pregnancy and when she is being contacted by someone asking to be conceived -- or found. Holly writes:

Several years ago, we adopted two little girls out of Romania. For about a year before that, I knew that I had children over there. Before I left for Romania, I knew more convincingly than I've known almost anything, that we had two little girls waiting for us. Finding them was quick and I knew absolutely they were my children. When I arrived at the airport with them, my husband took one look at our new daughter with Down's Syndrome and said, "Oh, she's the right one!" Later he said that he recognized her, and knew he had known her before. Although not quite as dramatically as with Alexandra, he also knew our daughter Alina belonged with us.

A short time later, I felt there was a baby that needed to come to our family! My husband agreed after about a month to attempt a pregnancy and the next day, I felt the same type of "tingles" down my back as I felt when pregnant with my daughter, but I just knew it was a boy and that he was ready to come.

The next year was an unfortunate string of miscarriages, and about thirteen months after we had decided to try and have a baby, I spent a lot of time wondering about my feelings of the year before. I then had a spiritual witness that my son had already been born, somewhere in Russia! So far, we have not been able to "find" him and he is now around two years old.

We did, however, decide to adopt a little five year old girl from Kazakstan. As I was making preparations to go and get her, my husband and I both had very strong feelings about a baby boy wanting to come to our family (except, for my husband, it was twin boys!). As we debated our sanity, this baby (or babies) came to visit me. I felt the now-familiar prickles down my back, but this time, instead of being quite fleeting, the feelings (and the baby) stayed and stayed and stayed! The first time was about forty minutes, the second time, an hour, and the third time, another forty minutes. I certainly felt that this baby really wanted to come! We do not yet know who or where this baby or set of twins will be coming from.

I got pregnant with one baby in December, and am currently five months along, with all going well. I do not know if the child I am carrying is the same one who visited me. This child seems to be quite "mild-mannered" whereas the one who visited seemed so forceful! It will be interesting to see how it all plays out!

There is little difference between the "invitations" sent out by people hoping to conceive and by those hoping to adopt. In both cases, a kind of spiritual nest-making gives our inner world a receptive and welcoming shape. Lisa, an adoptive mother, writes, "When I knew for certain we would be forming our family through adoption, I consciously and unconsciously put out the message that we wanted a baby newborn that we would bring home from the hospital and that I'd be able to nurse. It wasn't something I necessarily meditated on -- but I carried this vision/thought with me all the time."

Another woman's experience with adoption parallels both the prayerful mood of pre-conception, and the long nurturing months of pregnancy itself, for Leslie's baby demanded a nine-month term of virtual physical union:

"I Sent Out a Silent Message:" Leslie's Story

I am infertile due to blocked fallopian tubes, but my husband and I knew we wanted a family, so early in the second year of our marriage, we set out upon the "adoption journey," fully expecting a long and frustrating experience. Our expectations were initially met as we explored agency adoption, but fortunately a friend pointed us in the direction of private adoption.

During the time when we were searching for our baby, we were aware that most private adoption placements take an average of five months from the time search letters go out until a baby is found. Therefore, I knew that our baby was alive, and existed "somewhere out there." Each night before I fell asleep, I sent out a silent message, something like, "We're waiting for you, sweet baby, and we love you."

Meanwhile, Elizabeth was growing in the womb of her birth mother, to whom we will always be grateful. She was a person who had had a terribly difficult life. At the time she became pregnant, she was living on the streets and had a drinking and drug problem. Within five weeks of our beginning an active search for a baby, we found Elizabeth, then just two days old. Or perhaps she found us.

We received a telephone call in June 1982 from a doctor in another city. A tiny baby girl had been born the previous day, weighing only five pounds and probably four to six weeks pre-term. No one was sure what the actual due date should have been, as the only prenatal exam had been performed less than two weeks before the birth. The baby seemed healthy, but was suffering from some withdrawal symptoms. Were we interested?

We arrived the next day, only because the doctor had discouraged us from coming that very evening. We met briefly with Elizabeth's birth mother, who was recovering from the caesarean birth. Even in the excitement and anticipation of seeing our baby (whom she had chosen not to see at all), we felt so sorry for her. Just looking at her tired face and frail form, we could see what her life had done to her. As she chain-smoked and admonished us in a tough voice to "love that baby," all I could feel was a sadness that she had never had a chance.

We brought Elizabeth home the next day. She was jittery from nicotine withdrawal, or so the doctors said; her little arms and legs trembled, and she cried constantly. She needed to be fed every two hours around the clock. So much for my expensive Lact-Aid* kit and dreams of nursing my child. Who had time to sterilize the tubing and set it all up?

Elizabeth was what was termed a "demanding baby." She was never content to lie on a blanket to look at toys or pictures. She didn't like the baby swing we bought with such high hopes; she hated any kind of carrying pack. She wanted to be held in my arms and walked. No sitting down, none at all!

Needless to say I was exhausted, often to the point of tears. My husband helped an extra amount with the housework, laundry, and bottles, and was wonderful, but since Elizabeth wanted *me* all the time, I was still overwhelmed. I had quit my job, and because going out with her seemed to upset her so much, we were home together most of the time.

I went through a period of having to defend my way of caring for her to many people -- friends and even our doctor, who felt I was "spoiling" her by not letting her "cry it out." I just couldn't. I tried to put her down and go outside or turn on the shower to avoid hearing her cries, but it never worked. I still knew she was crying, and I couldn't relax.

Don't think I was a saintly selfless mother. I was frustrated, exhausted, and even resentful at times. I questioned the wisdom of ever having become a mother; I felt urges to throw her out the window; it was pretty awful. But I could never bear to hear my baby cry. So I walked and sang to her and walked some more. We became almost physically joined, like some bizarre form of Siamese twins. She refused to be separated from me even when we were only a few feet apart.

This behavior lasted until she was nine months old and then magically disappeared.

Elizabeth is now five years old, happy, beautiful, smart, and quite independent. She will be starting kindergarten this fall, and each day asks how many more days until school starts. She has many friends, and loves to visit them.

Perhaps I'm being silly to think that she needed to re-live her time in utero, because she had not had a nurturing experience before. I can't help wondering if that is why she clung to me for nine months. Is it odd to think that my "silent messages" to her before her birth had anything to do with her pre-term birth and removal from a mother who was unable to nurture her?

$$*   *   *$$

Linda Heal, on her way to becoming a non-biological mother, had a series of dreams that enabled her to get to know her unborn daughter. The dreams gave her glimpses of her daughter's lively personality, and reassurance that their connection would really work. Her experience seems to me to be an example of the cooperative bond in action, dealing with our anxieties and smoothing the path to parenthood. This pattern, which is evident in so many stories of biological parenthood as well, may be one of the main "purposes" of pre-birth contact.

Says Linda: "It was through dreaming that I knew there could be a child at all..."

I came out as a lesbian at age seventeen, and beyond that, I'm terribly squeamish about all the bodily boundaries that get pushed so hard in reproducing; so for several years, I didn't think that full-time parenting would be part of my adult life, despite my involvement with kids' sports programs, despite my love for making kids laugh.

But when I was twenty-one, the first baby came in a dream. I was lying on my mother's couch, and in my dream my grandmother (her mother) came quietly downstairs with a child she'd just birthed. She placed her on my stomach, and the baby and I looked silently at one another, until she was ready to talk which we did brain-to-brain, circumventing our mouths and the messy mechanics of language.

"I knew you'd be the one," she said to me. "I knew you'd know that I could talk, that you would listen. I'm here now. I'm with you." And we stayed there for a long time, just looking at each other with the respect of equals. I don't remember how the dream ended, only that it was one of those dreams that change you forever, so in that way it never ended.

I don't think that dream baby was the one I've ended up with. I think she was a sort of spokesbaby, to let me know that inside me was the compassion and patience to nurture a deep connection with a child of my own.

Three years went by, and in late 1990, the woman to whom I had partnered myself became pregnant through donor insemination. During the first months of pregnancy, I had strings of short, quick dreams about caring for a baby -- always a bit hazy in detail, but always ending just as the child's gender was about to be revealed via a diaper change.

I'd been nervous about how it would feel, as a lesbian, to raise a male child. So for the year prior to pregnancy Amy and I had taken on "part time kids" -- we did daycare for a five year old boy and his three month old sister for a year, to practice parenting and to watch one another's style. Through my friendship with Michael, the five-year-old, I was reawakened to the knowledge that kids are kids, that gender doesn't have to predetermine the really important things. Once I knew deep in my body that what I really wanted was a *child*, and that gender was secondary, then I knew we were ready to go ahead with the insemination. But still, our preference was for a girl. And I suspect I was a bit shy about being challenged daily to abandon my strong womanist feelings about gender. Hence, the repeated near-diaper-change teases in the dreams.

Those all seemed like dreams to prepare me for parenthood, in a general way. But the dreams in which I made the strongest contact with the zealous soul I believe to be in my child, those dreams came later in the pregnancy. In about the fifth month, I dreamed of hiking down a long hallway of college classrooms, my child in a backpack carrier, a load of books in my arms. We were taking a class, something I long to return to. In this dream, my child communicated wordlessly, like the child in the original dream, and with that directness and force of will that have been characteristic of Dory since the days following her birth.

"Hey," said the child in the backpack. "Let's take that class... it has lots of teachers." It looked to me, in the dream, like it was just a very crowded classroom, with students crammed in along the front wall. I told the child that. "Let's go anyway," she said. "Hey, would you carry me?"

"My arms are full of books right now," I told her. (She was clearly female, my dreams had told me by now. It was something about the clarity of her communication and my dream appreciation of her puckishness that let me know that, I think.)

"So put them in the backpack and hold me instead. Check my diaper, while you're at it," the child directed.

Besides giving me a dose of her personality, in this dream my child reinforced many things for me -- first, that with a little work I'd be able to parent *and* do the things that really mattered to me (like taking classes and carrying around lots of books), a balance that I had feared impossible before birth and one that I step closer to with each passing week. Second, that my child would be clear about her needs and wants, if only I leave myself open to listening. I'd been worrying about understanding a baby, so hearing this child give such clear directions eased my worry. And there was, as I mentioned, the sheer force of her will and her confidence in piping up with her suggestions. Since her birth, Dory has never been a suggestible child. She's always known what she wants to do, and she ensures that it gets done. From the very first, when she had to be held and walked *even while she slept*, to today, when the correct Mom must carry her up the basement steps, Dory has liked being in charge.

My strongest dream came at the end of the eighth month of Amy's pregnancy. In the dream, Amy and I were in the back yard, and she was waving her arms around to dramatize her latest set of landscaping plans. Landscaping is Amy's passion. I'm not drawn to it like she is, so in the dream I was doing what I do in real life: listening politely. That's when I noticed Dory's head, sticking out between Amy's legs.

"What are you doing here?" I asked, bending down to make eye contact with a fully alert baby while Amy continued to talk about self-pollinating fruit trees and burning bushes. Apparently, she was unaware of what was happening.

"It sounded *fun* out there," said the child -- again, talking without words, but this time in a very animated impatient tone. "So I thought I'd come out now."

"Don't," I implored. "You'll be smarter if you stay in longer."

"I don't *want* to stay in longer," she said. "It's dull and crowded in there, it sounds fun out here, and I'm ready. I want more fun." She and I discussed that for a while, with her sounding more and more childlike -- like a four-year-old who's mastered the art of argument. She reluctantly returned to Amy's womb, muttering about what she was missing, about how she couldn't wait that much longer, grumbling about being sent back to her room. Amy was still talking about gardening, so it was clearly meant to be an exchange just between Dory and me.

Amy didn't have strong dreams about the kind of child she would birth; I had the dreams for both of us. Our daughter Dory shares many of the characteristics of the child in the dreams: she looks and sounds like her, and like most kids she is drawn to active, giggly, all-encompassing fun. Even her natal chart is littered with it: all her major signs are in the house that governs play or the house that governs communication. It's a chart that amused and amazed the astrologer who made it. You can back up that chart by looking at Doe -- she's an engaging child who instantly made friends of people who used to be casual acquaintances. Her drive to communicate, and her will of iron that's not always willing to accept compromise, remind me of the "helpful" child in the classroom dream.

The fact that this dream child chose to come to me is the real honor that makes me think that this was *my* child, preparing me to be *her* parent. I was nervous about parenting, about my ability to understand and feel connected to someone to whom I have no biological link. By appearing to me in my dreams, my child seemed to be reassuring me: look. *I* will tell you what to do, you will listen, it will feel just *fine*, and we'll have a good time. Really.

Our child, Dorian Elizabeth Liem-Heal, was born on June 20, 1991. Her first joke was refusing to gently float down in utero to stop the gush of amniotic fluid, so when Amy's water broke in the local bagel factory, the generous (and eventually comical) flow of fluid never stopped. And even through a long difficult labor and eventually an emergency caesarean (which by that point we all knew to be necessary), we were all conscious and welcomed each other with open hearts.

Dory is a talky eighteen months old now, and when she can get away with it, she lives in the refrigerator on the bottom shelf next to the eggs. She is compassionate and communicative and we understand each other just fine, and as often as possible we launch ourselves into the realm of communicating with just our hearts.

CHAPTER FOURTEEN
HELP AND REASSURANCE

The baby in the womb might seem to be a helpless passenger, unable to exert any effect on people and events. But in stories of pre-birth connections, we meet beings who not only can communicate but perhaps can even help and reassure their parents in times of need.

When the baby seems to provide reassurance, a parent in response feels, "You are strong and you comfort me." Can this be a valid impression? Or do we create these experiences out of a need to believe that the baby is in charge, or is at least sharing with us the tremendous responsibility for its welfare?

Some mothers describe a sense of receiving guidance from the child in decisions that affect them both. Vivien Beirne explains:

> When I figured out that I was pregnant, I spent a great amount of time communicating with the baby's spirit and the angels for guidance on how to be the best mother for this child, and most decisions were now being made through this communication -- that is, what to eat, what to name the baby, and so on.
>
> I don't remember dreams of communication. Mine was mostly just a heightened awareness, and an understanding which I could easily block out if I got anxious about anything. There were many times when I could not figure out what to eat for the developing baby -- I don't believe in a standard nutrition plan that fits all pregnant women. I asked from within, for the right foods for the baby, and was able to choose quickly after that, and often in surprising ways. I didn't eat the prescribed amounts of the foods from each food group each day, but I must have eaten what we needed, as he was born big and healthy.

There is some interesting corroboration to Vivien's impression that she received guidance from the baby. It is found in the testimony of people who have apparently been regressed to their pre-birth existence. *Life Between Life* describes the work of Dr. Joel Whitton, a psychiatrist who uses hypnosis to explore these memories:

> Many of Dr. Whitton's subjects have mentioned "hovering" over

the mother, encouraging her in choices of food and music, discouraging smoking and the drinking of alcohol, and generally directing behavior that will enhance their mutual welfare.

ARE YOU ALL RIGHT?

Anxiety about the baby's condition is often the prelude to an experience of contact. Reassurance comes in dreams and reveries, visions, inner voices, and almost physical feelings hard to name.

My two previous miscarriages had conditioned me to dread any sign of bleeding in early pregnancy. A few weeks after conception, I wrote in my diary about an odd happening:

> Last night a friend came to dinner. I felt a bit tired after all the preparations. After supper I rested on the couch and petted the cat and her fur got me coughing. I spotted a bit and jumped into bed, to huddle all night in a sweaty sleep. But before going to sleep -- something seemed to grip my arm. "I'm in the grip of something very strong," I thought. It was both scary and reassuring in a way.

At the time, I didn't put a great deal of faith in the sensation; but ever since my daughter came into my life through that pregnancy I have surely been in the grip of something strong.

Some of these reassuring experiences come at times of real danger to the baby, while others are small daily messages of comfort that "I'm still here..." Nikki Lee describes how such messages helped her through a pregnancy that followed three miscarriages:

> I spent the first trimester regularly nauseated. As time went along, I got less and less nauseated. On days that I felt completely well, I would panic that I was no longer pregnant. I would turn inward and silently ask Clelia, "Are you in there?" or, "Are you okay in there?" I would get a message back, a feeling that I put words to: "I'm okay, Mom." The messages from her felt like little bursts of sunlight warmth that radiated out from my womb; they filled my whole self from the inside.
>
> We regularly were able to have this exchange during the whole pregnancy. I would check in with her if I hadn't felt movement in a while, or if I just wanted to contact her. I would always get a sunburst back that told me all was well. Even when she wasn't born until three and a half weeks past her due date, and there

was some concern about my being thirty-nine and her being so late, I always got these great messages from her. She was so responsive. Sometimes I would send her messages of love and gladness that she was there inside me.

Susan Sitler felt she connected with her two children in many ways during each of her pregnancies, but her strongest memories are of communications regarding the babies' health. She says:

> With Luke, my first, I had been very sick for four months and hospitalized for severe vomiting. I also had heavy spotting. Needless to say, I was worried. At one point I got a message that "I" (the baby) was okay and not to worry. I was able to relax (mostly) after that.
>
> During my next pregnancy, at four months, I severely injured my back in a fall and had to take five days of narcotics to kill some of the pain. I was very anxious about the drugs and how the fall might have injured the baby. I asked Daniel if he was okay and "felt" the answer was that he was all right. By now, I had learned to trust my "talks" with my kids. I believed it fully, and the rest of my pregnancy I was worry free and confident right through our home birth.

Margaret Birnbaum was warned that she had a large uterine fibroid which might interfere with either conceiving or carrying a baby to term. She decided to go ahead and try to bear a child, and had no trouble becoming pregnant. But during the fifth month she began having contractions:

> I was advised to take it easy and reduce the stress in my life (I was working full time at a demanding job). By the seventh month I was advised to stop working and stay off my feet to avoid pre-term labor. I was given a device for monitoring my contractions at home. Nurses called daily to check on me. It seemed everyone around me was sure I was going to deliver prematurely. I didn't think so, but not being experienced at this sort of thing, I didn't have much to go on.
>
> Then, toward the end of the seventh month, I got a distinct "communication" from the baby. Here's what I wrote in my journal at the time:
>
> "Had a very emotional night last night... When we got into bed I was crying again. Too many people are telling me what to do -- and they all expect the worst. It's hard to retain my

confidence when no one else shares it -- except Davin (my husband). He comforted me. Then the baby spoke to me -- said she was all right and would hang in there with me. That meant a lot."

From then on I had a calm confidence that everything was going to work out fine, in spite of the fears of my care providers. I continued to have lots of contractions, but I didn't go into labor prematurely. I delivered my baby at full term by scheduled caesarean (necessary because the fibroid had grown to the size of a baby's head during pregnancy and was blocking the birth canal). My baby, Jessica, was and continues to be robustly healthy.

Alisha Buchser wasn't yet sure that she was pregnant, when she and her fiance attended an outdoor concert:

Ten minutes into the concert a tree limb fell forty feet onto my head, an ambulance arrived and I was rushed to the emergency room -- scared, confused and throwing up. At the hospital a serum test revealed that, yes, I was pregnant.

At that moment I knew all would be fine, in spite of all the negative input coming from hospital staff. I knew I would not die and that my baby would be healthy. I tried to avoid drugs and other medical suggestions about CAT scans and so forth.

Everything went fine until my second month -- the day after my wedding. I woke up in this beautiful hotel suite only to start vomiting and not to stop for six days. My husband and midwives were all very worried, but somehow I was seeing my baby and he was okay. Knowing that my son was okay was simply a feeling and a reassurance from the baby. Needless to say I got better and in the end the twenty pounds I had lost turned into seventy pounds gained!

Janette Patterson had been ill during her third pregnancy and had also suffered a fall, so she was concerned about the baby's wellbeing. Although in real life she had no medical tests done with any of her pregnancies, in the seventh month she dreamed of receiving a sonogram to check on the baby:

In the dream I could see the little baby on the monitor. I could see the head, arms, torso, all the organs, her little heart was just beating away. It was absolutely amazing. I could see that she was totally healthy and doing fine. But I could not see her genitals. It was as if she was saying: Mom, I am okay. See, you can even see inside of me, but you can not see if I am a boy or a girl. That you have to wait and find out later.

When I woke up, I felt overjoyed. It was as if I had had a direct conversation with the baby. And I laughed when I realized she was teasing me about my curiosity over whether she was a boy or a girl.

At a certain point in pregnancy (typically in the second trimester), some women find that their worries and anxieties are suddenly dispelled and a sense of calm and reassurance comes over them.

The change may come mysteriously, with a feeling of having been comforted on an unconscious level. A mother recalls: "We began planning for our first home birth. I was still worried about the 'what ifs' until my fifth month, when I unexpectedly became very calm and confident about the birth. I don't know how, but I recognized this was because the baby had reassured me in my sleep."

Sometimes the transition from anxiety to calm is associated with a definite experience. A mother writes:

> Up until the time she started kicking, I'd been scared of my pregnancy (it was unexpected), but when I felt that tiny person moving inside me for the first time, it was as if a peace had come over me, as though she was telling me, "Don't worry, Mommy -- everything will be okay."
>
> In one of my dreams, I saw the image of Jesus Christ. I was never overly religious, so I couldn't understand why he would appear in my dreams. Like all first time mothers, I was nervous about my pregnancy and worried about the health of my unborn child. But after that particular dream, I felt as if a weight had been lifted from my shoulders. Suddenly, I felt that everything would turn out all right.
>
> Today, Rebecca Lee is almost eight months old. Occasionally, I think of my dream, of how the image of Christ had calmed my fears and brought me reassurance when I was worried. I don't question it, I am just thankful that Rebecca is so very healthy.

A beautiful dream brought calm to Ruthie Ervin in the sixth month of her first pregnancy. "So vivid and moving was this 'contact' with my child," she says, "that I *knew* upon waking that I would deliver a son (previously I had thought I would have a girl) and what we would name him:"

In my dream, I am walking down the main street of my

four-block, rural Mississippi town, Crystal Springs. I am carrying my newborn baby boy. The town appears just as it would in reality, except that vintage pickup trucks line the street and a solid stream of old farmers blocks the sidewalk the entire length of the block. (Crystal Springs has always been a farming community, reaching its zenith in the thirties and forties as a "truck-crop" town and the "Tomatopolis" of the world -- it produced more tomatoes than any other spot in the country; I come from a long line of "Tomato Queens!" My great-grandfather, my grandfather and my father all farmed in this area. I no longer live there.)

As I watch these old-timers, both white and black men, most of them dressed in overalls and work clothes, I realize that they have gathered to welcome my son into this life. They have all worked side by side with my father Julian Ervin and his father Glen Ervin, both long deceased, and they are genuinely interested in this child.

I am very touched at all this attention. I have named my son Julian after my father, a man who sired three daughters, no sons. Without exchanging a word, I hand the baby to the first gentleman in line. He then hands the child to the next man, and on and on the child is handed down.

The striking image of this dream is that of gnarled, work-worn hands reaching out to this infant, then tenderly, almost reverently holding him, silently rocking him, then passing him along to the next set of strong, brown hands. All of the men are approving of Julian, as if the tribal elders had gathered to initiate a new member. The atmosphere is one of quiet import and warmth.

I awake with a profound sense of calm and assurance. Without doubt, I know I will have a son and that we will name him Julian.

After this dream, I never again suffered the normal worries and anxieties about having a healthy labor and delivery and child. I am convinced that this was a healing, psychic gift -- that for a time, I was allowed to glimpse another plane of existence.

HUGGED BY A FIELD OF LIGHT

Research has given us important information about the unborn baby's sensitivity to stresses in the womb environment. One result of our new awareness is that mothers often worry about the effects that "negative" moods in pregnancy may have on their child. Without minimizing the value of a peaceful pregnancy, it is delightful to find stories in which the baby apparently speaks up to reassure a worried mother! A woman writes from Germany:

> I am now seven months pregnant. In about my fourth month, I was up in the middle of the night after having just conversed with my sister in the U.S.A. about past emotional family issues. I was concerned that my negativity or what I see as unhealthy thoughts were affecting the baby. This disturbed me greatly. I went back to lying alone on the living room floor and drifted into a very relaxed but conscious state. I felt for the first time my aura expand outward and I went consciously to the outer border with my aura as I imagined it cleaning out with colors. It was a very strange feeling to be out of my body.
>
> After about five minutes, when I was back to normal but still deeply relaxed, the baby started communicating with me. Not in words but thoughts. The words I use to express what was said are my words for the communication that came full force across during our communion.
>
> The baby expressed to me not to worry, that he/she was strong, a strong, bright light. "Yes," it said, "there are fragile parts to my light as well which make me sensitive and vulnerable but the central core of my light is *strong!*" Then I "asked" this spirit, in an intense flow of love and communion, several questions. The baby expressed further that it had more of a "karmic" connection with me and that my husband would teach him (we believe it's a boy) how to live in this world. The baby or the soul of the baby also expressed that he could see his whole life before him but that it had no meaning or importance until he experienced it, actually lived it. In other words, there was no point in talking about future events because they are only significant in the moment they are experienced. One last thing I remember was that the baby said that our next child, a little girl (what a shock for me to hear of a next child!) would have more karma with my husband.
>
> With that I came to full consciousness and wonder at what I had just received.

Vivien Beirne recalls:

> There was a period, about five weeks before my due date, where I was feeling really badly about something related to my pregnancy -- I think it was because I had my third cold since

getting pregnant, and just couldn't eat the amounts and types of foods that I "should," and I couldn't control my negative thoughts, and I felt even more guilt because of these. I was apologizing to the unborn baby, in a state of deep shame, and all of a sudden I felt like I was being hugged by a field of light, and an unheard message appeared in my consciousness, which told me, "Don't worry -- I'm fine!"

Another remarkable story of reassurance is related by Cynthia, who doubted her ability to be a good mother.

A Night-Long Vision: Cynthia's Story

I come from a dysfunctional family: my father has a terrible temper and alcoholic tendencies, and my mother always bowed to Dad's wishes to create a "unified front" for the kids. As a child I promised myself that I would never treat children as Dad had treated us. Because I have Dad's temper, I felt for years that I shouldn't have kids.

Then I became pregnant! My husband Kurt is very good with children, so he convinced me to go through with the pregnancy -- he'd always wanted kids and was overjoyed. I, on the other hand, still wasn't sure.

We both grew up in the Midwest, so we decided to move back home to surround our new child with as many loving relatives as possible. So we packed our stuff, sent it on ahead, and spent four weeks (during my second trimester) seeing the Southwest on our way home.

That's when my son made his appearance. We were in Bryce Canyon National Park, a beautiful place! We pulled in late in the afternoon, set up camp, saw the sights, and then settled down for the night. I slept peacefully, but I had this vision of a young boy of about three, who stood before me, smiling and radiating love. He introduced himself (without speaking or gesturing) as Bryce, and he let me know that he was very pleased that I had had enough faith in myself and the powers that be to follow the flow my life was taking into motherhood. He expressed excitement at being a part of our lives, that we were very special people and he had specifically chosen and waited for us. This vision/visit lasted all night, and I can still picture it clearly, three years later, it was that strong an experience!

I told Kurt about it the next morning and explained that, for the first time, I felt very relaxed and at peace with what was happening. As my due date approached, we made all the necessary arrangements, but we never picked a girl's name "just in case." We knew it would be a blond-haired little boy named Bryce!

Bryce is now a healthy three-year-old, full of wonder and love. And he is the spitting image of the boy who visited me so long ago!

MY COMFORTER

In some mother-and-child couples, the baby seems to be taking on a role as helper and comforter. It might be easy to dismiss this as a fantasy on the mother's part, but after seeing so many examples of a child apparently giving reassurance from the womb, such a relationship doesn't seem impossible.

The following two stories illustrate how a child may be a comforter both before and after birth. Both women had special circumstances during pregnancy that made the comfort they received from their babies particularly heartening.

For Danielle, it was the stress of being without a partner:

Four years before my son was born, I started having dreams and urges to have a child. At that time I developed a keen interest in working for world peace, specifically in the Middle East, and also wanted to bear a child by someone from the Middle East.

The next man I was with was an Egyptian. I started to have dreams about having a child, before his conception, and dreamed it was a boy, a beautiful and happy child. Unfortunately the relationship with the father was a destructive, abusive one. We broke up before I even found out I was pregnant, and when I told him I was pregnant he chose to stay away, so I went through this alone without the support of family. None of my friends had children, so I was on my own for quite a while, and my sole source of support was God.

I told God, "If I'm supposed to have this baby, You will provide. If I'm not supposed to have it, I'll have another miscarriage and accept it and know it's God's will." In this way I placed my life in God's hands and it was shortly after this that I started getting the communication from the soul of the child -- it was when I really committed to allowing the pregnancy to go forward.

Early in the pregnancy there was considerable communication.

While waking up I'd get the sense that the soul of the baby was talking. In the mornings I'd feel the soul of the baby was waking up. And I started to talk to him before he was born.

I asked him, "Shouldn't I get married? Shouldn't I find a father for you?" And the soul of the baby said to me, "I just want to be with you, you're all I want. If you want to marry somebody, don't do it for me -- do it because you want somebody to keep you company. But I don't have to have that, because all I want is you."

Once I had a vision during meditation. In the vision, the baby was a few months old; I was crying and wanting to tell him why his father wasn't around. I was trying to be positive, being very careful about what I said, aware of the imprinting I would be giving him about his father. In this dream-vision, I was lying on my side and the baby was sitting up so our eyes were level with each other. He got me to look at him, and he looked me right in the eyes with a beautiful, soulful expression and said, "Oh, don't worry, we're going to be just fine. It's okay." This little baby gave me comfort!

Another time, I was wondering what it would be like after he was born. He communicated to me: "Just show me -- tell me where the hot water is, tell me where the cold water is, show me where everything is. After I'm born just talk to me about what you're doing, because I'm interested in learning all of that as soon as possible."

The spirit of the baby also told me he wanted to be home-schooled and have a classical education (something I'd never been aware of) and wanted me to teach him everything. And he expressed a desire to be out in the world -- "When you go to Israel and do your peace work, put me in a back-pack; I want to go with you." He also expressed a desire to be with me nonstop. Now how was I going to do that and support myself, one might ask?

Later in the pregnancy I heard about a program called "Sound Beginning," a way of using music to help the bonding.* That was a powerful thing to do, and as a result of it my son didn't cry for six or seven months after birth. Every time he started to cry I'd sing the Womb Song to him and he'd immediately settle down.

I started teaching music again when my baby was only three weeks old -- I carried him in my front pack and he sat there through several thousand lessons. I played concerts and traveled and took him everywhere I went, and he was incredibly adaptable and really easy. He never interfered with a lesson until he was over a year old.   So it was true!   Everything that was communicated to me before he was born was true.

Most of the communications were up until the fifth month of pregnancy.   After that, there wasn't any communication on a word level with the soul of the child.   He was kicking at that point, responding to the music by dancing inside in time with the rhythm -- that kind of physical communication.

My son is a beautiful, wonderful child, nineteen months old now.   He still reassures me with a hug, or he just stays real cheerful when I get stressed out, smiling as if to say, "Hey, it's not so bad!   Let's have fun."

✳   ✳   ✳

Susan Stout, also a first-time mother, was in great need of reassurance when she was confined to bed for several months to prevent premature labor.   She felt that her child took on a comforting role, both during pregnancy and after his birth:

At twenty-two weeks, I went into active labor and almost delivered Joshua.   After about three weeks in the hospital on complete bedrest and an IV drip of magnesium sulfate, I was very depressed that my "natural" pregnancy and birth plans were ending up this way.   I was told that I would need to stay on bedrest for the remainder of the pregnancy -- three more months!

Going off to sleep, feeling sorry for myself and scared for Joshua, I felt the most wonderful presence fill the room -- it was like nothing I have ever felt before.   It was all love and goodness and light and peace.   I felt the presence surround me and enfold me in itself, and I went to sleep feeling so comforted.

I knew it was Joshua's higher self.   It was not Joshua, the baby body within me, but rather who he was beyond his human body -- his essence, soul or eternal being which was existing beyond humanness.   I was fortunate enough to feel this presence in the same way one other night.   When I told my husband what had happened, he was delighted and said, "Of course Joshua would come to comfort you.   He has an interest in keeping you calm so he can be born when he is supposed to be born!"

My husband did have an experience with Joshua before his birth.   We were doing a guided meditation called "Communing With the Spirit of Your Unborn Child."* Part of the meditation was to ask the baby if he had any messages or things that he wanted to say to us.   My husband felt the baby tell him to play a particular song by Michael and Maloah Stillwater. Terry hadn't listened to that tape in years and spent the whole night looking for it. He thought initially the baby wanted to hear the tape or have the song sung for him, but once he listened to the words, he knew that the baby was giving him a message through the words of the song to help him with some struggles he was having. Another instance of Joshua in the role of helper/comforter?

Despite medication and bedrest, Joshua was born prematurely but did well. Susan adds:

My husband was questioning a psychic for me as to why I had such a difficult pregnancy. One of the things she told him was that Josh chose to be born seven weeks prematurely and subsequently spend two weeks in the hospital for his prematurity because he wanted to make things easier for me. I had been extremely sick a week or two before he was born when my electrolytes had become unbalanced. I was very depressed from it and from being hospitalized and completely confined to bed for three months. The psychic said that Joshua felt I had endured enough and that he was willing to take on the pain of being hospitalized instead. It broke my heart to hear that Joshua would do this for me because I spent those months saying I would rather be hospitalized than have my baby need to be in the intensive care nursery, and I did everything I could to keep it that way.

There was another unusual experience I had with Joshua *since* the pregnancy. One night while going off to sleep with my husband, I was thinking of Joshua and what a wonderful threesome we were. Then I felt his presence on the bed with us and got the message that the three of us would always be united as a family. I feel he has a very strong bond with my husband and me.

And there was also one night that I was terribly upset because of a fight with my husband. In the midst of my sadness, hurt and upset, I felt two small hands on my heart, caressing it and telling me it was okay. That blew me away and I have never told anyone about it until now. After my first experience with Joshua in the hospital before he was born, I am very surprised at the role he seems to be taking on in my life -- that of a comforter. It is real surprising to me since he is the child and I'm supposed to be the parent!

How far do the child's powers extend?

A cooperative bond is possible only if each person has some power of choice and action. Can this really be true of parents and their children yet to be born?

Stories of persuasion, help and reassurance do indeed suggest that the unborn soul has a certain power to affect things, to communicate love and other qualities, and to work on the situation before conception and during pregnancy as well. How far might these powers extend? The possibilities are surprising.

We hear many stories of rescue and protection attributed to "guardian angels." Is it possible that some of these "angels" are actually children waiting to be born? Here is what happened to Celestia Jasper, three years before the birth of her first son:

> My husband and I were returning from Minnesota to Montana after spending a disastrous Christmas with my family. (My mother had died the summer before.) We were anxious to get to our cabin in the Swan Valley so we drove night and day -- even though the weather was extremely cold. We stopped in Great Falls for gas and were warned not to cross Rogers Pass because there was wind and extreme cold. Being young, we went along anyway. After crossing the pass we stopped for a cheeseburger and fries -- it was about 9:00 P.M.
>
> As we started up the Swan Highway we encountered a snow packed highway. As we came around the corner, down the hill toward Salmon Lake, a large amount of snow blew off the bank above us causing a glare of snow and lights. I thought a car was coming toward us so I swerved, over-corrected, went into a spin and flipped once, and landed on our wheels in the Stillwater River (we were in a Volkswagen bug).
>
> Jasper tried to paddle the car with the snow shovel but we were in a small whirlpool and just went around in circles. He climbed out the window into the river and got the spare tire out of the trunk for me to float on. He swam for shore and I tried to push off from the car on the tire. Unfortunately the tire was attached, so that I couldn't use it for flotation as it was going down with the car.
>
> By this time I was ready to give up, death seemed a treat (I thought I would see my mother again). Jasper hollered at me from shore and then seemed to disappear under the ice. I resigned myself to an easy death.
>
> Then I heard, "But I haven't even been born yet." This didn't

seem relevant at that time, but a hand or force or whatever seemed to grab me by the collar of my jacket and much as a cat carries a kitten, propelled me to shore.

Later when we had broken into a cabin and were running out of energy I woke up and seemed to hear the same admonition -- "I'm not born yet." We were rescued in the morning.

In 1971 Frank James was born. The first night I was home with him he woke in the night to be fed. As I nursed him I had a vision back into the past of my mother, grandmother and so on nursing their children and I felt connected to this pattern or plan. Then I knew it was Frank James who had spoken the night of the accident.

If future children have such power to intervene in our lives, what might be an appropriate attitude on our part?   The following story presents one intriguing possibility:

Before I conceived my son, I sensed a conversation in my head where a "baby soul" wanted to come to us. Although I was eager to become a mother, I told this being that now would not be a good time. "I would like three things to happen before I get pregnant," I told him. "First, I want to make sure I have enough money to stay home at least a year. Second, I want to do a little more acting to 'get it out of my system.' (I had majored in Drama at college, but hadn't done much acting since graduating a year and a half earlier.) And third, I want Mark (my husband) to approach me with the idea of having a baby." (I didn't want him to ever feel pressured into becoming a father.)

Shortly thereafter, I won the equivalent of a year's salary on a gameshow; I got cast in *two* plays, and my husband said, "I think I'd really like to have a child soon." The night he said that, I conceived. Seventeen days after my husband suggested he might like to be a father, we found ourselves looking at the bright blue tip of a positive pregnancy test!

During the pregnancy we both agreed on the name Adam for a boy, but about half way through we both became inspired to change the spelling to Atom. Atom was born under water. He first laughed aloud at the tender age of nine weeks old, and it's a wonderful adventure raising him.

Now a female entity has been intruding on my thoughts. "Let me come!" she says. The time doesn't seem right. My husband (theoretically) is dying of cancer, although he looks healthy and robust. My gameshow money (which I've stretched for almost two years) is running out, and I need a way to bring in a little extra income while still being a full-time mother. I tell this entity that if she is to come, I'd like to see Mark have a long term remission (five years or more) and I need an enjoyable way to make money while raising children. We'll see what happens now.

Ellen Stanclift and her husband Jeff wonder whether the soul's power might include choosing the time of conception. After years of infertility, Ellen conceived shortly after Jeff had resigned his commission as an Army Captain. She says:

Despite his unhappiness with military life, Jeff thinks that had I conceived earlier he never would have resigned his commission, because it was a steady, well paying job. He is now a graduate student and loves it! He'll have his master's degree in the spring, at which point we will probably be embarking on a whole new life. Despite all the trouble we had with infertility, having Josh when we did was ideal. My parents are close by, Jeff is pursuing his personal goals and I feel like a much more centered person now. Josh was even born during the one month that Jeff had off from school! We tend to wonder if it was somehow possible for Josh to pick his own conception and birth time to maximize the good things in our family. It is an incredible idea to contemplate!

Is the baby's sphere of action during pregnancy confined to the small world of the womb? Isadora Paymer and her husband had a strange experience that suggests otherwise:

When I was three months pregnant with my son, there was wild thumping and bumping in the walls at night. It sounded like pictures were falling off the walls, but nothing had fallen. The first time it happened, my husband sat up in bed and said, "What's that?" and I said, "It's just the baby. Go back to sleep." Normally hearing a noise like that would have caused him to search the house for burglars, but he believed me. After a few nights of this we were getting fed up, so he talked to it through meditation and told it to stop. It did.

My son is three years old now, and I recently asked him about this. He has a wonderful memory, and remembers his experiences in the womb ("I swam around and drank water. It was red in there"). He said that he banged on the walls of the house because "he was bored." He was a very active, colicky baby, and I think that this was just another way for him to exercise his overactive nervous system. I think people come and go for a while until they settle down in their new body.

If the baby can affect the world beyond the womb, more subtle interventions might include rearranging circumstances to benefit both parents and child. Vivien Beirne noticed the serendipity at work in her pregnancy, and wonders if her child played a part in it:

> As I was looking through my old journal entries from pregnancy, one of the most frequent thoughts was a yearning to spend more time in quietness, contemplation and meditation, and in nature. I frequently described a discord between this yearning and my actual materially active focus.
>
> Although I felt perfectly healthy, the midwife put me on activity restriction for three weeks, as there was a risk of early labor. That meant no work at my job, nor on our house, nor running errands for the upcoming holidays. I really felt this modified bedrest was a gift orchestrated by the little ego and his helpers to help me make a much-needed shift in focus.
>
> An area that is somewhat confusing to me is the whole cause and effect cycle. Were we led to start studying about a certain kind of education, or diet, or form of healing, because the little one chose to be born to us and was directing our ways? Or was he attracted to us because we were studying and applying this specific information and life style? There are many such questions.

Of all the powers the child-to-be may manifest -- to help and reassure, make some choices, alter circumstances and cooperate with our requests -- to me the most impressive is the power to convey love. While other powers are like those we exert in our lifetime, the power to transmit love seems to be one we lose, only to regain through much experience and ripening.

Perhaps in our efforts to hear the communications of our children-to-be, we will get back in touch with the wisdom of the unborn soul, whose message is so often a transmission of love.

CHAPTER FIFTEEN
THROUGH THE BIRTH DOOR

Is there any connection between our pre-birth contacts and our experience at birth? For example, does the sense of communication in pregnancy lead to a better than usual labor and delivery?

Not necessarily.

As Nancy Cohen ruefully remarks, "I wish I could tell you that all this communicating and love resulted in a blissful delivery -- but it didn't! I had a long, painful labor and a nightmare delivery in a traditional hospital setting -- and I was full of fear!"

Pregnancies rich with contact and assurances can end in difficult births with complications. But there are also signs that by "listening" to the child within we may gather information and guidance for the birth and beyond.

Inner messages can help with decision-making at the time of birth. This mother felt she received clear instructions from each of her children before they were born:

> My older boy, Mac, had me understand that he was a boy, that he would be beautiful and in a world of his own. At his birth there were difficulties. As his heart rate dropped the doctor said a caesarean would have to occur. Mac told me NO. He told me the cord was wrapped around his neck but he would make it. It happened.
>
> Harry, my younger boy, also told me he was a boy and when he would arrive. He told me that I was going to deliver him easily and that I should delay going to the hospital, or stay at home to deliver him. My husband and I walked five miles to the hospital while I labored. Harry was born forty minutes after we arrived. He weighed nine pounds but took only four pushes.

Midwife Diane Gregg teaches couples to use their psychic awareness to begin bonding with their child while pregnant and to check on the baby's condition in the womb. When Diane was expecting her fourth child, her own well-developed intuition was combined with communications from the baby to prepare her for some unusual circumstances at birth:

Early in my pregnancy, my very close friend, Cathe', came to say she was pregnant for the first time. She had been my birth assistant and we'd talked of her future birth for years. Cathe' and another friend and I were all due at the same time. I trusted Divine timing and agreed to help them both.

During the pregnancy I had strong feelings about these three births. I felt Cathe' would be first and it would be so exciting that I would go home and shortly afterward have my own. On February third I went to be with Cathe' and Doug. After twenty-three hours, she gave birth to a beautiful baby girl. It was quite intense for all of us and I went home exhausted. After four hours' sleep, I woke up in labor.

This child had told me her name many years ago: Ruah Mitra -- Spirit of the Earth Mother. She told me her father's name too, and this was true though unfortunately he has not chosen to remain involved. I had also felt for years that my last birth would be family only. When the father was not involved, I felt it would be just me and my other children, twelve, eight and four years old. There was quite a lot of social pressure about this. In November I had moved to the ranch I'd seen for years as the birth-healing center. It was out of town fourteen miles and so I too felt more comfortable arranging to have my apprentice come for the birth.

Due to my intense exhaustion, I slept, only waking for contractions, for four hours. Around 4:30 A.M. I had to cop to no more sleep. I woke the kids, had Jeremy build a fire, and phoned my apprentice. The labor was very intense and I prayed it wouldn't be long as I had no energy reserves.

All through the pregnancy, this little one had let me know she wanted to be born in the water. We filled the tub and I got in when it was only six inches deep in hopes of relief for myself. Very soon, my breath started to catch and I knew I would be pushing soon. The water bag came out first and the pressure was so intense, I tore it open with my fingers. She flew out when the water barely covered her! My friend was just then driving up and came in a few minutes later.

Ruah Mitra's spirit has been with me for sixteen years and it's wonderful to have her here at last.

Michelle Veasey feels that communication with her baby helped bring about a good birth situation:

> We were faced with a hospital birth and possible caesarean on August 29, 1991, because our midwives believed that Ian was too big. I asked him to please come August 28, if he did *not* need a hospital, at approximately 3:30 A.M. (start of labor) and arrive quickly before 8:00 A.M. I mentioned 7:00 A.M. would be good.
>
> Guess what? I went into labor at 4:00 A.M. August 28, and Ian was born, in our home, at exactly 7:01 A.M. He pushed too!

Even when we have felt contact with the baby during pregnancy, the circumstances at birth may be very different from our expectations. We cannot afford to be complacent and to assume that our efforts at communication will produce the desired results. Nettie Lessmann writes:

> I have contact with my unborn baby much of the time. The baby is four days overdue now, and we just found out on his due date that he was breech. Two days ago a doctor was able to do an external inversion, so now we are just awaiting his birth.
>
> The night before, I talked with him about cooperating with the doctors and doing his part to turn. I visualized what I wanted him to do. By the time I was done, he was impatient with me since he'd said yes, he'd do his part to turn when I first asked.
>
> Normally I initiate contact by "thinking" at him. Generally he talks back to me silently. He's got a sense of humor and his father's laugh. Basically, we talk to each other all the time.

Nettie's next letter describes "an extremely hard labor." The baby (who turned out to be a girl) "had been breech long enough to refuse to tuck her chin, and to want her head in the wrong position for birth. After pushing for six hours with microscopic movement on her part, we went for a caesarean."

Experiences like this would have me questioning whether the earlier contacts were real or illusory. Perhaps there are limits to what we can alter, even with the child's cooperation. Or perhaps the baby is less "available" during labor, when the powerful and often turbulent energies might be like a storm interfering with communication.

Contacts with our child in pregnancy cannot guarantee that the delivery will be exactly as we wish. But they help us to see the birth as only one event in the continuum of our connection, and not as a win or lose-all proposition. The birth may not be ideal, but it is not the beginning of our relationship.

Stacey Mott's first child, Emily, was born by caesarean after a long and difficult labor. Approaching her second childbirth, Stacey needed reassurance as she faced the unknowns of a different kind of delivery:

> Before Emily was born in 1985, my ideas about pregnancy and birth were mainly "mechanical" -- I just didn't give much thought to anything else. I was very apprehensive about the birth, and I read book after book, hoping I'd find one that would predict how my experience would go. I felt that if I "studied" enough, I was sure to pass the "test." I avoided books that sounded at all "radical" because I felt threatened by the notion that medical science might not be able to rescue me. So you can see I set myself up for a pretty bad experience.
>
> When I became pregnant again I slowly realized that this time things could be different. I became committed to the idea of a vaginal birth and to doing whatever was necessary to improve our chances for a safe vaginal birth. We found a childbirth instructor who would work with us privately. It was a very challenging time, with so many decisions to make about what course of action we would take. I felt almost overwhelmed, as though one wrong step could cause a real tragedy in our lives.
>
> We had weekly sessions with Nancy, our instructor. Each one began with relaxation and visualization. Nancy would talk us through a process of relaxing, letting go of all the tensions in our bodies starting with our heads and going down to our toes. Usually that part ended with our imagining our bodies filled with warm, white light. Then we'd do a creative visualization. I don't really remember many of the other ones, they've faded. But there is one I will never forget.
>
> Nancy told us to go to a place where we were happy and safe and relaxed. I chose an idyllic place I'd gone on family vacations as a kid. It was a river in New Hampshire with a covered bridge, huge boulders extending from the riverbank in toward the middle, and a small waterfall that made a lovely natural whirlpool bath. I went there in my mind. Nancy told us to see a book there in front of us. I saw on the boulder, lying in the warm sun, a very old, thick book. It was like an old pulpit bible -- well worn, with gold pages and a cushiony leather cover. Nancy told us that inside the book we would find something we needed to know, and to go ahead and open it when we felt ready. I took a few deep breaths, stepped up to the book on the rock, and

opened it.

At once I was in the embrace of a child. It was a shock -- I gasped. The sensation was very sudden, very detailed. It was a child about two years old (the age Emily was at the time). It was not Emily, though. Emily has always been a very sturdily-built child. The child by the river was quite delicate. The arms were around my neck in a very cozy, loving hug. While this whole thing was completely nonverbal, the message came through quite clearly. It was this: "It's okay, Mom. Do what's best for you. Everything will turn out fine. I trust you. I love you. You're my mom." It's hard to explain how I could get that all nonverbally, but I really did. I needed to hear it, and I could only hear it from my child.

Both Nancy and my husband knew that something significant had happened. I was crying audibly, in total shock, relief, and amazement. As a result of this experience I felt the confidence to commit to what I'd long felt was the best course of action for us -- home birth.

Alissa's birth was not without complications. I had a rather long second stage (about six hours of pushing) and she aspirated meconium. Within five minutes of her birth she was on her way to the hospital in an ambulance. She was quite a determined little baby, though, and after a forty-eight hour stay, came home "as good as new." Having had her "okay" before the birth, I was able to come to terms with the fact that her birth was not the experience we'd hoped for.

I should mention that the physical sensation of the hug was completely accurate. Alissa is a sweet, slender thing and when she hugs, she wraps her arms around your neck tightly. It's almost as though she gave me that signature hug so that later I'd know it was really her there, by the river, and not just my imagination.

Despite our best plans there are sometimes disruptions at the time of birth; then the connection we have already made can become a talisman of our link with the baby. If there is separation, it helps protect the bond. This was Denise Boggs's experience:

On February 4, 1990, I was doing my meditation and I was "warned" that someone was coming. A couple of days later I met this stranger in my meditation. The stranger was formless but had eyes of blue (I'll never forget them). I was a little scared by this presence and at the time unaware of its meaning. However, soon afterward I noticed a problem with my period. Having worked in an OB/GYN office as a nurse I ran a few tests on myself, only to find out to my surprise and shock that I was pregnant.   That meditation had taken place just prior to conception.

I then went back to my meditation in hopes of clarifying what was happening. There I was greeted by a small child. The actual picture was that of a child waiting for someone, by pushing their face up against a window. Needless to say I welcomed "the stranger" this time with open arms. I seriously believe that the pregnancy would not have continued had I not welcomed it.

The birth itself wasn't as I'd hoped. Because of one thing or another I ended up with a caesarean, then they wanted to do a full "septic work-up" on the baby. (This included a lumbar puncture -- I refused it.) Anyway my baby girl -- Michelle -- was born three months ago. She was seven pounds eight ounces and perfectly healthy. There are many things about the birth I have yet to settle.

When I was finally allowed to see my daughter, some ten hours later, there were those eyes. The very same eyes I had seen in that early meditation. It was a wonderful connection and a wonderful affirmation of my sense during the pregnancy.

As the days go by, I feel closer and closer to this new life. We've known each other for just over a year now and with each day there is an ever-growing love.

Intuitions about our baby before birth can prepare us to cope with problems we may face later. One mother's strong impressions during pregnancy prepared her for complications with the birth and for her daughter's special needs:

First of all, I was positive that my baby was a girl. Second, I had a great fear that the birth would not proceed as I wished, even though I interviewed over a dozen obstetricians in order to find one who I felt truly supported natural childbirth and who worked out of a hospital known for its progressive policies. In the end, I discovered that the problem was not to be a struggle between me and the hospital or an interventionist doctor, but being pregnant with a breech baby at the wrong time in history.

Because of the high cost of malpractice suits, there is not a physician or a midwife in Arizona who is willing to attend the birth of a nine-pound breech, already-engaged first baby, and after trying an external version (as well as my weeks of yoga exercises) my doctor performed a caesarean section.

The third impression was that something was physically wrong with the baby. I thought I was being paranoid, because my husband is an athlete and I always wondered what would happen if we had a child who was not physically competent. Once again, I was correct: our daughter has a benign congenital myopathy, which is another way of saying she suffers from an as yet undiagnosed disorder of the muscles. Fortunately her neurologist thinks she will have caught up to the other kids by the time she is four, and he does not want to put her through muscle biopsies and other nasty tests yet. And very fortunately my husband loves her to death and doesn't care if she doesn't become an athletic prodigy!

A dream prepared Stephanie for difficult decisions she would face at the time of her daughter's birth. "I hold sacred the mystery of life and of living," she says, "and often get information from dreams."

Stephanie was seventeen weeks pregnant when she first heard her baby's heartbeat. It was arrhythmic. Stephanie, herself a midwife, researched the condition and learned that ninety-five percent of arrhythmias spontaneously heal themselves. She was confident that such would be the case with her child, but in her sixth month she had a dream, which she records as a poem:

> I was looking at my belly, six months big
> when suddenly I could see through it
> and there was my baby
> in my arms, beautiful eyes
> and soft red hair
> I knew it was too soon
> but I wanted her so much
> and she seemed okay
> So I began to feed her at my breast.
> Then the EMT's came rushing in and said
> You can't do that!
> She's not ready, put her back
> So I got a friend to boil some water
> and I gently put her back into the bag
> with the sterile waters around her
> and I put her back into my womb
> A minute passed
> then a few more
> And I suddenly realized the cord

had been cut!
She could not breathe!
So I brought her out again and
there was the meconium
and she was limp.
The doctors rushed her out of the room
then came back in
I'm sorry they said
there's nothing we can do
your baby is dead.

After this distressing dream, Stephanie decided to have a sonogram. It revealed a severely malformed heart. She continues:

> The prognosis was very poor and the recommended course of action was to hospitalize me at thirty-six weeks and to take the child by caesarean as soon as possible. They assured me that everything possible would be done to keep her alive, but they gave her chances of survival to be eight percent at best. I felt like a test tube rather than a mother-to-be.
>
> The next three months were a daily struggle between hope and despair.
>
> Our daughter was born eleven days before her due date, at home, into the hands of her father and myself. A very courageous midwife/friend assisted us. When she was born, she was the same child I had seen in my dream. Just as the dream had told me, she was our daughter. Her name was Nyima Loisann -- Moon Warrior Woman. She was held and loved her whole life by her father and myself. We took her in to a nearby hospital where there were neonatal cardiac specialists on staff, to make sure the diagnosis had been correct. They diagnosed it to be worse than originally suspected and gave a one percent chance of survival through tortuous (their word) operations and brain damaging medications. We declined and after jumping through many legal hoops, we brought her back home. On her fourth day of life she died in my arms with her father nearby, in the same bed she had been born in. She had had a brief but good life, and relaxed into death with a smile on her face.
>
> We felt very strongly that the quality of her life was more important than the quantity. We both thought it would be supremely selfish to put her through the kind of medical procedures that would be done to her. We knew that even though it broke our hearts beyond comprehension for our

beautiful baby girl to die, we had to let her go, and we could not allow her to be tortured. I feel that the dream was given to me to allow us time to prepare and make clear decisions.

CONNECTING IN LABOR

Some mothers experience a strong, reassuring connection with their baby during labor, even in situations where attendants are worried about the baby's condition. Several have described how despite indications to the contrary, they felt a certainty that their child was safe. Judy Goodale writes:

> It was a long labor, and we wound up having to use a hospital delivery room instead of the birth center. A series of risk factors popped up: I had been laboring for forty hours and was only two centimeters dilated, my blood pressure rose and I started passing protein in my urine, the water broke and had meconium in it, and the fetal monitors were worrying the doctor. It was a very tense atmosphere, and everyone was very concerned for the baby.
>
> I was in tremendous pain and very tired when I sort of "checked out" for awhile -- and I saw him, my baby, looking exactly like he looked when he was born. I only saw his face in the vision (complete with misshapen head), his big eyes and his brown hair, and he was fine. And I *knew* he'd be fine; I relaxed and delivered him not long after.
>
> As soon as he was born there was some general furor; he was taken from me to be suctioned and checked -- he was limp and depressed (my sister told me later that she thought from the looks of him that he'd been born dead). But throughout all the excitement I remained calm and secure in the knowledge that he was fine -- the impression stayed with me in spite of some practical evidence to the contrary. The message I'd received when I saw his little face float above me was that everything was just fine, and it was. He is now a very happy fifteen-month-old, and we share a wonderful closeness.

For another woman, connecting with the baby helped her to endure a thoroughly unpleasant situation. "I was aware of the baby intensely all during labor," says Patty:

> "Aware" is a very inadequate word. I knew exactly where she was every moment -- had the sensation of the contours of her face

pressing against the birth canal as she was passing through. It was wonderful, wonder-full in every sense of the words. It was also the only thing that kept me from being completely hysterical.

I felt that my labor was being torn from me at every chance. I was being over-managed and, at the same time, ignored. To preserve my sanity I turned way inward -- almost trance-like. I wanted to feel the contractions from the inside out. It was then that I lost track of the dimensions of my body. I was conscious of my eyes, my left hand, and the baby.

She became clear to me. I felt her to be self-contained inside her own energy, mine outside hers, suspended. She was patient, not struggling. With our energies (mine and hers) around her, the contractions were not doing any violence to her (to me, maybe!). She was floating above it.

When a ten-pound baby girl "splashed into view" and was taken to be suctioned, "they said she was fine," Patty recalls. "But I knew it all along."

Carla Sunderland had a recurring nightmare during her first pregnancy:

I had no complications with the pregnancy, but kept having this dream of myself hanging by a rope around my neck, and a baby girl dangling between my legs still attached to her umbilical cord. I could see the baby's face very plainly. I told my doctor about this dream and he said that women expecting their first baby often have dreams about their inner fears of childbirth.

While this dream seems to have foretold actual events at the birth, Carla felt a much more reassuring contact with her baby during the delivery itself:

We had planned a nice, quiet home birth, but I ran into complications. My water broke with meconium staining; I knew something was wrong. The doctor tried to deliver her with forceps, but they weren't long enough to reach her. So he cut me twice with scissors and pulled her out. My baby was grey and lifeless, her cord had been wrapped around her neck.

But at the moment when her head first appeared, she had her eyes open and was looking right at me. In that instant *I knew* my baby was all right, even though everyone else thought there was no hope. The doctor did CPR and brought her back to life!

I feel that she and I exchanged something at the moment of

her birth, something unlike any of my other birthings. A special kind of bonding, more intense.

*   *   *

Do experiences of contact before birth help us to bond with the baby when s/he is born? There's evidence on both sides. In their book, *The Earliest Relationship,* Brazelton and Cramer cite a study carried out by Elizabeth Keller at Boston Children's Hospital. She compared parents who knew the sex of their baby through prenatal testing with parents who did not know the baby's sex until birth. The authors write:

> One might expect attachment to, and early personification of, the newborn baby to be enhanced by foreknowledge of the baby's sex. Not at all. The parents who knew the baby's sex took longer to personify and recognize the individuality of the baby after birth. It seems there may be a protective system at work -- protecting the parents and the baby from a too-early attachment. The work of attachment to an individual baby takes time and early attempts to consolidate it may be rejected.

Perhaps with knowledge of the baby's sex we tend to build up too detailed a fantasy image -- an image that distracts us when we have to let it go and meet the real newborn. On the other hand, we have seen people who approached a pregnancy with a strong preference for one gender, but who were then prepared by their own experiences to love and accept the real baby. It seems the benefit of foreknowledge may depend on how it comes to us.

Perhaps there is a difference between receiving information from tests and gathering impressions ourselves. Maybe learning facts about our baby from impersonal medical procedures actually makes us feel a little distanced, and less likely to tune in to our own "internal monitors."

If our impressions of the child are based on projection and wishful thinking, they could set us back in the process of getting to know her. But if they are correct, they could give us a head start. For example, Mucbeah Robinson, who felt that she accurately intuited her babies' personalities before they were born, observes that "this was really lucky for me as I had no family connection to watch little nieces or nephews grow -- no experience with tiny ones."

Many of the people who experienced a connection in pregnancy feel that they truly began to bond with the baby before birth. Some of their remarks express this:

"I had the sense of expecting someone I already knew."

"I knew her the moment she popped out."

"By the time she was born I felt I knew her quite well..."

Others feel that even though the pre-birth experience was important, it did not help them bond at birth. Although I've spoken of the "continuum" of our connection, childbirth with its dramatic intensity seems designed to make a break in that continuum. Besides the huge shift in the mother's physical state, there is a shift from inner awareness to the more external senses. No matter how well we may know our baby before birth, there is a new beginning as we explore each other through seeing, hearing, smelling, touching. Karen Nelson explains:

> My dream of my daughter while I was pregnant pictured her at about six to twelve months old. I really can't say that it helped me bond or contributed to my sense of familiarity with her when she was born. Those two events seem to be different but very related. She did not feel like a stranger at birth -- I felt I had known her for years, that she had been a part of me for a long time and had just now arrived. As she grew and became like the child in my dream, it felt like a further confirmation that she was indeed mine, a part of me in such a profound way. I felt affirmed, very connected to her and very happy.

Another woman expresses the discontinuity between her pre-birth sense of connection and the newborn's reality:

> I got an image of my child when I was only four days pregnant: I couldn't stop seeing in my mind a little boy with dark red hair and blue eyes. I really wanted to have that little boy and I was hoping I was pregnant. The image stayed with me for the rest of the pregnancy and I tried not to set my heart on him, even though I loved him already.
>
> I did not feel as though the image helped me to connect with him when he was born because it was of a toddler with blue eyes and dark red hair, and when he was born his skin was yellow and his hair and eyes were black (why do people say "all babies have blue eyes"?). Nor did it help me tolerate the discomforts of pregnancy because, having never had a child, I did not associate pregnancy with its outcome -- the outcome was unknown and therefore frightening, and I didn't really believe in my heart that I would really have a baby and not be pregnant forever. I did not love the pregnancy -- I was very weak and sick most of the time -- and I did not feel affectionate toward the fetus at all. I loved Casey as soon as I saw him, though.

Casey is fifteen months old now. I was somewhat wrong about the hair -- it's dark, but brown and gold. But the sun has been making it redder every day, so while I wouldn't call him a redhead, I'd say I was pretty close. He has beautiful dark blue eyes and black lashes just as I imagined. Everyone said they would change, but they just kept getting bluer.

Like many people who have visual impressions of their future children, these mothers seem to have caught a glimpse of how the baby would look not at birth but some time later. The newborn, with his very different and often disconcerting appearance, is another experience altogether. But as the child grows and comes to resemble the envisioned image, those pre-birth connections are affirmed.

THE CONTINUING CONNECTION

Although birth can seem to interrupt the connection at one level, many parents feel that -- with a little effort -- it continues in a flow of empathic, telepathic communication throughout infancy and beyond.

"As to whether the communication continues after birth," says Vivien Beirne, "I think it does:"

We can block the information by thinking too analytically or by being too fearful, or by being too busy. When I'm in a somewhat quiet place, I am better able to see Oliver and his needs, instead of projecting my needs and pushing him through a day that is insensitive to him. It has occurred to me that I feel more connected to Oliver's "higher self" when we are breastfeeding, or as he is sleeping or going to sleep. We must be in a more receptive place during these times.

We can use these receptive times to connect with our children and even work out problems. A mother writes: "After my son's birth, I read that you can go into meditation while your child sleeps and ask that their soul or consciousness enter your space, and then talk over whatever it is you want to talk over. On several occasions (starting at about seven months or so) I did this with amazing results!"

Another woman, Danielle, went through pregnancy and birth without the support of the baby's father, from whom she had separated. Even before conception, her dreams foreshadowed a difficulty with nursing, but the problem was resolved in a surprising way. Danielle recalls:

In dreams where he was just born, I'd be holding off breastfeeding, saying, "Wait till your father comes, I want him to be here for your first meal." And in fact when my son was born, he would not take my breast. I ended up having to go to a lactation specialist. And spiritually I put myself on the prayer list and spoke to someone in my church. She said, "When the baby's asleep, talk to him and tell him that you're here to love and nurture him, and give him the assurance that you're going to feed him." So I did, and it worked and we turned the situation around!

Some mothers feel that their baby is able to guide them in decision-making after birth as well as during pregnancy. Nancy Cohen writes:

I've been thinking lately about this soul wisdom of children, especially in the early years (carried over from womb life and earlier) and how if you can connect to them as unborn -- shouldn't we also honor that connection as they grow? I often feel my daughter guiding me in her needs -- dietary, sleep, and so on. Now baby Gemma is fourteen months old. She communicates with me telepathically and also I occasionally ask her questions with kinesiology. For example when she was three months old she "told" me she was ready to sleep in her own room -- which she has done ever since with no waking problems. Her decision to start weaning also came to me telepathically -- and later, she told me she wanted all the stuffed animals out of the crib!

Patricia describes how her son seems to help her cope with the moments of uncertainty that she feels as an inexperienced mother:

I was quite certain that I would be an awkward kind of new mother, unsure of what to do and when. But when I feel like that, I feel he helps guide me through, giving me answers.

There are times I look at him and say, "How did I end up with a child?! I don't know how to do this stuff!" Then he looks at me, smiles, and "says" (this was at age four weeks), "Okay, take a deep breath. You can do this. Right now, you know my diaper isn't full because you just changed it. I've been looking at this same stupid mobile now for an hour, and I'm bored. How about we walk around the house, and you show me the pictures on the walls. You've never done that before."

He also did it when I was in complete dilemma over when to start solid foods for him. I'm interested in the tradition of Chinese medicine, and there are very different schools of thought about when and what foods to start children on. One day Luka "said" to me, "I'm ready. I'm *really* ready for solid food. Stop worrying about it. Try rice, and I'll love it." And he did!

Louise Richardson felt an inner reassurance about her baby during pregnancy despite worrisome medical tests, and after his birth she experienced a mental link with him:

As a result of blood tests during pregnancy, my doctor said there was a very strong indication of spina bifida in the baby. After my initial worry and fear, I relaxed a bit and somehow knew the baby was all right. I had to go for several sonograms anyway, but I had a gut feeling that gave me peace of mind through it all.

After my healthy son was born, I had the feeling of mental telepathy sometimes when we were quiet and relaxed. When he was ten months old, I had to leave him for two weeks, and although I left him in good hands, it broke my heart. A few nights before I left, I was rocking him before bedtime in the rocking chair. I was looking in his face and thinking how much I didn't want to leave him. All of a sudden I felt very calm, as if I knew everything would be all right. Just then, my son opened his eyes and reached his hand up to stroke my face. Although I missed him terribly the whole two weeks, somehow I felt at peace. Now that he is two we still communicate little mental messages in our quieter moments.

Louise was later able to use her telepathic experience to help her second child, a little girl:

When I was in labor with my daughter, the nurses in the hospital were particularly brutal. It turns out the nurses were in the middle of contract negotiations. What timing! My daughter was born vaginally, but at one point during labor one of the nurses was so rough, I had a strange feeling my baby felt it, although she didn't jump or anything. After she was born, I only held her about one minute and didn't see her again until four hours later. I can only hope they were more gentle with her than they were with me.

She was very jittery for the first six months. She didn't sleep through the night, she would jump at even the faintest of sounds, she would cry inconsolably when I laid her down or put her in her baby lounge or her swing, even in full view of me. She always cried when anyone else held her. She always cried in her car seat the whole length of a trip. I had the suspicion that this was because of the brutality when she was born.

After about six months of this behavior it became almost unbearable for both my daughter and myself. One night in the rocking chair, I had a mental conversation with her. I reassured her that I would always be with her, I'll never let anyone else do anything hurtful to her, and what happened in the hospital will never happen to her again, so how about if we call a truce? Do you know what happened? The next night she started sleeping through the night, and she was generally a lot more calm and content with life. At first I thought it was my imagination -- but my husband, the neighbors and my parents all commented on her change in behavior. My daughter is now eight months old and doing very well.

If I have any more children, they'll be born at home. It's amazing what kind of magic can happen in a rocking chair.

Many parents describe a telepathic connection that allows them sometimes to sense their child's situation while they are apart. In fact, one mother points out that we may need to voluntarily loosen this psychic tie as our children grow.

Fran's daughter is ten years old. "Since her birth," says Fran, "I have always felt a sort of sixth sense about her, where she is or how she is doing. This is less in the last two or three years, mainly because I feel she needs to become her own self, and that such a tie can become unhealthy without meaning to. I still have a strong hunch when she is sick or in trouble, and I hope that will continue, since it is so useful."

Beverly Hayes, an adoptive mother, writes, "I feel that my husband, my daughter and I are attached to each other by an invisible cord. Through that means we can check on each other while we are apart and also get messages like 'I love you,' or 'Call me.'"

Janette Patterson recalls how this invisible cord pulled at her one day when her baby Angelica was two weeks old:

She was asleep in the bedroom and I was working in the kitchen, when I realized that she was calling me. It was not that I heard her crying, it was a sense, an awareness that she needed to feel connected with me. I went to the bedroom immediately, where she lay totally motionless and not breathing (I know newborns do that -- long pauses between breaths). I touched her lightly and she breathed a heavy sigh and continued sleeping. I knew she needed to be reassured that I was there with her and that she felt better now that I had reconnected with her.

It was shortly after her baby's birth that Clare Adams felt and even "saw" the connection that may link us with our children and allow us to nourish them with love:

> I had a wonderful pregnancy, and a home birth at my midwife's home. Unfortunately, I had an infection at the time of delivery. My darling Madeline had trouble starting to breathe. She was in the room with us, but she had not decided yet whether she wanted to be in her body and join us on this plane. I rubbed her hands and arms and feet. I called to her, "Madeline, it's your mama. Come on, sweetie. Join your body. You can breathe. It's okay -- I love you, and I've waited so long for you." My husband joined in, and she gave a gasp. Still, no more. The midwife was doing CPR, another was monitoring her heart rate and another was getting the oxygen. My husband got our van and left for the hospital with the midwife, Madeline and one assistant. I was left with the other assistant, Bobby.
>
> After I delivered the placenta, I was washed up. Bobby and I decided to visualize Madeline well and healthy. I sent her lots of my love and strength. All of a sudden I "saw" in my mind a healthy and happy Madeline held by her dear papa. She radiated joy and contentment. He held her close to his heart in the crook of his arm and tenderly smiled and cooed to her. There was a golden light that connected their two heart centers. I saw the light become brighter and larger; soon all I saw was beautiful golden light. I relayed this whole message to Bobby as I received it. It ended with the feeling that my baby Madeline was fine.
>
> I dozed and awakened to the phone ringing. My husband filled my ears with the words, "Madeline is okay. She's breathing on her own." We both cried and thanked our creator, and thanked Madeline for joining us.

CHAPTER SIXTEEN
RESERVATIONS

All things are to be examined and called into question.
There are no limits set to thought.

-- *Edith Hamilton*

Working with these stories has been an adventure, challenging me to find a balance of open heart and discriminating mind. I've learned of experiences so far beyond my ken that I can scarcely imagine them. The stories and beliefs of many contributors have opened my eyes to new possibilities and made me question my own assumptions.

I am more persuaded than ever that we need to value doubt, ambivalence, and the ability to question everything. We need to look at our perceptions from more than one point of view and consider alternative explanations, lest we trap ourselves in a world of illusion. I believe there is great benefit for all of us in sharing our experiences that suggest pre-birth contact -- and potential for harm if we respond to them in a superstitious way.

Superstition is beautifully defined as *an irrational abject attitude*: irrational, if we do not open our interpretation of the experience to feedback; abject, if we feel overawed or intimidated by our own impressions or those of others.

In this chapter I want to point out some hazards and some ideas to consider as we try to evaluate our own and other people's experiences.

WHAT HARM CAN IT DO?

What possible harm could there be in taking everything at face value and believing whatever we like?

Perhaps I can explain my concern by telling the story of how it first arose -- and how I almost didn't write this book.

Nine years ago, I started gathering records of pre-birth contact with great enthusiasm, certain I was on to something that could only be of benefit. Besides wanting to know of other people's experiences, I hoped this focus would help me realize my dream of a second child despite my early miscarriages. And then two things happened that stopped me cold.

I was finally pregnant again, only a few weeks along. One morning after a cold, sweaty and uncomfortable night, I had a vivid dream:

> I'm holding a baby boy and I say, "Down's Syndrome." He has brown hair and low set ears and a typical Down's Syndrome face.

The dream shocked me. "Of course it's natural to dream of something I've worried about," I wrote in my diary, "but it's a nasty trick to play on myself as I get into my project on communicating before birth. That dream image was too vivid." Over the next few days all the symptoms of pregnancy flickered out, and I waited miserably for the miscarriage I was sure would follow.

Around the same time, I received an unusual story:

> I was four months pregnant, and in a dream the spirit of the baby I was carrying came and said she was sorry but she had made a mistake and now wasn't the right time to come, so she was going to leave. It scared me so much I went and had an abortion because I didn't know if I could bear miscarriage. I wanted that baby so bad.

This, I felt, was carrying trust in dreams too far. The coincidence of this story and my own dream caused a "Caution" light to go on in my mind, and it has never turned off.

Meanwhile my own pregnancy continued, and when amniocentesis revealed that my baby was a normal girl, I thought hard about my responsibility in sharing the stories I was gathering. Interesting and wonderful as they were, could they encourage someone to take drastic action based only on a dream or an intuitive impression?

As far as I can tell, no one knows how to separate truth from fantasy unerringly in these realms. Intuition springs largely from connections made at the subconscious level, but the subconscious mind is pressured by our desires and full of the innocent misunderstandings of childhood. Its voice may sound like revelation, but is it a sure guide in decision-making?

Ambrose Worrall, a man who embodied both intuitive and analytic skills in his dual roles as healer and engineer, has this answer:

> Intuition is the searchlight that points a way. It is not a roadmap, a defined plan of action, not a course that can be relied upon for definitive action. It is the indication of an area to be explored -- with care and wisdom and responsibility.

The danger is not in the experiences themselves but in how we interpret them, and what happens as a result of our becoming bound by our interpretations. Fantasies can be dangerous when we act on them, mistaking them for reality.

We tend to suppose our "imagination isn't good enough" to create visions and voices that seem to come from another source. Yet we all regularly create entire landscapes, characters, and storylines in our dreams, and we take this ability for granted, perhaps not realizing that the same capacity is available to the waking mind. Under the right conditions, the full range of our senses is available to give substance to our fantasies.

Just as we tend to underestimate the mind's creativity, we overestimate its accuracy. Our senses, memory, and thought processes are not perfect tools. We need a certain humility in admitting how limited and distorted our perceptions may be.

And so, what are the dangers, the downside of taking our impressions at face value?

One obvious hazard arises when we experience apparent past-life memories. Identifying people in past-life visions with our current mates and children could pose a real problem for the present relationship -- whether or not the memories are accurate.

One woman describes such an event, involving communication with her unborn child. "I think the past-life experience has brought a new context to my marriage," she says, "an understanding of why we are together and what we need to heal." While respecting the meaning that she finds in her vision, I wonder whether it may not be too much to ask of a man to accept his wife's view of him as a past-life villain:

> I was recently participating in a healing for myself with a facilitator. I began to have a past-life vision of being with a man, making love -- producing a baby. I discovered that the soul of that man is my husband today. In the past life, when I discovered I was pregnant I was very upset, because I was this man's mistress. It seemed my lover was of a wealthy, elite family and I was a poor woman.
>
> When the child was born, it was a boy... and my lover killed the child. At that point in the vision I realized that that baby is the baby I am carrying right now. The baby spoke to me and told me he forgave me for the past experience. He told me he was back and that he was glad I was healing so I could be a better mother for him. He expressed some fears about coming into the world -- because of his past experience with me and my husband.
>
> My husband is very fearful and scared about my past-life experiences. He tries to be supportive, but it goes against his traditional religious upbringing. He has expressed a fear that if

he did murder this child, that the child would be back to hurt him -- or "pay back." I explained that I thought the baby was back so that my husband could now "take care, nurture and love this baby's soul."

As we develop new potential abilities such as past-life recall and communication with our unborn children, we begin to see these are powerful tools -- two-edged swords requiring careful, responsible handling. We will have to learn the skillful and compassionate use of them.

EXPECTATIONS

A positive result of pre-birth contact with our children is that we come to see them as our spiritual equals rather than as lesser beings to be molded by us. But there is a risk to this attitude.

We may expect too much, lean too hard on the "wisdom of the soul" and not see our child's needs, not allow her to be a child, and neglect to play the parent role with enough confidence to give her security. We may even unconsciously reverse roles and treat the child as if she were our own parent.

With my Roselyn, identifying her (perhaps mistakenly) as the powerful being I "met" before her conception, I sometimes forget she is also a little child who needs a strong, calm mother. I let too much of my own problems burden her unfairly, because my perception of her is that she is "stronger than I am."

Thomas Armstrong warns of a related hazard, in his book *The Radiant Child*:

> The danger in any transpersonal philosophy of childhood is that the darker and more selfish attributes of the child will be ignored or sidestepped. This is often a problem in "new age" communities, where parents want their children to live spiritually pure lives and fight against any trace of selfishness or "low desire."

Pre-birth communications often involve impressions of our child's nature. I believe we need to be very careful, when these intimations of our children tempt us to assume we know their personalities or what their special destinies may be. It might be wise to file our thoughts away under "Wait and See," lest we forestall our children's self-discovery. There is a danger of forming a prematurely fixed notion of what this relationship will be and who this person is -- and then perhaps finding that we are not as open and available to the real child as we need to be.

If our ideas about the child are illusions, they may prove harmful. Will we subtly pressure him to live up to the image we hold of him? Will he be free to develop in his own way if we have identified him (whether rightly or wrongly) with someone from our past?

If visions and dreams are not confirmed in reality, we face disillusionment. There may be a huge contrast between our gratifying premonitions and the real baby! Life after childbirth may be less glorious than pre-birth experiences lead us to expect, and all of this may bring disappointment and difficulty in bonding with the child.

One mother describes how hard it was for her to deal with the fact that her second child was not the daughter prefigured in her vision. She lost faith both in her vision and in herself, as psychic ability was an important part of her self-image:

> I would like to share the vision I had of my children before either of them was born. In January 1983, I came down to Mexico on an intuitive hunch that I would live here. The day I arrived in Mexico City, I went to Chapultepec park to the museums, and stumbled on an area of children's play games and grounds. As I wandered about, I felt-saw? the presence of two children accompanying me.
>
> It was a strong feeling and yet part of me doubted it as a wishful fantasy. The children were a boy and a girl, about two years apart, maybe seven and five at that time, and I had a strong feeling of it being a premonition of a future. The children held hands and stayed by my side, and I felt them as spirits, which I could see in human form but not physical, made of light or a cloudlike hazy substance. The children were definitely of my Caucasian race, not Mexican. At that time I was neither married nor had a special boyfriend, was involved in midwifery training and had a very strong desire for children in the near future.
>
> Two weeks later I (re)met my future husband and father of my children in Oaxaca on the southern coast of Mexico. We had known each other as acquaintances for seven years. My first child was born in just over two years after the vision. I practiced natural family planning/breastfeeding and when my son was fifteen months old I conceived my second child. At that time I remembered the old vision and felt it was a confirmation of my faith that my children would be two years apart, as I'd trusted the second would be conceived at the exact right time following this method of family planning. For that reason too, I assumed the second child would be a girl, as in the vision.
>
> When my second son was born, I felt a tremendous lack of

faith in my own intuition and personal power. I didn't know how to integrate the sex of this second child without dishonoring the validity of the vision. I have not come to any conclusions but resolved it only by focusing on the present, and the intuition and insight I see at work now. As I said, the vision at the time it came to me felt very clear, I felt very happy and focused. After Gaby came out a boy I went through some of the roughest years of my life and I lacked a daily spiritual practice which I feel would have helped. Luckily continued psychic experiences reaffirmed my faith and got me to where I am today.

An interesting sequel to this story is that she later learned her husband had definitely not wanted to have a daughter, and she speculates, "My insight is that the soul of our pre-baby had to consider both parents in choice of sex. Maybe he felt he needed to be male to be born to both of us."

This thoughtful woman goes on to muse: "I seem to have both in me, faith and doubt. I didn't have my first child till thirty, and there were some years I wondered if my strong feeling that it was my destiny to be a mother was a delusion. Again that conflict between various parts of myself, positive and negative. I do believe that all our important relationships are here to help us learn something in this lifetime. Also in bad times I don't believe anything and I feel despondent and *scared* -- scared that it's all for nothing, that faith is a farce."

THE VALUE OF DOUBT

Although faith has a much higher approval rating, I want to affirm the importance of doubt. The touch of doubt is not a killing frost, only a cool breeze that keeps the mind awake and helps to keep us honest.

In an insightful editorial, New Age Journal editor Peggy Taylor warns of our tendency "to accept...certain assumptions about the way the universe works, without checking them out in the 'real world.'" She suggests that we need "to open our life systems up to feedback, so that they can transform and evolve; to be open to speculation, wide ranges of options..."

But why bother to doubt experiences that are so comforting simply to believe?

Some say it doesn't matter whether an impression of contact with our unborn child is true or illusory. My own initial impulse was to present these stories without raising the question of their validity. But as I realized their tremendous implications, I came to feel a dual responsibility: to open the door for sharing our experiences, and to point out that illusion is possible.

When doubt is allowed, there can be discussion, and we have a real chance of learning something. Because I believe there is so much to be learned from these personal experiences, I am concerned with opening them to question.

How do we open our experience to question and feedback?

We need to become aware of the common ways that we trip over our own perceptions. The more we learn about the mind, the more it resembles a brilliant professor whose vision roams the stars but who often ties his shoelaces together. And the more we see how mind and brain shape our experience, the more we need to increase our tolerance for ambiguity.

We need information about how the brain works, how our senses can deceive us, and how we use psychological strategies to protect our self-image and our picture of the world. Without such basic working knowledge of our own systems, we are easily fooled. Unfortunately this kind of essential information is kept at a distance as though it were esoteric, instead of being required curriculum for every high school student.

We need to know that we are capable of "entrancing" ourselves and creating simulations of reality; that visions, inner voices, invisible touches and the sense of presence can all be produced by the brain itself. Even the convincing feeling of deep personal meaning can be induced by stimulating an area of the brain.

When visionary encounters arise in connection with breathing techniques, we should be aware that changing the levels of our blood gases will alter consciousness. People volunteering to test the effects of various mixtures of oxygen and carbon dioxide have reported experiences that sound familiar:

> Some of these people saw bright lights, had out-of-body experiences and relived past memories. Some faced terror and some ecstasy, some cosmic understanding and universal love... {A young woman} first described a rush of colors and continued:
> "Then the colors left and I felt myself being separated; my soul drawing apart from the physical being was drawn upward, seemingly to leave the earth and to go upward where it reached a greater Spirit with Whom there was a communion, producing a remarkable, new relaxation and deep security."*

Sometimes we simply need to peel away the layers of interpretation we have added to our experience. When we strip an experience down to its essentials, we may discover that we know less about it than we thought we did. For example, when at thirteen I felt the touch of an invisible spirit, I told the story over to myself and gradually incorporated an assumption about "who" my comforter was. But the truth was that I had nothing to indicate an identity, just a simple sensation and the joy that came with it.

Memory is a storyteller. As we retell our stories it is easy to add definition, sharpen the outlines, and change "I think" to "I know." It is hard to be faithful to the fuzzy edges and element of mystery that may have been a genuine part of the experience.

We have other ways of subtly deceiving ourselves. We tend, for instance, to recall impressions that turn out to be correct, while forgetting the mistaken ones. Unless we keep careful records throughout pregnancy, will we remember the dreams that gave incorrect indications of our baby's appearance?

We need to acknowledge that our thinking is prone to logical fallacies. One of the commonest is "after this, therefore because of this" (the classic illustration being the hypothetical rooster who believes his crowing causes the sun to rise). For example, suppose that babies in the womb are completely unaware of requests for them to change position, say from breech to head-down. There would still be occasions when such a turn, just by chance, would come soon after we had asked for it. We would be inclined to believe that our request had caused the child's action.

Opening our experience to feedback is problematic when the experience is an apparent contact with a person before birth or before conception. Since the baby can't corroborate our impressions, there's no easy reality check for these events. But we can at least submit our impressions to the arbitration of time. In the case of the woman who dreamed that her child announced its imminent departure, she might have chosen to submit the dream message to the test of time. Would she really have miscarried?

We can also compare the visions and messages before birth with the realities that unfold afterward. It can be hard to let go of our pre-birth impressions, even if they are not supported by later events. We may tend to distort our perceptions of the child rather than give up the "specialness" of the experience. It takes courage to face the possibility that a cherished experience may not mean exactly what we want it to mean. In fact, it takes faith to doubt.

Because self-deception is possible, we need to keep several alternatives in mind as we evaluate our own and other people's stories. An experience may be exactly what it seems, an actual contact with the soul of an unborn child. It may be an illusion, like a waking dream. It may be a coincidence of events to which we have attributed meaning.

There is another intriguing possibility: our experience may be a kind of translation. It may be the way we interpret and "show" ourselves a contact taking place on another level. Just as a painting tells us both about the artist and the subject represented, our experience may be created by the interplay of our own needs and beliefs *and* the impressions we are receiving from the soul of our child.

OPEN A CHANNEL

There is much to be gained in sharing these private stories with each other. They both inspire us and offer us glimpses into life's secret workings. Under certain conditions, we can learn even more from them: for example, if we are not leaning too heavily on them to support beliefs.

If an experience must be true on our terms or else our sense of meaning will be lost, we can scarcely consider other ways of looking at it. Nor can we safely question other people's interpretations of experiences that have become the foundation of their faith.

We can learn more from our shared stories if we are not too polite to question each other and ask, "What do you mean?" Communication is difficult with people speaking so many different metaphoric languages. We need to go deeper into common but indefinite terms like "higher self," "old soul," and "intuition" -- words that we now use to mean a variety of different things. Without clear definition, words become blind spots that obscure thinking and communication.

For example, the meaning of an experience is often stated as something intuitively known. This seems to place it beyond question and stops discussion, for "intuition" has an aura of mysterious authority. By claiming intuition, we may stop ourselves from looking deeper into what we know and how we arrive at our impressions.

There is a parallel between information we gather through prenatal testing, and the insights that pre-birth communication may give us. Both present us with new powers and thus new responsibilities. Are we as careful about the inferences we draw from our own experiences as we expect scientists to be with their test results?

I am in favor of taking down fences between the "scientific" and the "spiritual," and having access to information from all directions. As the scientific and spiritual become one field of inquiry, we see a much wider range of possibilities -- and we are better able to provide each other with useful, accurate maps to the realms of experience we have traversed.

PART III

DOOR OF DEATH, DOOR OF BIRTH

Many of the most moving accounts that people have shared with me are about babies who died before birth or soon after it. To read their stories is to experience a small fragment of the parents' grief and bewilderment.

What is the meaning of such short term relationships? What could be their purpose? I sometimes felt almost angry with these elusive children, who often announced themselves and won their parents' hearts, only to disappear in miscarriage or infant death. "Why all the fanfare?" I would wonder. "Why all this preparation if you're only going to leave?"

The parents who endured these heartbreaking experiences have searched for answers, and in the stories presented here they speak for themselves. Among other things, they have found that death does not always end contact with the soul who was their child.

It seems that our connections with each other have little to do with the length of time we spend together. Whenever we really feel the presence of another being, we touch something powerful that seems to exist in a timeless dimension. And whether we are meeting someone who has died or someone not yet born, there is a similar quality to the experience, as though the dead and the unborn may be sharing the same "place" or at least be neighbors to one another. (In a few published accounts, people who have had near-death experiences tell of seeing children waiting to be born -- most commonly their own future children.)

And so I think the stories of meeting after death and meeting before birth belong together. Together they extend our idea of the parent-and-child connection way beyond old boundaries, and shine some possible light into the mystery that surrounds both doors of our life.

CHAPTER SEVENTEEN
MEETING BEYOND DEATH

There is very little that one can add to the stories in this chapter. They are sad and beautiful at the same time, for each story involves both an infant's death and a continuing bond that outlasts the brief life of a small body.

Writing about her two children, Julia Toth reveals how she connected with them in the dreamworld before conception, during pregnancy, and even following the death of one.

"A Rose That Tangled In My Hair:" Julia's Story

I was eighteen years old, newly married. Alone, really, my husband was busy and wealthy, meaning he worked and he played largely in places where I was not included, except as a wife. Boring! Not in my plans! Nor was becoming pregnant in my plans. I used birth control, I still had my cycles, but I kept on gaining weight. I felt wonderful, physically.

Then, when I was walking uphill in Seattle, I felt her, a rocking inside me. I lay down when I got home and felt my stomach. There was a round, hard ball there -- how had I not noticed? The doctor confirmed what the baby had told me, plus adding the information, beginning of the fifth month!

It was a good month. This baby, a girl, I thought, was a quiet person, only becoming active when I was very active. She was a peaceful sort of person, and I'd dream about her -- a dark-haired little girl with a cupid's bow lip. I did not plan her, but from the first time I felt her, she was very, very wanted.

She would say in my dreams, holding on to my hand, that we are a forever family. Over and over. We would be in a field, and we would walk through the wild roses, and she would put one in my hair. And that is what I felt when I first felt her move, the first impression, that she had chosen me. My husband says that I would be cradling my stomach and smiling, when I would dream that I had her on my lap.

I went to the San Francisco Gay Rights parade in the beginning of my sixth month and got gassed. I believe looking back at it that that was the trigger. The police didn't care who they hurt, and if you could have seen the violence that police and "fundamentalist" people were doing to other women's children, you would be forever changed. I myself got spat in the face by a man wearing a clerical collar. I laughed it off at the time, because I didn't think anything could happen to me, you know, the imagined invulnerability of the young.

Three days later I had her, right in the middle of a party, giving up her and a good deal of myself. It was a hard, ugly fight for my life. I woke up four days later.

I didn't understand it when they said that the baby (they wouldn't call her that -- she was a spontaneous abortion to them) had been born dead.

I had dreamed, in the hospital, of her and me, like two hands, gripping on for all we were worth, and finally of her saying that she was too tired, and then, I thought, I woke up.

When people began consoling me for the death of my baby, I realized that she had been alive at least long enough to get to the ambulance. I confronted my husband, and he admitted that she had died a few hours before I regained consciousness. He had wanted to protect me from grieving for a baby. I soon found that I needed protection from him, from his kindly lies and his absorption in his business.

When I left Seattle, though, I did not feel the same. I have never felt without her. In that sense my dreams told the truth.

When I became pregnant again, I asked the hospital for any information about my child, using a doctor friend's name, by permission, as my pass into the world of truth. They sent, among other things, the autopsy photos. Grisly things, no one should have only that as a record of the life of their child.

But there she was, a little girl with long, soft, dark hair, taking after her Eurasian mother, not her Irish father -- except for the cupid's bow mouth. She was just as I pictured her, exactly...

Nicholas

I had wanted a baby for years. Badly. I had had a baby, but everyone said, "You should get over the first one so that it doesn't just replace the other one." Never saying the words, death, or gone, acting as if one child can fit into the slot where another one was, just as you can replace a wrecked car with another, and still get to work on time.

I followed that advice for six years, before the pressure got too great. I kept on dreaming about sunflowers, dandelions, yellow pumpkinseed fish, long before I conceived. I had wanted a girl but the images I dreamed about were male, and Nordic. This was silly, I thought, I'm dark eyed and haired and so's Robert. I was hoping that, if reincarnation was possible, to get my first child back, somehow. I didn't know why, and I knew how bizarre that was, but there they were, in my drawings, yellow columbine and spurge, not the images from the first pregnancy, where a fair child would have been, if you pardon the pun, conceivable.

Nicholas was active, right from the start. I knew that I was pregnant long before the doctors believed that I was, because like the first time, my cycles stayed with me. Again, I found out medically in the second trimester that a baby was on the way.

He was so strong that he put a ring of bruises on the outside of me and dislocated one rib by the time he was born! Very different from my first pregnancy, I stayed up the night with him dancing inside of me by the sixth month. He liked Art of Noise, turned up loud, and German opera, which I can't stand, before and after he was born.

When they handed him to me, I saw -- red hair! White skin! The slate blue eyes of a newborn, but he's three now, and they haven't changed. He's got ice blond hair now and he looks like the kid on the Dutch Boy paint can. Where he gets it from, I don't know, but he's a beautiful little towhead boy who still likes Gotterdamerung and Euro Beat over Sesame Street.

Children are people, after all, with their own tastes and personalities, from before they are born, too, maybe even before that. If my dreams are anything like what really happens when a child is conceived, we go picking children like we go to pick flowers. Nicholas was a sunflower I chose for myself, and Ariel was a dark red rose that tangled in my hair.

I've taken to dreaming about her again, and she's the age she should be, if she had lived. Except that she's blond now, and she's in the field, laughing, saying, watch for me, watch for me, I told you that I would never leave you!

I don't think that I'm pregnant...

*   *   *

Patricia's first child was stillborn. Like baby Ariel, she seemed to stay in touch with her mother after death. And later, much as Julia Toth sensed a second child coming to be born, Patricia met another child in her dreams. (That story is told in Chapter Eleven.) It seems as though the same "channel" that connects us with the unborn may link us as well with those who have died.

"Grieving is Hard. . . But Necessary:" Patricia's Story

In February, 1990, our child died in utero during the thirty-second week of pregnancy. We were devastated. Her name was Hannah Marie. Within a few weeks, I started hearing from her in my dreams. I had one persistent question: had she died in pain? Of course, I also wanted to know why we lost her, but for some reason, I was fixated on whether she had suffered. She said she was okay, that she had not suffered, and that after life wasn't so bad after all. This helped me considerably.

I continued to hear from her. I really didn't document the number of times she entered into my dreams, but it was often. As sad as I was, it was comforting to hear from her. Often, it was just a feeling of her presence, no verbal communication.

When I dreamed of Hannah Marie, I had no visual image of her. But I felt her presence very strongly. She was innocent, yet wise; loving to me, yet not belonging to me anymore, and far less fragile than she was when she was with me. In fact, she seemed like a very sturdy entity: something that could not cease to exist. Far less fragile than I, I must admit. I took comfort in knowing that she was okay, while I didn't understand exactly what state that was.

I find the fact that I didn't have a visual image of her in my dreams rather unexpected, since I had seen her after the birth and knew what she looked like. Her physical image was burned into my memory, and I can still recall it. But during the dreaming, she was not a physical being. My only explanation of this is that we are really only embodied during our stay on Earth. Between lives, we are present in a different form.

My husband Peter and I went on a vacation to Ireland for the first two weeks in June. We really needed to get away. During the second week, I noticed that I hadn't heard from her for a week or more. I didn't take it badly, but weirdly enough, I noticed it. Ireland was a peaceful place, and we found it quite calming to be there.

In July, a friend introduced me to a woman who had moved to the area. It turns out that she's able to connect with (as she calls them) "the Guys." She's able to ask these "Guys" about people who are currently in limbo between lives. (As a point of validation, she has also helped the police find lost people and details of murders.) I don't necessarily believe in this stuff, but I don't disbelieve it either. Anyway, I let her do a session for me. I asked her questions, which she'd ask "the Guys." One question I asked them was why I hadn't heard from Hannah. They responded that she had been re-embodied. That made sense.

As for Hannah helping me understand why we lost her, all I can say is this: It happened the way it was meant to. As a result of this experience, I became more open to spiritual things, and through that I might someday gain an understanding of what happened and why. It's not something that I'm supposed to understand yet. According to "the Guys," death truly is just a transition. It's really no big deal. They said that. It hurts that I miss her. That I didn't have the opportunity to know her, or to carry out the commitments I made. But the path I'm on (which I'm not entirely clear about) is the important outcome. I was also told the following by "the Guys": Know that the entity that was briefly a part of my life was prepared for this outcome. In a weird way, that also helped me face it all. And they also said that she didn't suffer in her death. That was important for me to hear.

As for this path I'm on... I know that I've changed. I've been more creative. I've explored more of me, and the world around me. I've opened up the boundary of my world, the possibilities of my life. I'm not doing anything magnanimous with it, but I'm mostly enjoying the journey. I say mostly, because sometimes new paths bring endless possibilities, and it's hard to sort out what to do when. And also, grieving is hard, but I've learned it's necessary. It's required to heal a part of us that we rarely experience.

*   *   *

After the death of Sharon's infant son, his continuing presence was felt not only by Sharon, but by her mother, who had played a special role in her grandson's brief physical life.

Messenger of Love: Sharon's Story

In the spring of 1985 I gave birth to a seemingly normal baby boy. The doctor told us we had a perfect baby and we should go home and enjoy the rest of our lives together. That was a very happy day for us, but our joy was short lived. Our seemingly perfect son did not want to nurse. When I voiced my concerns, the hospital staff reassured me that the baby was just sleepy from the drugs I had been given during the birth. I finally got one nurse to take me seriously when I pointed to my baby's depressed fontanel. Our son was becoming severely dehydrated. Dr. Sexton examined Christopher carefully and then told me that although he could find nothing wrong, he had a feeling something was not right.

A specialist was called in from Children's Hospital and during his more in-depth examination, Christopher went into heart failure. After they resuscitated him they discovered that the baby's kidneys were shutting down. When he was finally stabilized on full life support, extensive and ongoing brain damage was discovered. Our son lay, unresponsive, in a coma.

Since I had hemorrhaged shortly after the birth, I was kept in the hospital an extra day to recover. If we had been sent home on a normal schedule, our son would have died suddenly at home. Because expert medical care was available, his suffering was prolonged for six days. The diagnosis? Ornithine transcarbamylase deficiency. Our son's body was unable to break down ammonia, and since ammonia is a by-product of protein there is no way he could have survived. There is no treatment, there is no cure. As soon as the umbilical cord had been cut, Christopher had begun to die.

Once he was diagnosed, my husband and I went to visit him in the neonatal ICU. Between the beeping, graph displaying machines that crowded around him and the tubes, catheters and electrodes attached to his small body, there was no room for a mother's hesitant caress. Every time I looked at him I became weaker. Every time I touched him I felt the very life being drained from my body. I had walked into Children's Hospital under my own power and had to be taken out in a wheelchair. I was young and unprepared to watch our baby die. I never went back.

On the fifth day, we conferred with the doctors by phone and agreed to remove Christopher from life support the following day. Unable to sleep, I stayed up late by myself watching TV and tried not to think about anything. I was sitting in our living room watching a comedy show when Christopher came to me.

These visitations are hard to describe because I have nothing to compare them with. The TV, our living room, even the couch I was sitting on seemed to drop away. It seemed I was inside of his little body, experiencing everything from his innocent point of view. There was no sound, and yet I could hear him in the same way one "hears" a remembered melody in one's mind. He could not communicate with words, and yet he demanded answers to three specific questions in a terrified scream. "Where am I?" "Why aren't you here with me?" and "Why does it hurt so much?"

The next moment I was back in my living room, sitting on my couch, and weeping. I knew then that the doctors had been wrong when they said the brain damage was so extensive that our son could no longer feel pain. The time was 12:12 A.M. Days later, a night nurse confirmed our son had briefly regained consciousness shortly after midnight that night.

The next day my mother did for Christopher what I could not do. She went down to the hospital. When he was removed from life support, she rocked him in her arms until he quietly died.

Weeks after the funeral I told my mother about the disturbing psychic communication I had experienced. She then told me that she had been visited nightly by the baby since his death. She had repeatedly wakened in the middle of the night with the baby in her arms and the sweet scent of a newborn in the room. As soon as she was fully awake, he was gone. These comfort-seeking visits gradually tapered off over time.

Both my husband and I were obsessed with grief over his death. I cannot begin to describe how badly we handled trying to get on with our lives. About four months into this turbulent time Christopher contacted me again. I was at work one evening, trying to keep my mind on what I was supposed to be doing, when my surroundings dropped away much as they did that night in our living room. Again I seemed to be experiencing the moment from Christopher's point of view. I was inside his tiny coffin. I had the sense that although he was there with me, his essence had not been buried with his body. Wordlessly, he was trying to show me something. A teddy bear. Not just any teddy bear, but the one we had placed in the casket with him. That bear was wearing a T-shirt with "Messenger of Love" written across the front. To this day, that image still comforts me.

Years passed, and I was sure I had heard the last from our son, but I was wrong. About five years after his death he contacted me again. It was late at night and I had been studying for a class I was taking. I went to bed and tried in vain to calm my mind enough to sleep. Then, just as before, my surroundings seemed to drop away and my attention was riveted to our son's presence. This time Christopher used language to communicate with me. His "voice," which I am sure could be heard only in my mind, reminded me very much of the biblical "still small voice" usually attributed to communications from God. This was not God. This was our son. I did not "see" him, but my inner self recognized him immediately. He said, "You are blessed." In near panic, I called out to him to stay long enough to explain this odd message. I had so many questions to ask him, and I longed for further contact with him but he was gone as quickly as he had arrived.

It has been over two years since that last confusing visitation and I am still wondering what was meant. Four months ago, I finally gave birth to a healthy rosebud of a little girl. It is possible he was referring to her, but since she was born over two years after his "blessing" I cannot be sure. I am not a religious person so I am not inclined to make religious interpretations. The only thing I know for sure is that I did not imagine his contact with me and neither did my mother.

*   *   *

When Cheri Carlson's baby succumbed to Sudden Infant Death Syndrome (SIDS), Cheri called upon her pre-birth connections and her philosophy of life and death to sustain her. Despite the grief and anger, she was able to experience an altered but continuing relationship with her child.

Cheri's Story

Back when I hit age thirty I felt the "biological clock" thing, and planned a baby with the guy I was with. We had a chest of drawers with T-shirts and blankets and rattles and toys. I did not conceive, and eventually the relationship ran its course. I thought about intentional single-parenting (artificial insemination) but ultimately decided against it, not seeing my way past the ol' hospital job to support us versus wanting to be a stay-at-home, home-schooling mom. I could always eventually adopt anyway if I "panicked" someday.

The night I came to peace with the whole issue of waiting for parenting, I sat by my doll cradle -- and instead of my childhood doll, I saw the most perfect dark-haired girl baby. There was no doubt she would be in that cradle someday.

November 8, 1989. I was thirty-four. By now, that vision was quite distant and it didn't seem I *could* conceive. I wasn't upset that I never conceived, but was finally lazy about "paying attention to precautions."

Somehow I knew the instant I conceived.   I also knew immediately that the relationship would be over. I knew abortion and adoption were not options for me. And I knew I was single and working "per diem" (wages in lieu of benefits). And... I knew everything would work out. It took me a month or two to truly get my act together and feel like I could do it. I was nauseated, working extra hard, determined to keep a positive focus, and empowered by the presence of the "baby."   She was a wise powerful old soul. I felt very blessed by her physical presence -- and not sure to what I owed the honor! I dreamed of a dark haired girl and a blond haired boy. I named her Samara and bought neutral clothes.

I worked long and hard through the pregnancy. I went into labor at work one morning, two weeks early. I denied that it was labor; after all I wasn't set up at home. And it was a summer Friday and there was no one to call in to replace me. After my shift I drove home, set up my delivery space, called my midwife, and finally delivered Samara Lynne, seven pounds, perfect, adorable, tons of black hair, the cutest baby ever.

At her birth I bled, requiring IV pitocin (the midwives were very good with this) and I tore fourth degree -- pushed her out when her heart rate remained decelerated between contractions -- the midwives were also able to suture this. I did get infected and developed a fistula and "things" fell out. It kept me down longer than expected -- and gave me time to be with the baby.

I had felt communication with "star friends" for years -- and readily recognized the presence of "that" one soon after conceiving Samara. I remembered past time with her, and "knew" she had not incarnated for a very long time. When she was born, of course, the physical proximity made the communication easier and more intense. Once when we were shopping she picked out a lovely outfit (she was three or four weeks old). I said, "No Samara Lynne, you need a heavier material for that time of year. Where will you wear this party outfit then?" But she persisted. Turned out she had a use in mind I hadn't thought of -- a funeral party outfit.

She was always impatient with me as an "elderly crippled" mother. At all times she has been impatient with me over abstract concepts that I'm slow to grasp. Where I live used to be country (a few years ago) but "civilization" has moved in. When Samara was six or seven weeks old the "tree mutilators" came and in two days, three lots of woods was a flat dusty space, a few feet from me. For years it had been my woods. Blackberries, a swamp, frogs, raccoons, cat space. I was devastated.

The third day all was quiet, the machines were gone. And the air was "thick." I felt I could hardly move around, bumping into "someone" constantly. That evening, I was still baffled about what was happening. As we sat together, Samara was laughing at "someone" up by the ceiling. I finally said, "Okay Samara, I give up, who are they?" She looked at me, exasperated: "Tree devas, Mom..." "Oh, yeah, of course."

When Samara Lynne died I lost that feeling of contact. It had been there as many years as I could remember and then *she* had been here and then it was *all* gone.

She died Tuesday morning. I woke from sleep suddenly and knew something was wrong. She couldn't have been out-of-body too long because she had electrical activity on the monitor when the aid car arrived. I began CPR, my sister called 911. By the time we reached the Emergency Room the whole hospital knew the "code pink" arriving was my baby. The ER was jammed with people. It went on "forever." Family, of course, is not allowed in a code room. Three large friends were trying to hold me back but I was making headway when my ER nurse friend let me in.

A nurse/birth coach friend was one of the people present. As I said, I had lost that feeling of contact, but she saw Samara watching us and said, "We've got to let that baby go." Of course she was right and I knew it and the code team soon agreed.

I left the hospital with my friends... without my baby. Tuesday and Wednesday were empty, pointless, a complete void, angry, screaming, sobbing, busy busy busy. Friends were there by the handfuls constantly. Phone calls and more phone calls. Searching for a cemetery, planning a funeral loomed ahead. Who cared? A friend said, "Samara says you should eat." I said, "Why, who cares, I can't."

And then sure enough, that second evening I heard Samara again. Immediately that feeling of re-establishing contact helped fill the void. And immediately we started going round and round. She said -- first thing she said -- "Good grief, what are you still upset about?" (As in, "Hey, we had a great time but now I've got stuff to do. We always communicated fine before and now it'll always be even easier and more special.") I saw her point but had to argue my point that I was quite a bit more entrenched in physical body stuff than she was; she had to give me a little more time to adjust and be okay with this new rearrangement. She herself had not liked the limitations of an infant's physical body (or *any* physical body I assume). She was quite happy to be free to "fly" again.

In the days following her death, I saw her, and also a blond boy. I lit candles for them both, at the funeral parlor and at home. I didn't try to rationalize why; it just felt right.

After Samara died, in the weeks and months that followed, it occurred to me I had to have "known" on some level -- and had been "preparing" for the "SIDS event" for many years. Over many years of working critical care, being on the "code team," doing hundreds of codes, seeing hundreds of sad, unfair situations, I developed quite strong philosophies about life and death and karma and specifically, SIDS. If it was ever possible for someone to be prepared to deal with SIDS it was me. And yet consciously I never thought it would happen to me. (I am very glad I didn't waste any of our precious time worrying about it!)

Eight years before Samara's funeral I had been in that same funeral home -- the only other time I'd been there and the only other SIDS funeral I've been to, a three month old boy. That event was held "as usual" with rows of people in black in hard pews, mournful music, and so on. I sat in the back and thought, "This isn't how it should be" (dangerous thought). "Supposedly all you people believe in something 'better' after death, yet you are not acting in the least happy for the child, or the time you had with him." My friends and I had long discussed how our "funerals" should be (parties we would have liked, with our friends celebrating our life and our transition to afterlife). So there I found myself in the spot of having to do it the way I thought it should be.

The poor funeral home people had no flexibility to adjust the frowns painted on, on "funeral" day, to the group of a hundred or so assembled in a circle, holding hands, wearing white and pastel, playing lively music, telling fun Samara stories, burning candles and incense and having a celebration of her life. In reality I'm sure the frowns were real and due to the glitter and candle wax and incense smoke and overall alteration of usual atmosphere.

Samara Lynne is buried in a tiny country cemetery; cows behind, river below, mountains in two directions, under a fir tree in the baby section. It is a very peaceful place and I freshen it up every month or so with flowers, confetti, balloons, pinwheels, toys, whatever. It's not a sad place for me generally speaking, but peaceful and inspirational.

At least three of my friends have told me they "got messages" from Samara while she was alive, and many more since she died. One held her once briefly -- she said Samara told her, "Yes, I'd like to stay and play but I've got things to do. Take care of my mom." (She was here for me.)

Many people I did not know well have told me experiences of feeling her presence since she died! I have felt it since the day after she died when I re-established contact but it makes me happy that other people "see" her too!

I must tell you the story of the musical teddy bear. It was my old bear, from my childhood... he'd quit playing when I was about fifteen. I placed him below Samara's casket for the funeral, lit candles, and *the bear played* -- not just a note or two... he kept on. It was the night before the funeral, I was there "setting up" with a few friends. He played while we got things ready; he played while we "sat;" he was still playing when we left.

Cheri has another child now, the blond baby boy she envisioned so clearly. She writes:

My impressions and dreams while I was pregnant with Samara were much more intense than correspondingly with Trey. I feel that's because I had to jam it all into such a compressed time period with her. Some part of me knew that; with Trey I have a whole lifetime to discover it all and we can do it while we're physically together. Samara and I still add pieces to our discoveries, but it's different. She comes and plays here off and on -- by candlelight; fairy princess scenes -- and she nags me off and on...

Before my pregnancy and birth experiences I realized I was at the end of the "critical care nurse" phase of my life, but not sure what the next phase was. November 8, 1989 I began the next phase. I knew the instant that I was pregnant. And I also knew in that instant that nothing would ever be the same again. Pregnancy, birthing, with complications, death, pregnancy, birthing, surgeries, with complications -- it's been quite a journey (and all as a single woman). It's brought me to Now: a very enthusiastic Labor Support Doula, working towards my certification, community recognition for Doulas and more happy birth stories -- fulfilled mothers and happy babies, wanting to help wake up America and the world to gentler, more aware birthing, leading ultimately to a gentler more aware planet.

Four years later, Cheri still feels the presence of Samara strongly. "My angel daughter continues to keep me busy," she writes. "I've had some amazing experiences, including people seeing her with me and telling me so. Someone I'd just met, who didn't know about Samara, saw her 'working' with me." Samara seems to lead Cheri into new connections and ever-widening circles of caring and helpfulness, and Cheri speaks with appreciation of the "little voice" that urges her on...

*   *   *

The conception of Susan Bassett's first child was heralded by a blissful vision of light, as Susan described in Chapter Two. But the baby lived only twelve days. I asked Susan to share her thoughts about the meaning of his short life. She replied:

> The meaning of my son's life -- who knows? However, as you can probably imagine, I have given this a tremendous amount of thought. I do believe in my heart that all three of us (husband, son and I) have probably shared many, many lifetimes together. I think for whatever reason my son needed his last lifetime to be as an infant who experiences death.
>
> It almost seemed to me to be his last "good-bye" to earth, as I really believe that he has gone on to a much nicer place. In all of the metaphysical work I have done, he comes to me in a place where people talk with their hearts, so I refer to it as the "Heart Planet" for lack of a better term. I think João picked me and I him before this lifetime to fulfill this last agreement between us -- it is the ultimate sacrifice that a mother can do for a child.
>
> As to "why..." I once was driving along and heard Ram Dass speak to parents of AIDS children and he said something that really hit my heart, "In the moment of your own death, you will know the answer to the question -- 'why did my child have to die?'" For this reason, I look forward to my own death -- but at some point in the grieving the "why" becomes less a wail and more of a whisper. Ask any mother who has lost a child and I think you will find an answer similar to that. My son led a very exalted life for those twelve days he was here -- he was a very old soul!

Claire C.'s daughter, Andrea Grace, died at birth but soon afterward visited Claire in meditation and gave her a profound experience of love and healing. Since then, Claire and her husband have had two more children, and Andrea has continued to be a spiritual companion and guide for Claire. Her story points to another possible dimension of the parent-and-child bond. It suggests that someone who comes, however briefly, as our child may really be a teacher who chooses to help us from the other side of life. Claire writes:

Yes, I feel a continuing connection with Andrea. She made it clear to me the first time she "talked" to me that she did not have to take on a human body. It was a pure gift of love that she did so. She took on the experience of birth and death as a means to awaken me to my pain and to my spirituality. Not that I can always appreciate what she did for me -- in my "Higher Self" I certainly do, but in my grief I still feel the pain of the loss and wish to hold my little baby. On every anniversary of her birth I fantasize making a birthday cake and being with my little girl.

However, she is an ongoing part of my life in a spiritual realm. I found that I could "talk" with her whenever I wished. She is a continual source of wisdom for me. I ask her questions about decisions I am facing, questions about parenting, my growth, other people, anything. I listen quietly, and answers always come. She doesn't always answer me directly, and she never tells me what to do. She always envelops me in love and acceptance. She often responds with "this would be good" or "this would not be helpful." Always when I follow her guidance, it leads to greater good. She is like a spiritual mother to me -- infinitely loving and giving.

What I understand now is that everyone has such a spiritual being who is devoted to them. Some people call them "Guardian Angels." They call themselves "Master Teachers." My teacher must have decided to teach me through coming as my baby, Andrea Grace, because she needed to do it that way to break through my extremely strong denial. At the time she came to me, I was "locked" in my ego state. I could have gone on for the rest of my life sidestepping any real emotional growth. Or at least, for a long time -- who can know. Anyway, she did this for me, and it worked. I've been travelling fast ever since.

It all seems "ordinary" to me now, although when I look back over it, it's like a miracle gift. The healing in my life has been profound, but the place it is taking me to is one of simplicity and joy -- the miracle of the ordinary -- how life is meant to be. Without her help I could not have found my way to this healing. I think our Master Teachers reach us in whatever way we will listen -- there are many, many ways, no doubt. I feel so grateful that she found the way to my heart's unfoldment. I feel at the threshold of a new life.

CHAPTER EIGHTEEN
MISCARRIAGE: GRIEVING AND GIFT

> *A young falcon is in our house. I slip into the kitchen and*
> *prepare a mixture of herbs, and place the bowl in the*
> *hallway. The falcon enjoys eating the herbs, but then*
> *something frightens him and he spreads his wings and soars*
> *out my bedroom window into a sky so bright that I can't see*
> *him flying away...*
>
> *-- a miscarriage dream*

In the developed countries of the world, only a few parents must endure a baby's death. But many more experience the intersection of life and death that is miscarriage. Like other female passages, miscarriage has been largely silent and invisible for so long that even now a woman may feel alone in it and be surprised to learn that it is as common as one in six pregnancies.

There seems to be an unspoken message in our society that says we should not grieve too much for our miscarriages. Medical attendants and even our own partners may not understand the intensity of the experience, and we may find little support or recognition for the loss. We almost expect it to be "nothing," an insignificant event. After all, there was no one really to be mourned, was there?

In my own two miscarried pregnancies, I had no sense of anyone there to be lost. I felt no presence with the first and nothing at all with the second, a pregnancy I hadn't even recognized until it ended. So I supposed there could be little sense of presence with any pregnancy that ended in miscarriage.

Some of the stories shared with me tend to confirm that view. Roxi, for example, whose full-term pregnancies were announced and accompanied by powerful dreams, noticed that no dreams marked her three miscarried pregnancies. Lisa Ponder, accustomed to feeling communication with her unborn children, was baffled by the difference in her third pregnancy:

> I got frustrated that there didn't seem to be anyone listening (inside) or anyone talking to me or for me to talk to (inside). It was eerie. That one was a miscarriage of an empty sack at the beginning of the fourth month. I had been so sad that the baby

wouldn't talk to me, and then I finally knew why.

While in Lisa's case there was literally no one there, we can speculate that even when an embryo is growing in the womb, there may be "nobody home." Could some embryonic bodies go unclaimed by any soul? Strange as it seems, it is not inconsistent with the evidence of some people's experiences, as we shall see in a later chapter.

However, during some pregnancies that fail, people do sense a presence. An Australian woman whose pregnancy was ectopic recalls, "Throughout the short time that I was pregnant I was always aware of a presence with me, both of a child and a feminine 'presence.'" She is one of the mothers who found, to their surprise, that the presence they felt during a miscarried pregnancy was actually more intense than what they experienced with other pregnancies carried to term.

A mother writes:

> I conceived almost five years ago (and knew immediately I had conceived), and a few days later, while plugging in my iron, I had a split-second "flash" and knew it was a boy, his name was Luc, and I had a strong sense of his personality. The pregnancy lasted only a few weeks, but to this day all of the information I received about that child is clearer and more real than most other memories I have of anything. I feel privileged to have experienced this "bonus" of such closeness and intimate contact with another soul even if for only a few weeks.

Ann Wasserman and her husband Larry both felt contact with a definite personality during Ann's second pregnancy. "He was a trickster," Larry recalls. "He kept joking, even to the point of saying he was okay when he wasn't. (Was that a joke or the truth?)"

Ann had similar interactions with this personality. "I heard a lot of snickery sort of laughter in my head," she says. "There was a lot of tension of some sort, some anger. He was a joker and a trickster, but underneath that was a person in need of much love and attention."

This pregnancy ended in an early miscarriage. Now, Ann is nearing her due date with another child. Though she and Larry have felt impressions of a personality in each of her three pregnancies, they agree that the greatest sense of communication and contact was with the miscarried child. Ann suggests a possible explanation for this paradox:

> The man I go to for acupuncture says the Chinese philosophy of birth and death is that they are processes, rather than simple events. The soul gradually comes in and gradually leaves,

beginning and ending well on either side of the events themselves. So a baby begins its journey long before conception, and doesn't fully "get here" until well after birth. He theorized that my second baby was so clearly communicative because his goal was just those three months of contact here; he came quickly, did what he needed to do, and left. Now number three is taking the more gradual course and will be born and keep coming on in.

The one thing everyone (including me) is clear on so far is the personality. Everyone uses words like: stable, grounded, centered, calm, strong. This is certainly different from the sense of my second. But lately I've been feeling that this really is the same spirit. Maybe whatever all the tension was about has been solved as its part of the miscarriage. And I think I've heard that same little trickster laugh a few times...

"PHANTOM PREGNANCIES"

These stories reveal not only that parents can connect with a presence in a miscarried pregnancy, but that even an early loss may bring deep and long-lasting grief. The lack of permission to mourn a miscarried child, and the absence of customs for expressing our emotions, make it harder to cope with feelings that may linger on long after we "should be over it."

The emotional aftermath of a miscarriage may be connected to the time that we had set aside for the pregnancy to unfold. One mother, for example, relates how after an early loss her grieving lasted a full nine months. Some feel a need to honor the original due date when it arrives, with a special observance or even by going through a kind of spiritual birthing.

A mother's grieving can be acted out physically, as though the body is unwilling to believe the pregnancy is over. Clare Adams tells how her body maintained the semblance of pregnancy until the due date:

> When my husband and I were married for two years, I decided to go off birth control pills. I immediately became pregnant. I felt a soul come into my body during deep and loving intimate contact with my husband. I could feel the baby inside me from the moment of conception, but my husband couldn't believe me. I could sense another energy besides my own in my second chakra center, the womb.
>
> I had to have a rubella shot in order to work. I did this even though I felt strongly against it. Sure enough I miscarried three

weeks later. I was only six weeks along. I never got the pregnancy confirmed but I knew I had been with child.

The grief was overwhelming. My husband did not know how to comfort me. Three months went by. My tummy was swollen, and I had no menses since I miscarried. I went to a gynecologist, who could not understand why my body was "acting pregnant" when the tests proved I wasn't. He gave me pills to bring on a period, but still my tummy was swollen and firm.

Another three months went by. I repeated the same procedure -- doctor and pills. I was still grieving for my unborn child, and I still felt this soul inside me.

Sure enough, during the week I should have given birth, I did! I had horrible pains and "contractions." I mentally, emotionally and spiritually "birthed" my baby's soul. It was a healing experience. I finally bled on my own and acknowledged the loss of my child.

It took over six months to resume a regular menstrual cycle -- perhaps I was spiritually breastfeeding this little soul.

Midwife Sally Gartner calls them "phantom pregnancies" -- the aftermath of her two pregnancies that miscarried. She describes her strong awareness of the due dates and her need finally to "release the space in my body although the babies are long gone..."

Sally's Story

I believe I am a pretty rational person, but I had an emotionally repressed upbringing. Parenting my firstborn was very healing, and as I grew capable of deeper emotional connections through motherhood and the second pregnancy and birth I became more intuitive. Thus, after my son's birth I believe I was wide open to receive impressions from the spirit pair which I recognized as future children. Both pregnancies ended, but the experiences were so affirming.

Within a couple of months of my son's birth, I thought I was fantasizing about two future children. My husband and I always agreed to have at least three, so the idea of more kids was not new. I had no specific visions in terms of physical appearance. Indeed, their physical lives were fleeting. There was nothing to see, as it turns out.

My sense was that they would just "be there," filling my presence as I went about my daily routines. I was not ever in the habit of meditating. I would simply be aware of them, or not. I remember making brief mention of them to my mother when my son was only a few months old. Feeling foolish about it, I said sometimes I felt these babies just "followed me around." I made up an image of cherubs with their little angel wings, hovering over my shoulders -- one on each side. It is not really accurate of how I felt them, but for lack of a better image that one came to mind. I didn't really even believe in them, but I was confused because although I didn't believe it, I felt them anyway: just a vague sense that they were there, and they would be my children some day. It seemed so foolish, I didn't even tell my husband.

Off and on for over a year I would have these "visitations," which puzzled me but did not seem threatening. I didn't pay much attention to it most of the time. It was something to muse on. I felt very busy, and can't say how much time they spent with me altogether. As it turns out, I am sure they did not intend to stay, so with hindsight it is very fulfilling for me to understand they were spending as much time with me as they possibly could *before* the pregnancies. They have since moved on. I have not felt them since the last pregnancy ended.

All my life I fantasized about having children, especially twins. When I thought of these two, however, wondering if they must be twins since there were always the same two together, I just felt they were not. I don't know why. In my best fantasies I had twins, but after all, I don't think these two were a fantasy. I was open to them, but did not conceive until my husband was ready for the next baby. This is significant, I believe, because we had some opportunity to conceive sooner but his commitment was not strong. As soon as he was ready, the first pregnancy began.

I thought I was pregnant pretty soon in that cycle, feeling confident of my fertility signals and our timing. Symptoms were vague, but I definitely felt different; my body went through some early changes and a friend who helped me examine myself agreed with me that the negative reading on a pregnancy test must be inaccurate. When my second test was negative and my signs of pregnancy refused to develop stronger, I felt I would miscarry.

Lots of people would question whether I really was pregnant at all. I was confused by the negative tests, feeling sure I must be pregnant, and then doubting my feelings, doubting my body. Awaking with an intense uterine cramp one night made me feel sure it was a pregnancy ending, but when the delayed blood flow was less than I expected (I really didn't know what to expect) I thought it must be just a weird cycle. My sense of the spirit child was lost. I felt the presence only in confusion in the beginning of that pregnancy, with hope and doubt strongly enmeshed. It was a nine week cycle. Five weeks is normal for me.

My body built up to receive the second spirit right away in the very next cycle. I thought I should have conceived that March, but I did not feel symptoms, and then had my period on schedule. Actually the pregnancy was ectopic, and I had some minor hemorrhaging (no tubal rupture) within days of finishing my "period." I was in denial about being pregnant, but finally went in to begin testing to find out what was wrong with me. Only after the pregnancy test was positive (I cried immediately knowing it had to be ectopic) could I acknowledge the baby. Since this baby followed in connection with the other and clearly did not mean to stay either, I recognized for the first time that these were the two children who visited me so much.

Aside from the obvious grief and disappointment not to be able to keep these babies, I no longer felt so confused about all the visitations. I don't know what they were trying to tell me, but on some level I believe they must have told me a lot. For example, I told friends that I might have an ectopic pregnancy just before the pregnancy began. It was so much on my mind.

I named the babies for the feminine aspect of their experience within me: Myra and Desiree. Sometimes I think Myra was really a boy. I don't know why I think one way or another about their sex. It doesn't really matter. But they were a part of me, recognized only by me, so I give them feminine names.

I felt the presence of that ectopic baby most strongly. Desiree was very much a wanted baby, and the pregnancy was much stronger than the first, in spite of the ectopic snag. Sometimes I wonder if she thought she might be too tempted to stay, in spite of her agreement to rejoin her spirit partner. So perhaps that explains why she sabotaged her chances by staying in the fallopian tube. Or maybe there was some design to lead me into surgery so that I would have the experience I need to work with other women on these pregnancy issues. I see it as an overwhelmingly positive experience, with so much purpose and so much gained. The losses themselves are gains of another kind. I don't believe there was any accident with these pregnancies. I just don't understand all the details and reasons. But having these experiences furthered my understanding in the work I am pursuing, and I believe I helped Myra and Desiree in whatever destiny their spirits must pursue.

I feel like I'm finishing those two pregnancies, overlapping as they are. I don't really understand why I continue to fail at further conception during these "phantom pregnancies," but I really feel like I have to finish these non-existent pregnancies anyhow, somehow, maybe just by getting past my due dates. The first is in mid-October. I am surprised by an approaching sense of relief. I could have given birth by now, had I still been pregnant, and I feel like I am releasing a space in my body even though the baby was long gone. I guess I've been having trouble letting go fully until a time that feels reasonable, safe for parting. The safest and best time to part with a baby physically is through a full term natural birth. I am about ready to dream up a beautiful home birth for Myra. Desiree will be next, but she isn't due until my wedding anniversary in December.

After the surgery, I wondered if the three of us had attained a level of consciousness together, because I awoke feeling I had had good contact with them. Although my body hurt, I felt utter bliss or euphoria, absolute peace with having to release my baby -- a much wanted baby -- through abortion. I remember this feeling intensely and have been puzzled at how I reached this kind of understanding. Before surgery I was desperate and tearful -- not caring what they would do to me but only hopelessly sad that when it was over I would no longer have my baby. Rationally I knew I couldn't maintain an ectopic pregnancy, but emotionally I didn't care *where* she was, as long as I still had her with me. But when I woke up afterwards I felt not only that everything was okay, but that it was absolutely as it was meant to be. I felt as if there was a real spiritual contact, and this sense was so strong that I told my mother immediately about the previous visitations as she drove me home. It has changed my life and my entire perspective on our relationships with the unborn.

The power of spiritual connections is so real to me in a way I could not have believed had I not felt it. The meaning which is strongest to me is to trust and believe whatever connections I may feel in the future, and allow other women to believe in their own experiences.

In Sally's story and in those to follow, along with the grief there is a strong feeling that something precious has been gained. Even when pregnancy ends, there may be a kind of cooperative bond between the parents and the children who leave early.

Ann Wasserman, whose pregnancy miscarried at eleven weeks, writes that the truly amazing events followed the miscarriage. "When I woke up the next morning," she says, "I came through that twilight stage of waking up with the clear sensation of being hugged by him."

Ann continues:

> That weekend we took part in a ceremony a friend had planned. She had had to have a hysterectomy a few years before and was sorting out the emotions of that experience, in saying good-bye to the children that would never be, and honoring the other creations she would bring into the world during her life. Part of the ceremony involved some symbolic objects to be burned, and a stone that would come back out of the fire.
>
> A few days later was my birthday. One of the gifts I got, from one of the friends who dreamed about this pregnancy and felt a connection to this baby all along, was a stone, exactly like the one used in the ceremony (a piece of peacock rock, same size and shape even). She said she knew the baby helped her pick it out. These two women don't even know each other! If I ever had any doubts about spirituality, the soul existing apart from the body, miracles being real, and so on (and I've had lots), I lost them all when I opened that present!
>
> If you want to believe that all experiences in life come to teach you and help you grow, as I am coming to believe, then certainly one of the lessons for me in this miscarriage was this gift of belief in "magic."

A miscarriage can change us. Whether or not we feel a presence or go through a time of grieving, we must confront disappointed expectations and feelings about what we "deserve." From my own experience, I learned that the resulting changes may be deep -- or superficial. We may change course with the unconscious hope of avoiding such pain in the future, and this can lead to disillusionment. Altering the surface of life may lend meaning to one miscarriage, but how to make sense of repeated losses?

The days I spent lying motionless in hopes of stopping that first miscarriage were not just days of sadness and physical discomfort. I found that all my usual thoughts and plans gave me no comfort while things fell apart and death occurred inside my body. With my values in chaos, there was nothing to hold on to. My solution, the only way I knew to find a calm center, was to become more "religious." I rearranged my life accordingly, and all went fairly well for six months despite the lingering depression -- until a second miscarriage turned my system upside down again.

Thoroughly angry, I had to admit that I'd thought to make a deal with God: "I'll be good, and you'll please let me have a baby!" I saw that my "devotion" was all in my head, unconnected to any realization.

In a way, Lucy Kennedy's response to the pain of miscarriage might seem to parallel mine. But for Lucy, the decision to change her life came from a deeper level. An intimate experience of love and spiritual presence was the basis for real and lasting changes beginning with her lost pregnancy.

As a dream foretold, this pregnancy was about learning to nurture her own neglected spirit.

Light Blue Wings: Lucy's Story

I was in a very bad state of health and doing poorly emotionally as well when I conceived in November, 1982. My husband and I were not getting along well, either. I felt really pressured to get pregnant again simply because our firstborn was already three and we (I?) wanted our children to be close in age. From the very beginning, there was no true excitement over having another baby, even though it had taken several months to conceive. I never felt physically pregnant -- no morning sickness, sore breasts, or cramping as with Duke -- and I never felt that I would actually be giving birth. One day I went through my old maternity clothes and tried to get excited about getting a wardrobe together, but those were the only moments I can remember of actually feeling anything like anticipation.

When I was about two months along, I dreamed that I went into labor. I knew that it was much too early for me to be giving birth, but at the hospital they just put me on a gurney and told me to wait. I finally grew impatient and left. Somehow I got to a place which resembled the big old house where I was taking my little boy for alternative medicine. There I settled into a rocking chair in a large, dim room with green plants and soft, gray carpeting. The baby just squirted out with no pain or effort. There were other women there around me. I was delighted with the baby, a girl, and right away I tried to nurse her. My breasts were overflowing with milk, and as she suckled, she couldn't avoid getting too much milk in her mouth and was choking and sputtering. I was saying, "Poor baby! Oh, little baby!" and trying to help her as the milk washed all over her little face. I noticed that on her left cheek, close to her nose, she had a red spot. A few months before, just such a spot had appeared on my face.

Late in January, my husband John was to go on tour in California for about two weeks. Just a few days before he was scheduled to leave, I began to have spotting and sharp cramps in my uterus. I was shocked and upset -- desperate to keep the baby. I started taking massive doses of vitamin E and trying to rest, but the bleeding and pain continued. No one would say for sure "You are having a miscarriage" or talk about what might happen next. As I said good-by to John at the airport I wanted to cry out, "You can't leave me now!" but I felt that if he didn't care and love me enough to stay with me of his own accord, it wasn't of any value to force him to stay. I went home with my three-year-old Duke and waited.

I had never had any family living in Minnesota, and around this time all my friends seemed to disappear as well. I finally decided to go stay with the wife of one of John's colleagues, because I was fearful of miscarrying alone, in case I couldn't take care of Duke or I needed medical help. I had never felt comfortable with Sigrid -- she was on another wavelength in terms of lifestyle and worldview -- but she did welcome me to stay with her and her three daughters. In the last month Duke and I had both been sick with flu and I had nursed John through a bout of pneumonia. Now I was exhausted by the pain and worry.

I think it was the second night I was at Sigrid's that the miscarriage began. I was in such pain that I couldn't sleep, so I sat in a chair against the dining room wall -- just sat and looked at the kitchen and the dining room and living room, watching the clock on the microwave. A nightlight was on somewhere; the house was quiet except for the hum of the refrigerator.

I sat for hours in increasing pain, longing for resolution. And then I did something that reminded me of stories from Sunday School, where I had heard of saints and other people bargaining with God when they were in dire straits. They promised to dedicate their lives to doing His will if He would spare them. I had my own version. I acknowledged that I was doing nothing of any consequence with my life except tending to people's basic needs on a day-to-day basis. My life was fundamentally superficial and lacking any spiritual content. Somehow, between childhood and age thirty-three I had lost my sense of oneness with the Universe and my determination to make things better on Earth. I felt that I had lost my sense of purpose. What I promised, in return for resolution of my suffering, was to try to rediscover what I was on Earth to do, and to try to accomplish it. I promised to stop wasting my precious time and to devote the rest of my life to fulfilling my spiritual goals. I was very earnest and intense. I sat there and prayed to the Universe to accept my promise and help me.

In the wee hours of the morning I went into the bathroom to change my pad. As I sat on the toilet a huge clot of blood fell into the water. I gasped and retrieved it, thinking it was my baby. Then I knew that the miscarriage had begun. The pain divided into contractions which rapidly increased in intensity. My body felt like it was on fire. Duke woke up and came in to the bathroom. I didn't know how to deal with him. I felt that I might pass out at any moment. I asked him to go wake up Sigrid, who came and assisted me through hours of labor, but the fetus wouldn't come. Finally, after hours of dreadful pain and struggling to birth my dead baby, the contractions fizzled out and I went to bed for a short time. After getting the girls and Duke settled, Sigrid drove me to the hospital emergency room.

The doctor on call was the most horrid individual I have ever encountered. Totally insensitive to what I was going through, he sneered at me repeatedly. He asked me what my blood type was, and when I couldn't tell him sneered, "You've been pregnant twice and you don't know what your blood type is?!" He said I needed a D & C* or I would bleed to death. I told him I would rather bleed to death than let him touch me. I signed a release, and left.

That evening I got a call from one of the midwives at the hospital. She told me that a young woman doctor was now on call and begged me to come back and let her do a D & C. I really wanted to wait and try to pass the fetus naturally, but I knew that Sigrid had to go back to school the next day, and I was exhausted with the waiting. I decided to return to the hospital.

The doctor was kind and the midwife was angelic, holding my hand the whole time. I was very brave and sang a Welsh hymn under the influence of the Demerol. They gave me a book about losing a baby, and sent me home. I felt that I had been shown that love is abundant on Earth, that we need only to be open to it, that complete strangers can give us the love we need. I felt that I was on Earth to learn about love. I was totally grateful to those women for caring for me and caring *about* me and my baby.

That night I was still in some pain and unable to sleep. Again I sat in my chair in the dining room and observed the clock and the silent house. I thought about my experience of receiving love from people who didn't know me, who never questioned whether I deserved it. I thought about my baby and how its spirit was returning to the spiritual realm. I was peaceful, awake, aware, and very clear in my perceptions. And as I sat there I was aware of seeing, in my peripheral vision, huge wings of a beautiful light blue color which were open and encircling me from behind my back, but much taller than I was as I sat in my chair. Somehow I knew that I should not turn around and look, but just be still and feel the presence of what was clearly a spiritual being, and commune with the being.

What I came to understand as I sat there, enfolded in those beautiful wings, was that my baby's spirit had, out of love and compassion for me, helped to set up this whole experience of learning and being loved, so that its leaving me would not be an empty, painful event, but an illuminating, beneficial and beautiful happening. I think that "Light Blue Wings," as I called the spirit, really wanted me to know that it loved me and cared about me even though it was leaving, and that it wanted me to be assured that my "bargain" was being honored. This opening to Love and unmistakable, intimate contact with the Spiritual were the beginning of my new, rededicated life. At that moment I promised myself that I would never abandon my belief that I really did see with my own eyes the manifestation of my baby's spirit. I knew what I had seen and experienced, and I was happy and grateful.

The sense of the baby's spirit watching over me faded in the next few days. Duke had an asthma attack, and I headed home to take him to the doctor and resume our daily routine. When John came home from tour I told him all about my experiences, but there was no comment. It seemed that he was relieved that the baby was not coming. I was left to grieve the loss by myself.

In the next year after the miscarriage, I became interested in spiritual healing. I had many, many sessions of healing on myself. I knew that I was "coming home" to something that felt energizing, natural and "right" for me; I realized that healing was my calling and my purpose. I began to work with many people, mostly women and children, to share the healing energy. I began the long process of healing my own life, and I realized the meaning of my dream of giving birth. The little girl baby whom I had birthed and was nursing was *me*. I had given birth to myself and was nurturing myself, feeding and loving little baby Me.

Pregnancy and birth are times when the physical and spiritual worlds reveal their interwoven nature. I feel very privileged and happy to have had experiences which showed me this interconnectedness in a way I could both understand and believe in. It has helped me to accept the losses of my unborn babies and has also relieved my fears about my own death. This is the silver lining of my grief and pain.

CHAPTER NINETEEN
MAKING SENSE OF MISCARRIAGE

We have a need to find reasons for the things that happen to us. A loss like miscarriage is more threatening and harder to accept when it seems meaningless; finding an explanation for it gives back some sense of control and the confidence to go forward. So we may ask ourselves, as we try to make sense of miscarriage, whether we are really discovering a reason or inventing one that comforts us.

That said, it seems quite possible that at least some miscarriages do make very good sense. It even appears that some may result from an agreement between parent and prospective child. Although we can seldom trace cause and effect with any certainty in stories of miscarriage, we often see evidence that some communication is involved.

Sheila Sherman feels communication was the key to stopping a threatened miscarriage:

> I had two miscarriages in one year and now, pregnant again, I was determined to keep this child. And yet, I had engaged in intercourse in the first trimester, just as I had the previous pregnancies, and I didn't make a connection until I began spotting. I was scared and began to blame myself for being so stupid. I had confined myself to the couch, feet elevated, and prayed for my child's life.
>
> I decided to talk to my child. I caressed my belly and thought of my child. I told him I loved him and that I wanted him to live. I told him he *will* live, not to worry. I told him how he would continue to grow and we would soon see each other, hold each other. I let go of my fear and worry and put my belief in my body, my child and my God. We three became one. And the bleeding stopped the same day.

Miscarriage is common, but harmless "spotting" is also frequent in early pregnancy, so we have many opportunities to feel responsible when we lose a pregnancy, or to believe that we have saved the situation when ominous warning signs fade away. Yet there is no way of knowing for certain whether we have really influenced the outcome. And so, while I believe the cooperative process may well be operating in these experiences, I urge readers not to take on extra guilt over what they did, said, thought or felt during pregnancies that miscarried.

In the following stories, women describe miscarriages that seem to happen for a definite reason, triggered by quite specific communications. For example, Jean Fejes believes that her pregnancy ended because she asked her child to wait for a time when the environment would be more healthful:

> My period was a week late, and I knew I was pregnant. I had three months left in the Navy (what a horrid life) and was exposed daily to welding fumes, petroleum products, paints and so on. My husband and I would be moving to a small farm immediately upon my release. I sat down one night and explained to the baby (even then I felt that it was a girl) that I didn't want her to be tainted by the chemicals or consciousness of my Navy life, and I thought it would be much better for her to wait until we moved before coming. That night I started my period. Two months after we moved I got pregnant.

Clare Adams faced a similar conflict when she became pregnant while working at a job whose stresses she believed would be harmful to her unborn baby:

> When Madeline first entered my body, it was the end of August 1991. I felt a soul come into my body through my breath when my husband and I made beautiful love to each other. I knew I was pregnant. I was so excited. I knew she wanted to come into our life; I had felt her presence in my area for several months. She was in my dreams and "touching" me with her spirit.
>
> I convinced my husband to buy a house in the country in Pennsylvania by his parents. It needed total renovation, though we were surviving on my income in Massachusetts. There was a great debate over what to do -- should I work five hours away, while pregnant, while my husband works on the house or should I just leave my job and enjoy my pregnancy with my husband. With reluctance I agreed to keep working through the pregnancy.
>
> At that moment I literally felt Madeline leave my body through my vagina. I cried in frustration. I begged her to come back. Two weeks later I bled (about three weeks "late"). Well, I knew my baby did not want to grow in my body through the stress of my job with long hours, harsh chemicals and nasty "comrades."
>
> On Christmas Eve I told my husband that I was leaving my

job and leaving Massachusetts. That night, I took a long, warm bubble bath with candles and patchouli incense. I remember soft, slow lovemaking with my gentle husband. He agreed that we need to be together to be a real family. I gave notice two weeks later and bingo! I knew I was pregnant. Madeline was "back in." She had maintained contact with me in the intervening months through dreams, touch, and daytime visions.

Perhaps a pregnancy ends because the father isn't ready to take on the responsibility of parenthood. Felicia, a mother of five, recalls that she felt her first child's presence intensely before conceiving him:

Before I became pregnant with my first born son (now ten) I was living around Tucson, Arizona. I began running in the desert and feeling very in tune with the natural and spiritual world. Around that time I began feeling the presence of my son. He wanted to be born very much. He was hanging around me often pressuring me. I felt love for him but I kept telling him it was not time yet. One day I remember being in the house alone and telling him loud and clear to stop bugging me.

I had a close friend, Richard; we shared a lot together, we were more like brother and sister. Richard and I made love only once and I became pregnant. A few days later Richard announced he wasn't ready to be a father (he was only nineteen then) -- a day later I had a miscarriage, the only one I have ever had. For the next week or so the feeling and presence of my son was diminished; I could barely feel his presence, yet I still felt that I was not alone.

Felicia's son was born within the year -- with a different father.

A defective embryo is believed to be the reason for many miscarriages. We may have a foreboding sense that there is something wrong, as this woman did while trying to bear her second child:

One month, I was sure I was pregnant, feeling different, all those feelings that meant pregnancy to me, then as my period didn't come, I was sure. I was so happy, joyful, but kept seeing pictures of a Down's Syndrome child. I tried to shake it off, aware of the common anxieties that I thought I was falling victim to. But when day after day for two or three weeks, this picture stayed with me, I stopped fighting it and began to want to make peace with it. One morning I went out to the garden, lay down on the earth and simply affirmed, "If the child within is not healthy, let it pass." The next day I bled like a heavy period, interpreted this as a miscarriage, mourned all day... and went on.

Mixed feelings are normal in the early days of pregnancy, but Mary Halter Petersen feels her ambivalence may have caused her miscarriage. Her story is one of mourning -- and forgiveness.

Jonah and Aren: Mary's Story

Our third child, Jonah, died at nine weeks gestation, but this pregnancy was where my awareness of pre-birth contact deepened considerably. I was ambivalent about this pregnancy from the beginning, feeling very worn out with three year old Lukas and ten month old Hannah, often alone with them in a new city.

My pre-birth contact with this spirit person brought me to fall in love with "him." I felt from the beginning that this child would be another boy. I dreamed that he was the most beautiful child I had ever seen. In the dream I couldn't stop looking at him, but I was told that I had to bring him back to somewhere as the birth certificate wasn't ready yet. At the time I didn't understand this, though now it seems clearly to indicate the death.

I felt this spirit being was a very enlightened being. He would appear to me as an adult male, full of an inner strength and beauty. I often felt puzzled why this being would be coming to earth and why through me. I felt very unworthy of accepting the responsibility of raising someone who seemed so obviously farther along than I was spiritually. I felt great, great love around me whenever I sensed "his" presence.

I have some difficulty calling this being "he" although I strongly felt that the baby was a boy and the appearances seemed male. It didn't really feel like a "he" or "she." The enormous love was what brought me around to accepting the pregnancy and to feeling that I'd be able to make it through the next winter's isolation with two little ones and a new baby. Then I miscarried and stood in total awe over this one and a half inch long human being, so perfect, tiny, toes, hands, head, eyes.

The night of the miscarriage Gorm (my husband) had fallen asleep beside me for a moment, thinking, "Why is this happening? Why, why, why?" (which was what I kept wondering all those days from the first bleeding as well as for years afterward). It was then that Gorm "heard" the words, "It is for you to learn."

As a young child I had many instances of praying intently

about something and having it happen. At twelve or thirteen I remember my mom bought a Ouija board and we'd play with it. No matter whom I did it with the board would always spell out my thoughts. Actually this propensity to easily bring to matter things in the realm of the mind is what made the miscarriage so problematic for me. I had prayed that somehow it wasn't true that I was pregnant, that somehow it could not be. Well! Watch what I pray for, I must. Answers may come in a way unexpected! Of course, the miscarriage still might have been part of my experience, yet I feel very strongly that I did influence it to happen.

I felt almost as though I murdered my baby. And *no one* understood that aspect of it and not even the best books I found to support me touched on this kind of thing. No one could talk me out of my guilt by saying things like "Well, sometimes the answers to prayers are no" or "It may have been meant to be." None of that kind of talk was helpful because a part of me knew I *could* cause a miscarriage and in fact probably did. I had been so distraught at realizing I was pregnant. I was so tired and depressed that winter with my two rival toddlers. I prayed intently, never imagining...

Now I feel very accepting of the whole thing. I no longer feel like a terrible human being for not feeling ready for another baby. I would have accepted and loved the baby and I know this. Mechanical abortion would have been out of the question for me. Yet my emotional state was problematic and I believe it was for the best the baby died, though it was hard. I did learn a lot...

I mourned the death of Jonah for a year before we quit our midwestern middle class lifestyle and went searching for deeper healing. I had scoured the library for books to support my grieving and awakening process and then I just couldn't live the emptiness of what our life was any longer. We quit our "job" and travelled to a family vision quest, a healing retreat and a woman's gathering. I began gradually to be aware that someone else wanted to come into our family, but I was still very frightened. I felt a lot of guilt about Jonah's death. The miscarriage was such a devastating loss to me then after I had fallen in love with the baby. I was terrified that it would happen again.

I began to talk with my pre-baby, the spirit that I felt was hovering around us, to tell her to please wait, that I needed time to heal and I really wanted to be able to welcome her lovingly. I strongly felt this would be a girl child though part of me longed for the healing I thought I'd get by having another boy and accepting and loving him this time from the start. Often I had an internal vision of a young woman and a young man, so I wasn't sure at times who was planning on coming or if I'd have twins. These two always had a very angelic, translucent, "airy" quality to them. They seemed to be very playful, joyous, wise spiritual beings. I'd "talk" with both of them, through my journals, in my mind and sometimes out loud. Somehow we'd communicate, though they never really "talked" to me, I just knew we communicated.

Soon it became apparent that the young woman was always somewhat clearer than the young man and I felt my feelings of a girl next were confirmed. About every three months I'd feel intensely that this person wanted to come but I just couldn't conceive her. We were in the middle of selling our house in Wisconsin, running low on money, and very uncertain about our life.

Finally, about three years after the miscarriage I felt I wanted her so badly that I didn't want to say no any more. We still hadn't sold the house by then, but were planning our move to Utah. I was already calling the pre-baby Aren and thus we invited her in. Though I was one day past my peak fertility, we conceived and I "knew" when we conceived. I actually felt a surge of energy at 11:33 A.M. and I knew it was conception. Aren was on her way.

She was with me from the start as she'd been for at least the two previous years. I felt her presence strongly. I never had any attraction to "pinks" and "pretty" so sometimes I wondered if it was really a girl as those feelings had been so determined and strong, such an unconscious attraction, with my daughter Hannah. I dreamed often of eagles in the early part of the pregnancy, thus "Aren" was a form of a Scandinavian word meaning eagle.

Though I had periods of doubt and worry I felt this spirit's strong determination to be with us. I had feelings of a sprite, an elfishly light person and often sang a song I made up to Aren about my "little sparrow hen." Aren is here now, two years old, and a joy. She has an "impish" appearance, curly red hair and a smile that lights up her face. She is indeed rather spritely and dances about on her toes. I often think she is the same soul as Jonah -- she is so aware she amazes me.

Her middle name, Sameh, came from her brother, Lukas, who walked into the room on the day after her birth and said, "Sameh is a nice name." Never having heard of it before we looked it up in a baby book and found it means "forgiver" and as I felt so healed from all the pain and guilt of the miscarriage it seemed so perfect, so, Aren Sameh, she is.

ADVANCE NOTICE

One detail of Mary's exquisite story, her dream, is an example of the warnings that may precede miscarriage. We are not always taken by surprise when pregnancy fails. Often there is some advance notice, though we may not consciously understand it -- just as Mary did not realize the significance of hearing that the baby's birth certificate was not yet ready.

Warning signs can also come through strange moods, physical "telepathy," and perhaps direct communication from the child, as this mother experienced:

> Before the births of my two boys I miscarried a pregnancy. The baby told me a couple of days beforehand that the miscarriage would occur. I felt fine and discounted the message as common fears. It happened. The baby assured me that *she* would be back later and what she would look like. She has spoken to me during the years that have passed. My sons are not this child.

There is, I think, a kind of emotional mirroring that can alert us to the situation in the womb even though, like a dream, it may not be consciously understood. I had no thought of miscarriage at four weeks pregnant; I was full of energy all that day, when suddenly at nine-thirty in the evening I felt an awful sinking feeling of deep dismay that made me say, "Oh *no*..." My eyes were strangely caught by an insignificant corner of the floor, almost as though on some other level I was *seeing* the miscarriage that came only a few days later.

Suzanne's experience is a much more dramatic instance of the emotional mirroring that links us to the baby's state. She writes:

> In 1979 I was pregnant with my second child, Paul. He was born in May but died the next day. An autopsy report showed he had had two cerebral hemorrhages. One happened at birth, but the other was a few months earlier. At about that time in my pregnancy I had a very unusual experience.
>
> I had been feeling fine and happy, and my husband and I went out for dinner at the Officers Club. As we approached the door to the bar he left me to go get us both a drink (orange juice

for me). I had the one and only anxiety attack of my life. I am always a very outgoing, extroverted person. But I stood there in stark terror until I could regain myself enough to run to the bathroom. I sat on a chair in that bathroom for two hours crying my heart out. I have never cried like that before (but I did again after Paul died).

I was hysterical and didn't know why. My heart was being torn apart. I felt such a deep grief like I had never experienced before. My husband came looking for me and asked what was the matter -- did he do something? Was I sick? I said no; I didn't know why I was crying, I just didn't know. But for more than two hours I cried and I mean howled and sobbed. I wouldn't even leave the room to go home. My husband just waited outside the door, checking every so often. Finally I let him take me home, still crying for another few hours.

That was it. I felt all right the next day. It wasn't until after the autopsy report that I said to my husband, "I bet that's when Paul had his first stroke and my subconscious knew he was in trouble but my conscious didn't." It was the same grief I felt after he died.

Some time after Paul's birth and death, Suzanne had a miscarriage. This time, a strange physical reaction may have mirrored the crisis in the womb:

The doctors estimated the child died at about six weeks of gestation but I carried it until twelve weeks. At about six weeks I was sitting in the kitchen and my heart started beating furiously. It was pounding so hard and fast my blouse was moving vigorously. It lasted maybe sixty seconds.

I called the rescue squad. They talked to me over the phone and took it very lightly, asked if I had just had some caffeine or medication. No, I had not. It wasn't just a little activity, it was incredible. I went for an EKG some time thereafter and all was normal. Maybe it was just a freak experience and not connected. Or maybe the baby was dying and my body reacted.

Strange moods and inexplicable doubts are not rare in early pregnancy, but to Jeri Lermusiaux they seem to have been a message from her baby, preparing her for the loss. "I recently was honored with a sad, but very touching experience," she writes:

I have been learning over the last couple of years how important it is to tune into my body, and let my intuition and instinct flow. My maternal hormones are still heavily flowing in my body, because my son, Travis, now ten months old, is still nursing. That on top of a new pregnancy really tuned me in.

I knew I was pregnant the night I conceived, but no one believed it. Once it was confirmed, we were very excited. My five year old daughter, Leora, wanted a baby sister. So I began preparing, from the start, for nursing while pregnant, and then tandem nursing.

As I began to feel my emotions becoming pregnant, I noticed that I was one big raw emotion, and in tune with the whole universe. I also noticed that I got very strange vibes when my husband and I talked about this child. This didn't happen when I talked to anyone else -- only Tommy. Since I couldn't place where these feelings were coming from, I assumed that Tommy had reservations about the impending birth. I knew it wasn't me, and I couldn't shake the feeling that something wasn't right. I kept asking him, and he swore he didn't have any feelings of the kind. He was baffled by my insecurities.

Regardless, the feeling continued throughout the remainder of my short, six week pregnancy. It got so strong, I really became paranoid, and sometimes even accused Tommy of lying to me -- that he really didn't want the baby. I couldn't figure out what his problem was. I must have driven him crazy! Then, in my fifth week of pregnancy, I began to spot lightly. Tommy wasn't worried, but deep down my small life was telling me it was not going to stay. By the end of the week, I was bleeding heavily.

While Tommy hoped, I knew it was over. Tommy stayed so close to me. I told him I needed to walk. We took the kids, got the jogger stroller, and headed out of town to Grampa's. We walked in silence for what seemed like miles on the gravel roads, and I silently prayed for our family, and our baby's tiny soul. Walking hard helped immensely. I no longer felt the strange vibes from Tommy. I really felt peaceful -- but very sad. I cried off and on, but everything felt "right" in a strange sort of way. I felt acceptance that nature and my body were doing what had to be done.

I continued feeling very subdued, and at peace throughout the night and the next day. I was still contracting and bleeding steadily. Tommy didn't go to work, and rarely left my side. I napped and rested -- and meditated, I guess. I've never purposely meditated, but I prayed and spoke to her silently. I also tried laying my hands on my belly -- I guess hoping to somehow stop what was happening. It was wishful thinking. I knew the truth.

During this meditation time and reflection, I asked the baby if it was a boy or a girl. The answer I got was just a flash in my mind that told me she was a girl. It wasn't a picture, or a voice. It was more of a feeling of just knowing. She was Tess. I had chosen the name when I conceived.

The last day, we spent with friends. It was a good distraction. Our kids played together, and we barbecued. My friend and I made salad and talked. I was on my feet and bled quite a bit. I felt like I was having a bad period. When everyone was worn out, we gathered the kids and went home. We got the kids to bed, and Tommy and I relaxed. I realized I hadn't been aware of any contact all day. I had passed clots all day, and I began to think the worst was over.

I went in the bathroom to take a shower, and I had to pee. I sat down, and felt the most awful feeling. Something fell out of me. It wasn't big enough to hurt, just big enough to really feel it pass. I jumped up to look. It was a placenta the size of my palm. There was no identifiable fetus -- just a lump. I cried for Tommy and told him what happened. (I can't believe this still makes me cry.) I couldn't bear to flush what would have been our baby. I left the room, and Tommy took care of it; then we held each other until I calmed down enough to go to bed. In bed, I said a prayer to my lost child. I told her goodbye, and that I loved her. She answered me in my dream that night.

After Tommy and I cried ourselves to sleep, I had a dream I was swimming with dolphins. In my interpretation, I had a few very special moments to connect with my baby, and touch her, and be with her before she was gone. She left me with a feeling of finality by morning. I knew she was gone, and I let her go.

Since that night, I have had an insatiable desire to study our spiritual link to dolphins. Have I felt contact with her since? Not exactly. I haven't felt contact with *her* personally, but I have been drawn to dolphins, almost to the point of obsession. She sent me on a journey. I feel she opened the door for me, and she's guiding me into another part of my life. Many things have changed for me spiritually thanks to Tess.

A friend gave me the best words of wisdom after the miscarriage. She said that sometimes a soul is sent into our lives for a purpose, however short the time is, to gather or give information. When their job is done, they leave again. That's what I believe.

This experience has taught me a lot about psychic

communication. All those weeks that I received strange vibes, I couldn't place them. Now it makes perfect sense. The feelings I thought were from Tommy weren't actually from him; these feelings were between us. He just didn't recognize them as I did. So when only I felt them, I assumed he was putting them out, when actually, we were both receiving them. My baby warned me so I wouldn't be totally shocked when something went wrong. Thank God -- now I just pray for her return.

Jeri was pregnant again just a month after her miscarriage. Her continuing story, and her next contact with "Tess," will be found in the following chapter.

CHAPTER TWENTY
ANGELS AND OTHER FRIENDS

According to the evidence of many stories, the bond of parent and child is important and precious enough to attract considerable "outside" attention. Surrounding the parents and baby, there may be a wider circle of interested others.

Many accounts suggest that the dead are involved with new arrivals to their living families and friends. They seem to act as informants, helpers, and guardians. In other cases, help and information apparently come from entities such as angels, devas, and "beings of light." Equally mysterious are stories where it seems as though the unborn child may be enlisting elements of nature -- trees, for example -- as visible, tangible forms through which to communicate.

Perhaps the soul's journey into the world opens a doorway between dimensions. From the evidence, it seems that dwellers of different realms draw near, with what appears to be kindly concern for the traveller. If indeed "heaven and earth" join in support of the child, perhaps we need to become more aware of the help that is available to us from the worlds of spirit and nature.

Vivien Beirne is one of many who believe that a pregnant woman is accompanied by other beings -- angels or guardians -- who come to help her and her child through pregnancy and birth. She says, "It is hard for me to tell when I was being guided by the baby-in-making, and when I was being guided by the wise beings that assist the mother and child throughout the process." Another woman describes her own impressions of the spirit helpers attending pregnancy:

> Pregnancy was the most special time of my life, the most unique experience I have ever had. The bond between the mother and the child is extraordinary, defies description. The two are in a miraculous bubble of light and heavenly protection which is as strong as a fortress, guarded by a bevy of angelic spirits which attend, bless and harbor the two souls in their growing relationship. This is one of the reasons mothers have that "special glow" around them while they are pregnant.

These mysterious beings sometimes give specific information or reassurance, as if taking a friendly hand in the work of smoothing the way for parents and children-to-be. Lu Anne Balfrey admits she was "rather obsessed" with wanting a girl in her first pregnancy. But late in the pregnancy, she had a most remarkable dream:

> I really don't usually remember my dreams but this one I'll never forget. In the dream, a luminous being appeared. He (I remember it seemed male) told me that the baby would be a boy. I argued with him and told him I wanted a girl. After a short discussion in which I pouted and stamped my foot, the being shook his head and said, "I do believe you would argue with God himself!" He began to fade and I shouted out, "At least tell me why it has to be boy." Just a voice said fading, "Family reasons, for family reasons." About three weeks later our first son was born.

Alicia Russell-Smith tells how she was reassured during her pregnancy -- not by the baby apparently, but by beings she calls "garden fairies":

> This happened last summer when I was newly pregnant and prone to startling jolts of extraordinary, often psychedelic awareness. Morning has never been my strong point of the day and in pregnancy it became downright grueling. I found morning sickness much, much worse than the mild nausea I had been led to expect; and it lasted until nightfall!
>
> One of my (feeble) sidetracking techniques was to go out in the yard and wander around in my bare feet. The morning dew was unfailingly cool and soothing. I'd planted a bed of borage to attract bees, then learned the leaves of this herb are an excellent food for pregnant and lactating women (because the leaves are very high in calcium), so I made a practice of munching on some leaves during those morning perambulations.
>
> By August the grass was growing quickly. In fact, the whole garden was a bit wild from our lack of time and attention. (And a state of uncultivated growth is very attractive to the plant devas and other nature spirits.)
>
> One day, I decided to eat a few of the pretty, lavender colored flowers of the borage. As I did so I was worrying about the little life inside me. Was it safe and growing normally? In addition to the physical unpleasantness of early pregnancy, I had a bad case of new-mother jitters. What if the baby was a dwarf or didn't have a head or grew flippers instead of limbs? My mind raced

and then the air was awhirl with violet and silver light.

Suddenly I was surrounded by dancing, dark haired little beings. They were very beautiful but also a little frightening -- they were *really* there! Somehow, they communicated to me without speaking, to tell me my child was safe and well. They offered to show me and I looked down to see a violet-tinged, very small fetus curled in the grass. It was sleeping with a peaceful expression; I had (and still have) the distinct feeling I could have actually touched it, but I lacked the courage. Instead I freaked out and bolted away.

Later, from the safety of a work-bound bus, the experience seemed quite wonderful. I decided if I ever saw the spirits again and they tried to tell me anything I would listen without fear.

COMPANION SPIRITS?

Perhaps some of the presences we sense while expecting a baby are not the children who are coming to be born, but their accompanying friends or guardians. My old friend Gail, who surprised herself by becoming a mother at thirty-eight, felt that there was another child to come, a little girl who formed a "matched pair" with her son. Circumstances changed, and it seems unlikely she will have a second child -- yet her impression of that companion spirit might not be mistaken. Perhaps there are beings who do not intend to be born but who are linked with others on this side of life.

Some of our children's "imaginary playmates" might be of this nature. Ali recalls that her son Brett had "an imaginary brother who lived under the bed." Brett told her, "John used to be my friend, and he came with me to be my friend, and he's still my friend." Now grown up, Brett never had a real brother; whatever John was, he was apparently not what one might have supposed -- a child waiting to join the family.

Claire C. felt a rather remote male presence attending her during a pregnancy that resulted in a baby girl who died at birth. A few days after the birth, Claire came into communication with the spirit of her daughter, and took the opportunity to ask about this mysterious attendant, whom she and her husband had named "Reed." Claire says:

I asked her who "Reed" was. I had thought he was the baby, but that he had a mission to accomplish, and wasn't particularly attached to us. About a week before the birth, I went to see some psychic healers, and they were very good and very sweet people. They too felt the baby was a boy, and they described him in much the same way I had experienced him. Well, Andrea said "Reed" was there to attend the baby's body as it developed. She wasn't even there -- not until the last moment of birth. His "mission," it turns out, was simply to watch over the body for Andrea, I presume to safeguard its development.

While miscarrying an early pregnancy, Jeri Lermusiaux felt a telepathic connection with a girl she named Tess. Another pregnancy quickly followed and culminated in the joyful home birth of a baby boy, Sky. Jeri writes:

> When I was pregnant with Sky, I was pretty big, but not out of the ordinary. Lots of people asked jokingly if I was having twins, but I have a few psychic friends (and one psychic stranger who approached me in a laundromat) who seriously sensed two souls in me. I knew I was only carrying one child. I couldn't figure it out.
>
> Sky's birth was perfect. It was filled with love and peace, and I felt so safe birthing without an assistant. Tommy and I felt so intimate and close, being alone. We knew it was meant to be this way.
>
> After this birth, I talked to a friend who is psychic, and she told me that sometimes the sense of two souls could be the baby and a spirit guide. I know in my heart it was Tess -- the one I lost -- making sure that Sky was okay and made it safely into the world. He was born with his eyes wide open, looking around as if he knew what to expect.
>
> I don't feel Tess now. I think she stayed long enough to guide Sky to us, but another psychic friend (I have lots!) told me she'll come back to me again. I can't wait!

THE DEAD AND THE NEWCOMERS

There seem to be many connections between the dead and the children coming to be born. Some people believe, for instance, that deceased family members act as protectors of the family's children. One woman describes an incident involving herself and her great-grandmother:

> At eighteen, I awoke to see my great-grandmother (who died on Christmas Day, 1961) standing by the side of my bed, looking at me. She remained there momentarily, and then floated away,

disappearing through the wall. I told no one of this experience. Months later, I was listening to a tape of a psychic reading done for my mother. The reader said that my mother's paternal grandmother was looking after her second child. I am second-born in my family.

Kamille Smith has often felt protected by her grandmother who died when she was six, and she believes that her baby girl also has her own protector. She writes:

> I've had contacts with my grandmother since adolescence. But our communication has improved as the years pass. My protector has been a great help to me -- she's made sure I was around when someone needed help, kept me from getting badly hurt in an accident, told me when to be careful of "bad" people.

Thanks to her practiced ability to "hear" her own protector, Kamille also sensed communication with her husband's much-loved grandmother. The communication began soon after the long-awaited conception of Kamille's first child. She continues:

> After years of trying, I finally conceived three days after my husband's grandmother passed away. It was as if her spirit returned with him from the funeral. Within two weeks, I had heightened connection with the "spirit." She was the one who told me, "There's something inside you" a few weeks later. I had to wait to be able to get a pregnancy test -- she told me before a test could be given accurately. She and other "spirits" even cracked jokes of twins and laughed -- luckily I only had a single girl.
>
> On and off through the pregnancy the spirit world communicated with me -- helping to pick the name, telling me of future events and so on. My husband's grandmother was my main informant and protector during the pregnancy. But my own grandmother was also involved especially as the pregnancy progressed.
>
> Most of the information I received was as if spoken to me, but not audible -- it just pops in your head. Usually I receive information when doing monotonous tasks -- like milking cows or driving a car. Sometimes I'm contacted just after awakening, while lying in bed (I'm a slow riser). It's easy to miss the voice in your head; I've trained myself to hear it better.

Miscarried babies and those who die in infancy are sometimes seen as the guardians of other children in the family. Laurie Bolotin, for example, feels that her first, stillborn daughter watches over the twins she bore later. Another woman writes:

> Our first son was born and died long ago. Just days before his death at seven months, he appeared to me while I was holding him in my arms. The picture I saw of him was mature, with a man's beard growing on his cheeks and with the same blue eyes. It lasted long enough for me to comment to him at how handsome he was going to be as an adult. Since his death I know that he often functions as a guardian for his brother.

Stories of pre-birth contact reveal other connections between the dead and the newcomers. In visionary dreams and in waking communications, the dead sometimes bring information or reassurance, or introduce the coming child.

"I am not someone who has had any 'paranormal' experiences, or even particularly believes in them," says Jane G., "but this incident tends to make more of a believer out of me:"

> I had a friend, Neal, with whom I worked very closely between 1986 and 1988. (I am a lawyer specializing in securities litigation and Neal and I were on the same litigation "team.") Neal -- who was in his early thirties -- died of lupus in the late fall of 1988. It was a great shock to everyone.
>
> I became pregnant with my first child in May of 1989. It was not an easy pregnancy, and by the end of that year, I had taken off work and was staying at home. At that time I was under the care of an ob/gyn who was very rushed and distant and whose comments to me about the pregnancy were essentially limited to chastising me for gaining weight. Little did I know that the reason for the weight gain was that I had developed high blood pressure and was in the beginning stages of toxemia.
>
> In the very beginning of 1990, I noticed that the baby's movements, which had never been very strong, had slowed down considerably. From approximately January 3 on, the baby stopped moving entirely. I did not contact my doctor about this situation as my communication with her was so poor. I felt a terrible sense of doom, however, and from that time on thought that there was a good chance that the baby would die.
>
> On the night of January 4, I had the strangest dream of my life. I dreamed that my boss and I had travelled down to

Argentina (we *had* been in Argentina earlier that year) and were out walking around at night. We were in a large open-air market, and as we walked along I heard my friend Neal's distinctive laugh. I rushed around the corner and there he was, sitting with a group of people at a table drinking and enjoying himself. Neal had always been quite a bon vivant, so this was a typical scene.

I ran up to him and he threw his arms around me. I was overwhelmed with joy, and said how happy I was to see him, and that I thought that I would never see him again. Neal indicated somehow that he really had died (not just travelled away) and that I should understand that.

I started to tell Neal about how I had gotten married (he was also a friend of my husband) and that we were going to have a baby. Neal said that he knew all about it, and said, "Don't worry. Everything is going to turn out okay." I woke up with an incredible sense of well-being and *knew for a fact* that I had seen my friend. I could still hear his voice.

Two days later I went into labor and my son, Joseph Edward, was born via emergency caesarean. He was about six weeks premature. It turned out that because of the toxemia, he had not been getting sufficient nutrition. Large parts of the placenta had actually died. He weighed four pounds, eleven ounces, and spent two weeks in intensive care. It was a very bad experience for everyone, but he ultimately recovered and now is a healthy, normal three-year-old. I have never dreamed of seeing Neal again.

I have always thought that my dream right before Joey's birth was one of the strangest events of my life. I definitely feel that somehow he -- or possibly Neal -- was contacting me to tell me that there was trouble.

Isadora Paymer lost her father at an early age, but he seems to have remained lovingly involved with her and her family ever since. She says, "I think my father made special attempts to contact me because love transcends death." Among other communications, her father's voice told her of her two pregnancies. Isadora recalls:

When I was a child of about seven, a little while after my father's death, I began seeing a black and white spiral at night and hearing his voice. The voice told me about what my life would be like as an adult. After a year or so, I stopped hearing the voice. This was the last time I heard it until it told me about each of my two pregnancies.

I believe my father told me that I was pregnant with my first child, and to be very careful with my activities in order to prevent a miscarriage. This was before I knew that I was pregnant (I had been trying for a year).

When the voice told me about each pregnancy I was wide awake. The first time, I was at a meeting at IBM, where I was a systems analyst. The second time I was also awake, lying on the sofa.

My son Nicky, age four, has been talking to "round-and-around" since his infancy, so he tells us. My late father has been telling him about what his future life will be also, but Nicky won't tell us. ("Round-and-around says, 'Don't tell the family.'")

Barbara Sieradzki's first contact with her child, before she consciously knew she was pregnant, came in a dream of deceased family members she had not known but who held deep meaning for her:

I dreamed of my husband's father and uncle. My husband's father talked to me about my son. I first thought he meant his own son, but when I awoke that morning I knew I was carrying a boy and was not surprised at the test results showing that I was pregnant.

My husband's family is all from Poland. His father Moshe, uncle Abe (who both appeared in my dream) and mother Sabina and others survived the Nazi Holocaust. But many more died. Moshe and Abe spent four years in one of the cruellest concentration camps where experiments and executions were performed on pregnant women. My husband, Michael, was born in Frankfurt in 1946, in a displaced persons camp. Moshe, Sabina, Michael and Abe came to America in 1949 where they have lived until Abe's and Moshe's deaths.

Both my parents and all my relatives live in Germany and are not Jewish. My parents were teenagers in the war and came to Canada in 1954 disgusted by all that happened and was still happening in Germany as a result of the war.

My understanding of Moshe and Abe's appearance in my dream (other than a communication to me that Daniel was coming) was this: I do not believe that either of those men, who were often beaten, starved down to ninety-six pounds, humiliated and forced to see repeated cruelty, would ever have imagined that their son/nephew would marry a German descendant. That Moshe's grandson should be half German was probably not conceivable. Yet the issue was never raised in my dream. So it was not the personality of Moshe I was meeting, but his eternal presence -- that is neither Jewish nor non-Jewish. It simply *is*. Therefore it was significant that it was he and his brother who came to me. They were definitely Beings from another plane, which gives deep meaning to their communication. They were saying (really reminding me) that this is the plane from which Daniel is coming. He is not only flesh, with heredity and history, but he *is* and comes from beyond where none of this earthly trouble matters.

I've always known that I've "always been," right back to the beginning of the world. I know Michael from that time, too. And Daniel. I feel that the Being who incarnates has a deep spiritual connection with the parents who, at one level, know it. The incarnating Being always communicates spiritually and the parents hear or don't hear. I know that Daniel was talking to me through Moshe and Abe.

THROUGH THE WORLD OF NATURE...

"Daniel talked to me in other ways as well," Barbara continues:

> I was very emotionally volatile during my pregnancy, which my husband, Michael, found difficult to handle. I would get so angry, then a bird would come unusually close and I knew that was Daniel's doing. The anger would inexplicably vanish and my love for Michael would return.

The spirit of the child may be able to make its presence felt and communicate with us through nature. When I consider the passionate sympathy and identification that some young children have with the natural world, I wonder whether those feelings might be rooted in their pre-birth experiences.

Donna Kurtz recalls something unusual that happened during her pregnancy or shortly before it: "I was in my herb bed sitting next to the cicely, when I heard a velvet voice tell me she was here. At the time I thought it was the cicely deva. Now I'm not sure if it was the plant or the spirit of my daughter."

In the year before conceiving Roselyn, I had some of the oddest sensations of my life. Walking along the sidewalk and passing a tree, I would have a sudden sense of a presence, another consciousness near me. It was almost as though the tree was silently reaching out for my attention. This happened several times with various different trees, and I supposed I was becoming mysteriously attuned to tree consciousness. But once she was conceived it never happened again, and I have wondered whether the spirit of my daughter was calling to me through the tree's presence, playing hide and seek -- just as she does today, an eight-year-old calling to be found from halfway up a young pine tree...

OURSELVES AS FRIENDS

We ourselves may be able to befriend and help other people's children on the way to birth. In *Conscious Conception*,* Carol Bridges describes how she forms relationships "on the astral plane" with souls waiting to be born. Since she has already raised her own family and doesn't wish to bear any more children, she says she guides the souls to other women who are available, sometimes remaining in contact with the children during pregnancy and through birth.

In stories shared with me there are frequent references to friends and relatives who feel a connection with the unborn child. One woman received pre-birth visits from her sister-in-law's child. She writes:

> Although the baby's mother never knew the sex of her child until birth, I knew it was a girl, and she and I had several contacts until she was born, when they stopped. I had a very clear picture of her personality. She is now four years old and I believe is the same person who used to visit with me.

Beverly Hayes felt she was able to help and reassure an unborn baby -- to whom she was to be closely connected:

> Last November, I met with the woman who was carrying the child I would later adopt. She was seven months pregnant. After she returned home, I dreamed of the baby. I saw its face looking at me, a small, little face. I felt its confusion, so I sent it messages of love and comfort, telling the baby it would live with us soon and we would love and care for it forever. The next day I received in the mail the ultrasound pictures and they were of the face I had dreamt about! It was amazing. I felt I had truly made contact with the baby.

Beverly's sense of comforting her baby in a dream is strangely similar to some encounters with the dead. People tell of being visited in dreams or meditation by individuals who have recently died a sudden or violent death and who seem lost and confused. A woman describes two such occasions:

> One involved a close friend of my husband's whom I never met. He worked with my husband -- they are both airline pilots. While working, Jack died in a plane crash which killed all the people on board. My husband called to tell me the news and he was of course very upset. For the next few days after that, I had dreams of Jack lost in a tunnel, a big void with a small light at the end. I felt a very urgent need to keep telling him to go towards the light.
>
> The second experience occurred in 1989, after the San Francisco earthquake. We received a call in the middle of the night from a stranger looking for his wife and a friend of ours, John. They had never returned home after the earthquake. I returned back to sleep, very disturbed. In a half sleep, I dreamed of John in a tunnel with the same small light at the end. There were a lot of other people around -- a lot of chaos but I only focused on him. He talked to me like he always had -- just kind of shooting the bull with me like nothing was going on. I responded by telling him he was dead. And he said, "So that's what has happened here." And then I told him to go towards the light at the end of the tunnel...

The people who described such experiences have themselves been comforted at times by children before birth or after death, and now they are the ones offering reassurance to those on the other side of life. The will to *help* seems to come full circle. And even though none of us may really know what's going on in this mysterious existence that we share, still we act as lighthouses for each other -- or at least we whistle in the dark to keep each other's courage up. The cooperative bond that links parent and child may really connect all of us, across boundaries of death and perhaps even with non-human worlds.

PART IV

WONDER AND MYSTERY

Once we accept the possibility that we may exist before conception, some fascinating questions arise. For instance, where do we come from? When do we join our body? What sort of life precedes this one?

When we try to imagine life after death, we tend to project our current self forward into "heavenly" scenes. It isn't hard to do, however illusory it may be. But when we try to imagine an existence before conception, we find a mystery more elusive to our thinking -- like the Zen riddle, "Show me your original face before your mother was born."

What is that state or place or dimension from which we and our children emerge? Can we find hints of it in our experience? Perhaps we have memories that we express without "meaning" to. Perhaps I chose the word <u>emerge</u> because I remember that coming to conception was a separation from something in which one had been merged, immersed.

We may find clues in the impressions that come when we feel the presence of a child not yet conceived. The imagery and moods evoked in us might be echoes of the world in which that soul exists. In fact, if the pre-life state is real, we all must know it intimately; maybe we touch it with the mind of poetry, when we translate subtle perceptions into images.

For example, Teresa Williams describes a mood of austere power and mystery attending the "being" who persistently visited her thoughts before she conceived her son:

Primordial winds swirl in my womb
Hurricane force
I think of you
Sound out of silence

Lightning bolts
Begetting thunder
Conceiving you/sound out of thought.

You are here
Though not conceived
I speak of you
You are sound out of nothing
Thunder out of wind
I light my womb
My thoughts with you...

Clues and possible answers can be found in many sources. There are descriptions of pre-life by adults regressed under hypnosis, "channeled" messages, psychedelic trips to primordial places, glimpses of a between-state from children recalling previous lives. We find that state described in many ways, from a kind of soul soup in which we float without separate identity, to the rather comic recollection of "staying on a tree for seven years" like some invisible bird. We find accounts of comfort, beauty and peace beyond what we experience in our earth life. And in Helen Wambach's analysis of a large number of hypnotic regression reports, there is the startling discovery that sixty-eight percent of her subjects recalled feeling "reluctant, anxious or resigned" at the prospect of leaving the pre-conception state and coming to birth.*

My intention is to turn back to the experiences people have shared with me, most of them spontaneous encounters with mystery, and see what possible answers we can glean from them to the questions we might ask of a soul coming to be born:

Where do you come from?
When do you join the body?
Who are you?

CHAPTER TWENTY-ONE
WHERE DO YOU COME FROM?

Where do you come from, before I conceived you?

We can gather ideas and possible answers from stories of pre-birth contact, but some of the most charming possibilities are in the casual hints that children let fall.

Little children sometimes produce astonishing comments on their previous whereabouts. Exposed as they are to our multimedia babble, it's hard to be sure they are voicing their own thoughts and not something overheard in conversation or in a TV show or preschool story. But often they speak with a kind of innocent authority that makes their words unforgettable.

I remember a conversation with my son Devin when he was three years old. We were sitting together on the back porch of our house when he suddenly said, "Mommy, let's go home."

"Where's our home?" I asked.

"Far, far away," said Devin. Pointing upward, he went on: "Up in the sky. This the dirt place. Our home up there."

*   *   *

Where do you come from, before I conceived you?

. . . From the air? Ali recalls:

> Brett used to talk about "when he was air." He loved maps and was quite precocious, beginning to read at two years old. Once he asked me, "Have you ever been to Hawaii?"
>
> "No," I replied; "have you been to Hawaii?"
>
> "I used to go there all the time when I was air -- it's a beautiful place."

. . . From the ocean? Katryn Lavanture writes:

> At the time in my life when Kate wanted to come through I had no interest in becoming pregnant. I was at a bookstore when I became inexplicably drawn to the section of books on pregnancy

and babies. This was on May 3, and I remember wondering why I was so drawn there and hoping it wasn't an omen. I left there with a card depicting a fetus surrounded by dolphins above the earth, and I had no idea why I bought it -- rationally. Well, I got pregnant several months later and my due date was May 3!

I had a dream, when I was pregnant with her, that two dolphins swam up to the side of my bed. I was then moved to get the Dolphins Dream birthing tape, and cried the first time I heard it (and I don't cry *that* easily).

When she was about nine months old, we were at the beach. A group of dolphins swam right by the place where we were set up, and she crawled as fast as she could down to the water, and would have gone right into the water headstrong and fearless had we let her. This was at the New Jersey shore, and was the first time I ever saw dolphins there, and I've been going there my whole life.

I asked Katryn about the significance of the dolphin theme in her daughter's life. She says:

It is my belief that dolphins and whales are not only an intelligent species, but one that brings to the earth a very cosmic, spiritual, and psychic component that can teach us humans much, if we open ourselves through time and effort to what they can teach us. I feel that some souls, before they incarnate, have a special connection to the dolphin and whale dimension, and that they may always have it in their earthly lives. So, I think Kate is one of those souls.

. . . From other worlds? Katryn continues, "I believe some of us have spent some incarnations in other star systems, and maybe more in some cases than here on this planet, so that some of us have affinity for certain star energies." In this connection, we may recall the little boy who pointed out Jupiter in the night sky, telling his mother that he had lived there before he came to be her boy.

Doryan Dean Kasoff's vision of a being from another world took place long before the birth of her first child, a daughter:

At that time I was meditating two hours a day, living a very clean strict life and diet. On this particular day I had been rebirthed, which is a powerful breathing therapy that, for me at least, puts me into a place of amazing clarity of being.

I was standing in our library, feeling very still, when I felt a presence around and inside me, so to speak... like a hologram. In this holographic experience I "saw" a scene. In the scene there were three "people." One was myself, one was this being who was showing me the scene, and one is unidentified. Somehow I knew that this was a scene which had taken place "in a past life," and that all three of us were scientists working in a pyramid on some technology that had to do with earth and another planet. I also knew that the being in the middle was the one I could feel communicating with me, and that he was from another planet.

Having seen that -- the feeling of the hologram changed and I could feel a whole sense of relationship with their presence. Then there were telepathic "words," which I somehow already knew and had agreed to in feeling. This being "said" that he was going to be my son (a sense of asking, was that all right, and a sense of warm acceptance from me) and that his name was to be Nile. I agreed to this fully, feeling the rightness of it, and the being withdrew.

He did not say when he would come, but right now I am seven and a half months pregnant. I am not certain this is he, yet, though if my baby is a boy it will be Nile.

. . . From another life? Pamela Millar recalls:

I had three dreams while pregnant with my daughter, in which an old French country woman went about her day -- harvesting crops, cleaning. This woman was heavy and robust, and seemingly content. In one dream she made love with her husband. I sensed the simplicity of her life and also how physically difficult it was.

The morning after these dreams, I had a strong sense that this woman was somehow my child. Believe me when I say I am usually a level-headed, of-the-earth person. While I don't *dis*believe in reincarnation, or life-after-death experiences in general, I don't ponder these things as a rule.

Now whenever my child pronounces words differently than we do, I have to smile to myself and wonder if this is a bit of her French accent!

. . . From each other, by a kind of subdivision? Isabelle Kessler relates her husband's experience:

Scott did a past-life regression where he felt our son Abraham with him as this "cloud" of energy. Abraham then split from Scott and became an entirely separate being.

. . . Or from a place between the worlds?   Katryn Lavanture's daughter Sierra was three months old when Katryn felt a communication from her, part of which is reproduced here.   Katryn writes, "Sierra was lying next to me on my bed and I was doing singsong rhymes to her just out of my head.   She fell asleep and suddenly the words began to come in sentences, and there was an urgency to them like I had to keep listening for the next line.   Here is what came:"

Yes, said Sierra, there is magic in the air
Come with me Momma
And I will show you where

We can dance with the fairies
We can sing with the trees
We can talk to the spirits
We can fly on the breeze

I can see them with my eyes
I can feel them in my soul
If you listen with me Momma
They will tell us where to go

To feel Earth magic moving
In the cool night air
To feel ourselves tremble
As our senses take us there

And I know this place Momma
I know magic to be true
And part of why I came here
Was to show this place to you...

Because I go there often,
At more times than you could know
To that place between the worlds
Where the seeds of life are sown...

So when you watch me sleeping
Know I'm much more than you see
I travel to all kinds of worlds
And many welcome me.

✻   ✻   ✻

Where do you come from, before I conceived you?

Denise Shaffer, trusting the wisdom of her children, simply put the question to them. She writes:

> My children, as they grow, are very powerful little beings, as are all children of this generation. Without influence from me (I never place my beliefs on them) they have given me information I shall always remember. One of my favorites is this: at about age two I asked each one where they were before they came to me.
>
> My daughter said, "I was up there (pointing toward the ceiling) waiting in a white chair. Some of us had white chairs, some of us had brown chairs..."
>
> My son promptly replied, "I was floating above you like a whale in the sea."

CHAPTER TWENTY-TWO
WHEN DO SOUL AND BODY JOIN?

"I felt the spirit come into my body... It flew in from the Sandia Crest."

"At about three months pregnant, while washing dishes at work, I had a feeling of the baby's spirit coming into my body. The spirit was a girl -- the baby a boy." Comments like these are thought-provoking. Mothers report impressions of the soul's "arrival" at every stage of pregnancy or even after the birth.

What does such an arrival feel like? It may be different for each person who senses it. Dove Penn-Hamburg describes three elements in her own experience. She felt an inexplicable mood change, a definite physical shift, and the quality that is so often emphasized when parents describe their pre-birth contacts: a clear "knowing." She recalls:

> One night when I was five months pregnant, I was lying in bed staring at the ceiling. I was very depressed; my husband and I had been arguing earlier that night.
>
> All of a sudden, this *huge* smile came over my face, I couldn't understand why! I just lay there smiling for several minutes, and all of a sudden *I knew* that at that moment the baby's spirit had entered my body; well... her body.
>
> Before then I had never felt the baby kick, or for that matter, move around much at all... only small flutters very rarely. And after lying there for five minutes with this huge grin on my face, I felt the baby kick so hard, it scared me to death! And then she kicked again and again, and moved all around, for about two hours I lay there feeling the baby inside me. It was beautiful...

Some parents, instead of feeling a single dramatic arrival, have the impression that the child is able to "come and go for a while before settling down." For example, a mother writes when seven months pregnant, "I have the feeling that the baby's spirit is often not in my body or his body yet -- that he wanders about and takes up residence by choice."

Some mothers sense the child's presence in the womb from the time of conception, or even from a time before conception can have occurred: "I felt a soul come into my body through my breath when my husband and I made beautiful love to each other..." But many pre-birth contacts suggest that the soul is only loosely associated with its body, even well into pregnancy.

This mother's strange encounter came when she was six or seven months pregnant with her firstborn son. She and her husband were being visited by an old friend and his preschool-age daughter. Because they lived in a small apartment, everyone slept in the same room. The mother recalls:

> I woke up that night "dreaming" I was in communication with the being who was to inhabit my son's body. He was not really "in" the body. It was as if he became aware somehow of there being a child's body there, and he wanted to "incarnate" -- he was a bit distressed. What I communicated to "my son" was that his body wasn't ready yet, and that he couldn't have the body of the girl, who was sleeping nearby.
>
> This happened to me in a half-awake state, and I thought of it more as a dream, than reality. Later that day I mentioned what happened to our friend, the father of the girl. He said that he had experienced a "being" in the room in the early morning too! He had told the being to get away from his daughter, as she was already "complete" and had a spirit. He had told "my son" the same thing I had: that he had to wait for me to grow his body for a few more months!

Adam Tritt proposes that the child soul is able to inhabit other objects while its body is growing in the womb. He recalls:

> While my wife was pregnant, I bought her an Opus doll (the penguin from Bloom County). Opus is a symbol we embrace lovingly and we spent much time holding it. One day, the doll changed. It took on an energy unlike anything we had ever felt before. I went inside to investigate and discovered it was the soul of our child resting in the one object in our house which was held the most -- Opus. We were duly shocked and spent, needless to say, much more time holding and talking to Opus.

According to some accounts, the one who will "join" the fetus may not be determined for some time. A mother writes:

> When I was a few months pregnant with my first son Jamie, I became aware that there was a spirit "hanging around" me. I understood that he/she (how do you sex a spirit?) wanted to take over the body I was going to have. He seemed like a nice guy so I agreed. He was around until the birth and then took over the body. I know that my son *is* that spirit that was hanging around me when I was pregnant.

Is it possible that the final decision on "who" will become our child may not be settled until late in pregnancy or even at the time of birth? Lisa Oviatt writes, "I had an amazing experience during labor:"

> During the pregnancy I had been receiving massage from a good friend, who had been my labor support with my first child. This woman is very sensitive and quite open in a spiritual sense. We share a unique bond. During this labor my friend was again in attendance as labor support. Again I was experiencing a long and uncomfortable labor and the doctor was considering a caesarean.
>
> At that point, my friend and I went into the bathroom to get away from the labor room and all the "concerned/worried energy." There my friend led me through a visualization that culminated in my being offered four colors: burnt orange, lemon yellow, rose lavender, and lightning blue. I visualized these as orbs floating about three feet away and slightly above me. When my friend told me to choose one color, the blue literally thunderbolted into my heart. I felt I had opened and accepted the baby. That's also when I knew my baby was a boy.
>
> When we came out of the bathroom the birthing room energy had changed, with the doctor's attitude changed to a resigned acceptance that this labor was just going to take some time. I did labor intensely for several more hours, but without interference, and Paul was born.
>
> Several days later after discussing this experience with my friend she said she had done a "healing" and that the colored orbs I visualized were "baby beings" waiting to be let in to the baby's body.

Another woman, Tamara Thomas, also envisioned a light form entering her body shortly before the birth of her daughter:

While I was in labor, during late afternoon the sun coming into the window of the room seemed to change at one point, growing brighter. I saw what seemed to be a ball of light float through the window on the lingering sunbeams, over to me, breaking up slowly over the lower part of my body. I felt strongly that this presence made Rowan complete, that she was, at last, really all "there." I believe that it was her soul.

The next story presents a unique point of view that challenges us to question a basic assumption. If we suppose the child's soul to be "in" or "with" its fetal body, we must assume that two souls can share the same space, or one can be contained within another. This woman's experiences have convinced her that this is actually impossible! She writes in depth of connections with her children beginning well before they were conceived:

I have distinct prenatal memories of my two children, Holly Rose and Michael John, while they were as yet unborn. Even before I became pregnant, I sensed their presence on a higher level. I knew instantaneously the moment I became impregnated... Besides the obvious physical signs, I was very aware of the souls of my little charges still on the heavenly planes, connected closely to me through a streaming strand of light. I walked around conscious of this small soul connected to and following me in a bubble of light, much like a small balloon.

Almost immediately after knowing that I was pregnant, I started "talking" directly to my children. Actually I had been talking with them even before they were conceived, as they got closer and closer to my energy field and I realized they were "trying to get my attention" and permission to enter the earth plane through me. I not only heard each of them, I "saw" them in my mind's eye. I was aware of their individual vibration, sex and energy. I saw how both Holly Rose and Michael John were going to look at the age of about twenty months. The picture in my mind was exactly how they looked as toddlers.

Both of my children communicated with me as well. We laughed and talked, shared joyful feelings, anticipating being together as separate individuals after they would be born. Both told me the names they had chosen, which I honored.

As the fetuses grew, I could of course feel the physical movements, kicks and turns as the little body's cells multiplied at a rapid rate. I was aware of each of them responding physically to noises, sounds and vibrations, like a passing train and so on.

I also felt subtle and sometimes dramatic responses to my own emotional and physical conditions, especially during times of stress. I remember being very conscious and concerned about the few times I became angry during my pregnancy. I didn't want my own negative energy to have an impact on them. Most of the time I was happy and relaxed, enjoying the special energy and anticipation of the soon-to-be baby growing inside of me.

During the entire time that I was pregnant, I never experienced the actual energy of these beings -- their souls -- *inside* of my body. I always continued to experience the real energy of the individual in this sort of balloon suspended and connected on a strand of light. In comparing my experiences with two births, I feel grateful that I have gained a clear perspective about this charged issue of when the life of a child actually "begins."

My first child, Holly's, birth was such a laborious experience that I was totally absorbed in the work involved. I really didn't have a lot of extra energy to observe it. Although any birth is an extremely demanding, energy-filled time, my second birth gave me an opportunity to consciously experience this phenomenon. Both births were completely natural and occurred in the privacy and sanctity of the home, with the help of midwives and my husband. So I felt safe and relaxed in both cases. But with Michael's birth, I gained a clear understanding of the nature of this experience from a soul level.

My labor with Michael was much shorter and less intense. It seemed to flow along with a rhythm that was inexplicably soothing, predictable. I remember observing the contractions and how absolutely amazing this natural physical process was. I certainly was involved, but it was as if it was going on by itself, regardless of me and my contribution.

I was much more in control with Michael's birth, and much more effective in pushing his little body out. I was glad to be able to move around and squat in the Amerindian way until the baby was down so far that I had to lie back. Everything flowed along smoothly and methodically, gently and easily, until just before the moment of birth. At the moment that my son's head crowned and he was obviously ready to come out, there was a dramatic shift in the energy and momentum of the birth.

At that instant, I experienced the strand of light explode into a blast of light, which I now know was Michael's soul, coming in through the top of my head. But once this happened, there was so much energy that my eyes popped wide open. It was like the energy of a freight train inside of me, and there was no containing it. At that point the midwives were saying, "Stop pushing, start holding it," but there was no control over this explosion of energy. In a flash, the boy whooshed out of my body and was "born."

That word is exactly correct, for I know that it was at that moment, in that ball of energy exploding out of me, that his soul entered his body and he became an individual human being. The energy of each soul is so powerful that there is positively no way for one human body to contain more than one soul at a time.

Even birth may not complete the process of becoming fully embodied. One mother observes, "I have had experiences of sensing my son's soul-consciousness enter his body. I do not believe this happened all at once -- but rather in several stages, including some after birth."

It is not unusual to dream of giving birth to a child much older than a newborn baby. At least in a first pregnancy, this could be due to a lack of familiarity with newborns, although a common interpretation is that by picturing the baby as a three- or four-year-old, we soothe our anxieties about dealing with the needs of an infant.

Still another interpretation is possible, according to Deborah's experience with her first child, Fairity. While pregnant, Deborah had dreamed several times that the "baby" was born four years old. She never told anyone about the dreams, and had not even thought of them in a long time when, with Fairity now seven, she consulted a psychic:

> The psychic told me that because her father and I were going through a lot of turmoil in our relationship, she did not really "come into her body for good" until she was four years old. I have had more than one psychic tell me that we all choose different times to permanently enter our bodies, and that while in the womb we float in and out, until birth or later.

CHAPTER TWENTY-THREE
WHO ARE YOU?

At the heart of each person, there is mystery. When we seem to encounter the soul of our child before birth, we may begin to ponder the mystery of who this being is, and to wonder at the connection between us.

In this chapter, we will explore what pre-birth contacts may tell us about our children and about parent and child relationships.

Some parents are puzzled by the fact that they have sensed contact with only some or one of their children and not with all. "Is it because that child decides to make contact when another might not?" one mother asks. Of course, our receptivity and ability to pay attention vary greatly from one pregnancy to another, depending on other factors in our lives. But several parents affirm that the child whose contact they felt before birth seems particularly available afterwards as well. They speculate on the meaning of these psychic links.

Vicky had mental conversations with her son during pregnancy and found that he seemed quite telepathic with her as a small child. She writes:

> I haven't pinned down the exact cause of my psychic connection with my son but am considering it to be a simple matter of sharing similar brain patterns. His brain works "top-down" like mine, from concept to particular. It may be that we see things so similarly that we flash on thoughts at the same time. I don't think it's that easy though... With my daughter, the pathways don't seem to be as "open" feeling. I can't explain why. She did have some problems (meconium aspiration and three days in the hospital) when she first came out, and I know I felt that there wasn't a bond with her. It may have been due to a fear that she was going to leave us and I didn't want the pain of removal if she did.

Another mother describes the different relationships she feels with each of her two sons. She had experienced a powerful dream connection during her first pregnancy:

My son James will turn five in three days. We now also have a six month old son named Tommy. The two boys are very different in temperament and style, just as my two pregnancies were. I did not have the baby-centered dreams of my first pregnancy during my second one. And I do not have the unmistakable, visceral connection with Tommy that marks my relationship with James. I believe that my firstborn and I share something "other-worldly" that both enriches and complicates our relationship. My second son and I seem to give each other more psychic space, while James and I often still communicate telepathically, particularly during the night; we're often "in each other's face and space!"

Sylvia describes the daughter with whom she felt a strong pre-birth connection:

I feel my daughter and I need each other in a soul way. Not that my other two children don't need me, but we may not resonate on the same soul level as Magdalene and I -- this is intuitive -- I sit and listen inwardly -- I don't want to look for something that might not be there, but I also don't want to discredit it, and only time will tell.

Leigh McCune expresses a similar view that there may be a special resonance between certain people. While pregnant with her second child, Iris, she writes:

I was told by a psychic friend that Iris and I are twin souls and that our vibrations are very harmonious. This last, I had been aware of but had not put into words. My pregnancy has been so easy and without the usual even minor discomforts that I knew from the beginning we were "in tune" with each other.

When our children are very young, it's easy to imagine that our connection with each one will always have the same quality it has now. As they grow, we discover that not only do relationships differ from each other but also that they change, going through varying phases of intimacy and distance. There is more openness and flow now with one child, now with another. It is important not to define too rigidly our relationship with each one, but to accept the changes that occur in the currents between us.

It may also be wise to avoid attributing special value to the child who we feel has connected with us before birth. A mother writes of her wish that each pregnancy had held the same experience of contact which she felt with one daughter:

> The connection before birth gave me the insight that to be a parent, to be the doorway for another soul, is to stand on sacred ground. This one experience left me longing for that for the third child (didn't happen) and wishing it had for the first child, but happily it happened once, and I trust birthing my first and third children were experiences just as holy in their nature as this second birth. Perhaps when the veil between realities lifts, we can only take just a bit at first.

Do we really have special connections with some others, as the concept of twin souls or soul mates implies?

Claire C. received a lovely answer to this question from the spirit of her daughter. "At any particular level of evolution," said Andrea Grace, "all the souls that are evolving together are as twin souls -- they are that close." She added that "all souls in creation, from lowest to highest in their evolutionary path, are as brothers and sisters."

HAVE WE MET BEFORE?

Yet we continue to feel something unusual or "extra" in some of our relationships. Could these feelings be an echo from connections in another life? Or are they simply a matter of complementary personalities? For example, ever since her birth my daughter has seemed to be somehow wiser than I am. She often treats me ("silly little Mommy!") as a sweet but not-too-bright child. Does this suggest that she has once been my mother (or grandmother, as she announced one day)? Or is it the way her self-confident, nurturing personality interacts with me, and the way I respond to her?

Susan Stout finds that her child manifests a protective role towards her, and she feels that a past-life relationship might be a reasonable explanation. She writes:

> I have no idea if you believe in past lives but we certainly do. I do not have any of my own remembrances but have been told of my connection with Joshua by the psychic that we sometimes go to. She, by the way, told us when Josh was going to be conceived and his name which we already knew. Anyway, she said that in a past life, middle ages, he was some kind of priest or minister and I was a poor starving peasant girl. He took me under his

wing and introduced me to God and took care of me by feeding me, making sure I had clothing, and so on. We became very close and he was like a father to me. Now I have agreed to give him life and take care of him -- his physical and spiritual needs. As I write this, it all is becoming a bit clearer to me. Although I am the "mother," Joshua is sometimes still in the role he had in the prior life of taking care of and comforting me at times. That's the only way I can explain what is happening in the instances where I have felt his comfort.

In some stories of pre-birth contact, there are hints of pre-existing relationships in another world or another life. Deborah Prince recalls:

While pregnant with my first daughter, Fairity, I dreamed several times that she and I were sisters living in England, sometime in the late seventeen hundreds or early eighteen hundreds, I would guess from the architecture and dress of the period my dreams portrayed. I found myself attracted to old English names, and hence I chose Fairity, which I loved partly because it means fair and just.

When she was seven years old, a psychic told me that in a former life we had been sisters, living in England some time around the period I described above, and that we were so close we wanted to come back and be together again.

The following stories provide a more detailed picture of how present and past relationships may be woven together in the bond between parent and child.

Carole's Story

I have twins. They will be twenty next week, and they are wonderful, spiritually deep, fascinating, unconventional people. Lauren is an accomplished actress and a dancer and her goal in life is to bring everyone in the world together in harmony. She believes this can be done through participation in movement and dance and some sort of participative theater. Morgan is an artist in two-dimensional media and a student of art history and architecture. She has not shared with me her goal in so many words. She is a quiet and private person who is amazingly well grounded and self-motivated.

Coming from a background where there was much to overcome including a lack of funds to use for college, they have already done extraordinary things. I know, I'm bragging. But it's the truth; they are very special people. And I believe they have important missions in life. Who they have become already is confirmation for me of who they were coming in.

My story begins when I wanted to get pregnant. I was in graduate school studying psychology. My husband had given up rambling from one job to another and was trying to make it as a freelance writer. He was good but lacking in self confidence and did not earn much; we lived on my stipend mostly. The biological clock was ticking right along with the schedule inherited from family culture, and I was determined to do it anyway. I went off the pill and because the timing wasn't quite right (he wasn't ready) I got an IUD. This was 1972; I was twenty-eight. We had been married nine years.

After four months with the IUD, I experienced the abortion of a pregnancy, which was probably only a couple of weeks along. There was dizziness, discomfort and heavy bleeding, but I was told this was how the thing was supposed to work.

A couple of nights later as I lay in bed not asleep and not awake, I experienced a presence like a tiny ball of light which expanded and made itself felt as a soul. I don't know how I knew this, but I perceived it to be the soul which was to be my child. It promptly had a temper tantrum and asked, "Why did you do it?" I was quite taken aback and tried to explain. I reassured the presence that I would try again. I think I had already made an appointment to get the IUD out, but if there was any hesitation, that experience made up my mind!

We didn't actually try for a pregnancy until summer of 1973 and I got pregnant right away. I experienced some dizziness in the first couple weeks and would lie down and meditate or visualize in a receptive way trying to create a perfect attitude for the incoming soul. One of those times I thought I would try to visualize the child. I did, but it wasn't clear so I tried again and I got a clear vision of a pretty, dark-haired girl. I didn't think that this vision matched up to my previous sense of the child's energy. Much later (after they were born) I realized that she was the second child. The first one, whom I had not seen as clearly visually, but had a clear sense of at another level, turned out to be Lauren (who was blond as a child). This was also the soul I had experienced in the contact two years before.

After they were born, I remember waking up in intensive care and looking into Lauren's eyes. The nurses had put both of them in one bassinet right beside me. It was like looking deep into the eyes of an old friend. She knew me and was studying the situation and getting reacquainted. It was very clear to me then that these two children were the ones I had seen when I first got pregnant. (I was convinced from early on that it would be twins although no one else was until the eighth month when I had a sonogram.) I also knew exactly which one was Lauren and who was Morgan.

When the girls were close to a year old, I had several extremely vivid dreams of a time in Scotland probably in the late seventeenth or early eighteenth century (deduced from the prominence of the Rob Roy tartan). I was involved with a priest (my husband now) and was trying to save him. We both ended up getting killed. There was also an awareness of the girls as my friends at the time. It was startling and frightening -- fully experienced, not like a dream at all.

I also had at least two other startling dreams of deaths I had experienced, but those dreams did not come again and again as did the Scottish experience. One was of a ceremonial sacrifice where I threw myself off a cliff and flew free of my body which crashed below.

I think the theme of death was something I needed to explore because I had a difficult time with delivery ending in a caesarean birth for the girls. I realized that in any other time I probably would have died. I realized that had I been anywhere except a major women's hospital, I might have died even today. I was thirty and facing my own death. I was feeling quite overwhelmed. I didn't feel capable of caring for two children. My recovery was good I suppose, but I had some depression and a very hard time losing weight. After the dreams and some working through to process them, I was very clear that death is easy. It's just jumping out of your body, flying; I've done it lots of times. I was never afraid of death after that (I'm still a "wuss" when it comes to pain). And once I had cleared my fear, I never had the dreams again. While I can remember them clearly now, I haven't been able to add to them.

The dreams seemed to fit quite well with my growing understanding of reincarnation phenomena. Before that time I had found that I was able to recognize the paintings of a certain sixteenth century artist whether I had seen them before or not (I'm not generally good at the names and dates game). Several times I had visions of a person in my life as a person in one of his paintings -- sort of superimposed. One of these people was my daughter Lauren; another was a minister who was a friend. And once when I went to the National Gallery for the first time, I saw a painting across the room as we entered an exhibit area and I thought, "I didn't paint that, but I supervised it." It was painted by the nephew of the artist. I don't have any direct data, but I have a strong sense that Morgan and I have been friends before and have worked together in the arts somehow (probably painting). The relationship with Lauren from that lifetime as an artist is one where I felt that I could have been a better parent and I am trying to do that now.

When the girls were two and a half or three -- talking pretty well -- there were a couple of experiences where they referred to their previous lives. I remember Lauren saying, "Remember when I was a boy, Mom, and I used to fight all the time?" I was stunned, but I asked her to tell me more about it. She couldn't; that was it. I think it refers to the life I mentioned in the sixteenth century when I was an artist and she was my son. She does have a feisty nature and we went through some problems with temper tantrums with her as a three- to four-year-old.

I think that there is a plan, which we participate in making as well as carrying out, which may entail some compromises both beforehand and when the unexpected occurs. For example, I think I probably would have had Lauren a couple years before Morgan had I started sooner. I'm very glad it worked out as it did, however; and maybe it *was* the plan -- I always wanted twins. It's been very interesting seeing the differences and closeness as they grew up together.

From Lover to Daughter: Katryn's Story

I am now almost eight months pregnant with my fourth child. I myself am very psychic and intuitive, and am an energy field therapist by profession. I am therefore predisposed to receiving information in other ways, and am generally oriented towards a very expanded, alternative way of life.

Looking back over my pregnancies I can see that I became more open and more aware with each one -- I guess that's not all that unusual -- so it would make sense that I had a more open connection with these last two souls.

This baby was a surprise, yet not so much a surprise. I had felt another female soul around me for two years after Kate was born, who clearly wanted to come through me, but I was very ambivalent. This soul would be so strong around me that I became very familiar with her energy and presence, and felt very comfortable with her, like she was already a part of my life, yet I couldn't commit to another pregnancy.

In May of 1991 I went to Santa Fe for the third time to do work at the Light Institute. My friend who came with me looked up at me one day there and asked me, out of the blue, if there were twins in my family because she felt twins around me. I also had strong feelings of the presence of galactics around me during that visit, which was new for me.

The galactics are beings from other star systems, they are extra-terrestrials essentially. They travel in and out of the Earth "dimension" and interface with us for a variety of reasons depending on who they are. Those who have a higher consciousness than others seem to wish to help us open our hearts and release fear, as I understand it. Some people, like me, have a connection with them on a subconscious level and have different kinds of experiences with them. Mine seem to be that they want me to bring information through that would assist people in an accelerated healing process emotionally. (Some animals seem to be connected to them as well, like owls and dolphins.)

Their presence stayed with me even after I returned to Pennsylvania and I had many experiences of their energy opening my heart in profound ways. In June, during the time I was ovulating I became obsessed with conceiving this child, and it was not a conscious, rational state I was in. This was really only one night where I wanted my husband to make love unprotected, as I was in this haze of "Do it now." He refused to do that, but we still made love and I hoped that night for conception. Afterwards, I cried as I was infused with the energy of her soul, *and* of the galactics. It was very profound for me, and frightening for I knew this was an altered state and I'd have to face the consequences in the morning. I did not get pregnant that month.

In July, my husband and I and our two oldest sons went out to Santa Fe to check it out as I want to move there and they'd never been. We did not have sex the whole month of July before our trip, as we fought and grumbled the whole time and I completely lost interest in having a baby. When we got there everyone fell in love with it, we decided to move there, and my husband and I reconnected. Two days after we got home I looked at the calendar and realized I was to have had my period while we were in New Mexico, and hadn't. That day I found out I was pregnant.

Six weeks into the pregnancy I went to Massachusetts with a friend, as I used to live there and periodically visit. One morning I woke up and felt a presence in the hotel room. It became clear that it was the soul of this man I had had an incredibly strong past life overlay with -- he had been my lover and husband in thirteenth century England -- and I yearned for him desperately for several years before I released him in this lifetime. If there is a soulmate, he is the closest thing I've ever felt to it and I wanted him back, but it was clear he wasn't coming into my life as my lover again this time. I had not felt him around me for a year, since I'd let him go consciously.

In the hotel room he told me psychically that he was coming as this child I was carrying. He said he would be closer to me as my child than even lovers were, because there would be a bond there that could never be broken by another person, and to just trust this. I thought he was coming as a boy; my friend felt he would be my daughter. Mostly I was thrilled, but confused because I wondered where the other soul had gone and I grieved losing her for I knew she was not him.

This whole pregnancy has been a huge personal and spiritual journey for me. I was deathly sick the first trimester, and cursed any soul for coming, no matter who it was. Then I found out I had placenta previa, so I've been forced to deal with my fears around my difficult childbirths, and other fears I didn't even know about until I began to work on myself again to try and change the placental position.

I went back out to Santa Fe to do more Higher Self work in December, and this soul came in one of my sessions. He/she brought to me an understanding of what our soul connection is in its highest form, and helped me experience it consciously, physically, and energetically. It was exquisite, incredibly profound, and something I will never forget. I got to see us without the trappings of sex, status, familial relationship, or anything except the pure form of our souls in relationship outside of the physical, and could experience the deep, unconditional love we have for each other.

Since then I have gradually been able to make the transition from him (as my lover) to her (as my daughter -- per the sonogram) and to accept our new relationship to be as mother and daughter. It may sound silly, but it was a very real, and sometimes unwelcome, transition for me. I've not heard anyone else talk about feeling a past life so intensely (other than a real negative overlay), much less having that soul to face again consciously in a very different situation.

I have been working hard to make myself as clear as I can be of old fears, victimization, and constriction, so I can have a home birth, not a caesarean, and a healthy pregnancy. So far it looks good, I've gone from a complete placenta previa to a partial now, and I'm still working on moving it completely. I've reclaimed powerful parts of myself I'd given away, and I feel very connected to this baby, and extremely honored and excited that this soul would choose me for its mother, and that we'll get to be together again.

I didn't have my baby until April 13. It was a very profound and difficult time for me -- those weeks before her birth. She was ready to come two weeks before she was actually born, but I got into such a fear space about giving birth again that I held off labor, even as my body kept trying to start it. I ended up needing to be induced as I was leaking amniotic fluid by then, and I agreed as I knew I could hold off labor for months at that point! The whole experience was full of spiritual help and grace when I look back on it -- the two or three weeks before and the birth.

My new daughter's name is Sierra Katryn. She's six weeks old now, but appears to be two months or more as she is so big and mature. She is a sweet soul who has transitioned into earthly life very easily. I almost feel like I can't get a handle on the reality of life with her, as her soul was so familiar, and closer to me before the birth, yet now she's here and I get confused with her earthly, physical form, and the vast soul history we have together. It's very incongruous to me right now. And it's sort of uncanny how much she looks like me, much more than my other children. When she was just seconds after being born and they were lifting her to put her on my stomach, I looked at her face and saw *my* face -- almost like it was an energetic overlay of what she would be like. It startled me because it all happened so clearly and so quickly like a flash, and then we were back in the commotion of post delivery concerns. I dismissed it as wishful thinking until my husband remarked on her uncanny resemblance to me as well.

So she's now here, that journey is over, and I'm starting a new one. I am clearly not the same person I was before the pregnancy, and I'm struggling to get clear on what my life is about now and where do I go from here.

*   *   *

Denise Shaffer endured many painful procedures to bear her children, sustained by her contact with them and her apparent memories of previous lives together.

"Love Carried For Centuries:" Denise's Story

After my son Johnny was born I found I was infertile after trying to have a second child for several years. I gave up when the doctor said adoption was all that was left.

When Johnny was seven and I was in a second more successful marriage, I was in the shower one morning when a girl came to me. She said, "I am your daughter. I want to come to you but I need help." Okay. Whatever I can do, let me know, I will do it.

One week later we were having dinner with some friends who were going through In Vitro Fertilization (IVF). In the course of our conversation I realized that like my friend I was eligible for IVF *paid* by Kaiser Insurance as a result of a class action suit which I didn't know I was part of. At the time IVF cost five thousand dollars, which we could never afford.

I went through it twice. During this time I was extremely influenced by Native American Indian -- Dakota. I finally went to a hypnotherapist and regressed into my past life as a Sioux woman with my daughter. It was so special and beautiful. During the regression I would say to the therapist -- "This is the one -- the daughter who came to me in the shower. She's here now, I'm pregnant with her now." Sure enough one week later I had a positive pregnancy test -- nine months later -- Mimi.

Although always spiritual and clairvoyant, I never gave extensive thought to the preparation the spirit goes through before entering a body. I just had a "knowing" about my children coming. These experiences enhanced what I believed and encouraged me to do some serious spiritual growth. I have had similar experiences since a child, one being a near death experience, and I remembered my past lives as a child. Trance and meditation come easily to me, however, I wasn't aware of this until the experience with Mimi.

The form of visitation is best described as a "knowing." I felt the presence of a female, young, yet "adult." I heard no voices. I just felt her words -- clear as if they were a voice. Her presence came in around my left shoulder and ear -- as if she were whispering in my ear. She felt very feminine. She said she was coming to bring Michael and me warmth and joy -- and yes she does.

I was thankful to have had her. At last, my two children. I felt complete. In Vitro was an extremely intense and painful procedure. I don't know how I did it, twice at that. I said -- never again. Until last year. I was brushing my hair when a son tapped me on the shoulder. He said, "I want to come to you." I said, how could I? Kaiser only covers one successful IVF and we have no savings. IVF now cost ten thousand dollars. I told him -- okay, if it's meant to happen God will supply the money.

I was shocked a week later when my husband came home with a surprise ten thousand dollar bonus! Again I mustered up what courage I had out of love and went through IVF. I was stunned when my pregnancy test was negative -- this was my only chance; it was my only money to my name. Luckily I have four embryos in the freezer.

Again my son came to me. He said, "I'm okay. I've entered one of the bodies in the freezer." During this IVF I drove an hour each way to the hospital. Each day I had clear visions of past life memories, eventually revealing this son was also from the Sioux life but died as an infant. His father (from the past life) told me, "Have you not carried the spirit of this child in your heart long enough and have you not waited long enough for this child to return to you?"

I am scheduled to return in October for my frozen embryos. The odds of success from this method are almost nil. However, I know that the power of love between mother and child carried for centuries far outweighs those odds.

Recently Mimi and I were walking and she said, "Mommy, remember when we were Indians and we used to hold the bunnies?" This is with no prompting from me...

I did not get pregnant in October, however, the experience held great value for me. "Failing" was very grounding and added a great understanding to my awareness. It has enabled me to do a better job helping others going through infertility procedures. I find much of my work is helping women with a desire to conceive to get to know their baby beings first with the help of my psychic awareness and reading. It's sort of a spiritual adoption service.* Now we can make a conscious effort in connecting with our babies. Anyway, I look forward to another In Vitro attempt in March with enthusiasm I did not quite enjoy before.

Is it true the spiritual realm knows no time? I think yes -- as after being spiritually pregnant for two and a half years I am finally physically pregnant. The forthright spirit of a son has hugged me with big arms as a more subdued daughter stood back. (I'll know how many soon.) A big difference in this IVF process was that instead of receiving each medical procedure with fear and violation, my body received each shot, blood test and surgery with love and care and I was deeply aware that I was taken care of. Before and during IVF, my husband and I meditated together and he participated more in the "fertility" process. I saw the embryos implanting in a vision and in trance my spirit is no longer alone in its space. Of course along with joy comes overwhelming feelings...

I didn't hear from Denise for two years after this last communication, but when we got in touch again the reason for her silence was clear. The final In Vitro procedure resulted in not one, not two, but *three* baby boys!

One night in mid-pregnancy, Denise felt enormous pressure and the onset of labor. Following her doctor's instructions, she called immediately for an ambulance. On the way to the hospital, something extraordinary occurred.

"I was shaking and in pain," says Denise, "when a huge calm like a warm blanket came over me. It was as though I went somewhere else, and I found myself face to face with the three of them. I told them, 'It's not time.' And the labor, the pressure and pain all stopped. When the staff at the hospital wondered why I had come in, I didn't even try to explain!"

The boys were born two weeks later, premature but old enough to survive, and now they are a trio of healthy toddlers.

MY COMPANION

Some parents see their child as the embodiment of a being who has been their "companion" in this lifetime, without necessarily referring to past-life connections.

Cheri was brought up in a repressive environment. Her secret companions gave her some relief from the oppressive atmosphere around her. She recalls:

I was born into a radical cult -- kind of a cross between Jim Jones (follow the leader) and Hutterites (isolate from others). I was "brainwashed" for hours every week from infancy that the only way to heaven was through this group, specifically the preachers. I remember questioning about all the people who never met a preacher (of course they were condemned to hell). That's one example of a lifetime of "stuff they said" that just didn't fit inside my head.

I remember as a young child having very good-feeling experiences with "light beings" who arrived at my window during times I was really wondering. Not knowing another term I have called them "star friends." As I grew older I quit seeing them as light beings and felt their presence more when I looked at the stars.

I started trying to pay attention to these star-friend communications about ten to fifteen years ago, along with a conscious attempt to live more by intuition.

When Cheri became pregnant with her first child, she felt that the baby was one of her old companions -- "one of my spirit friends from way back. We'd played in the stars for as long as I can remember, now and then, but now with the pregnancy I saw that friend and felt the presence much more often..."

Mucbeah Robinson also felt the companionship of a future daughter for many years before conceiving her:

I knew I would have "Danika" always -- and I named her and talked to her spirit (now and then) since 1984. I wondered if she would evolve as I did, but she is the simple sweet little happy soul I saw in my mind almost ten years ago.

I was an only child who had little exposure to other children and even less exposure to communicating adults. I guess I never did well fitting into groups -- even spiritual ones. As a child I played dolls a lot -- and then from my teen years to 1980 I didn't focus on children -- my own, that is. In 1980 I decided I wanted to marry and have children. I did a meditation exercise with a woman. She told me to close my eyes and imagine myself as a rose and to see how many buds were on my rose. I imagined -- and saw a yellow rose open with two buds -- and it came to me I'd have a boy then a girl.

Still I focused on having a girl and hung out with my friends' kids -- girls -- a lot. Not having any family or any family guidance, I was really reinventing the wheel of parenting, or working up to it -- thinking about it -- getting practical experience -- seeing if I had the patience to do it for years.

So anyhow being with these girls I began to think to myself

when I was alone about "her." I began looking for a name for "her" and when I found her name it was like finding a dear old friend -- I felt great love and a sense of happiness -- love -- well being. Some part of me wonders if time overlaps like cloth in a pleat, and somehow I got hold of the thread and pulled.

Mucbeah's first child was a little boy, Kahlil. She continues:

Then I saw the same scene hundreds of times -- from the time I got pregnant with Kahlil. I saw Kahlil standing, walking beside me and Danika in my arms. And I knew her father was there too.

In July of 1991 I was praying. Danika came to me in a vision and said she would soon be in my arms. I said -- look I have been a single mom with no help -- I'm afraid to raise two of you alone. Then I saw an Indian (native) man holding her. Her Dad showed up less than two days later. She was conceived in late November.

I had visions of an Eskimo baby and couldn't figure it out. I knew she would be blond and blue eyed -- I'd seen her off and on in my mind for years. But when she was born she was bluish and very dark looking. She was the baby in the vision. She was really beaten up by the birthing. Within a few weeks she looked lighter and very different.

From eight months in utero on, I knew her nickname would be "Sunshine." At her own choosing she has always migrated to the yellow blankets, toys, even clothes, and she is up smiling every morning with the sun.

Yes, she looked just the same as how I saw her as a little girl of two or two and a half: blondish curly hair, dancing eyes blue or bluish, and I would say very stable according to my vision -- now I know it wasn't stability but rather, she is very physical, a very strong child.

You know the weirdest part of Danika in retrospect is how simple -- simply happy and joyful she was in my mind and heart -- like an invisible presence. I had never been that happy continuously so it was hard to imagine. Now she is my teacher, and has modeled a happy grateful joyful outlook on life for me.

And I am "Becoming" because of it -- her -- all from a vision long ago -- a vision that gave me hope.

Some "companions" first appear during adolescence, a time of heightened sensitivity and often of loneliness. Donna Kurtz felt the presence of a companion throughout many years, beginning in adolescence:

Once upon a time, right around the time I must have reached menarche, I became aware of a loving, guiding female presence. I think I always knew she would be with me as my daughter. I don't remember analyzing much; only accepting. I decided then that my first child would be a girl and her name would be Kirsten.

Later I decided wed*lock* was a horrible idea and I'd never bind myself thusly, nor would I ever bear a child. Still Kirsten was with me. Certain places, certain people would bring her to mind. A blond girl would appear, spontaneously, in my mind's eye. As I approached my twenties, I began to "see" her as a four-year-old. I could "see" or be aware of the little girl in my peripheral vision -- and only as long as I didn't look.

A few more years and the desire to have babies struck. Suddenly marriage seemed tolerable.

My first child was a girl. I named her Kirsten. Once we were home and settled in and starting to learn each other, I realized that this little person wasn't Kirsten. After a bout with colic we fell in love and still are.

Two different people predicted I'd eventually bring a daughter, two sons, then a daughter through. I did have a son, another son, then in spite of my insistence that I was carrying a girl, another son. Once I had the planned four children I felt finished. I thought maybe my last son was the female presence I'd always been aware of.

As the kids grew, I started having the emotional freedom to start meditating again. When I relaxed, I began noticing a glowing white disc with a lavender rim. It was always waiting. I read a book about guides and found that guides could be perceived as glowing balls. This "guide" was always available.

Then I read *Models of Love** and was overwhelmed at one point by the beauty of childbearing and childrearing. As I was glorying, I saw a pillar of light next to me, and I knew I would have another child. I told my husband who was astounded. He thought he'd never hear me say the word pregnancy in relation to myself again.

I really didn't want to get pregnant too soon. Two years later, before I was ready, life hit me hard. Labor Day weekend we were told that my mom had cancer. A long night of prayer and I knew that I wasn't ready to be a motherless child. During the night I was drawn into a tunnel past my mom, my grammy, her mother, her mother -- it went for a long way. And I felt, strongly, that I needed to add one more female to that line. I was caught in my daughter, my sisters, my nieces -- in a very female place.

I ovulated three times in the next week and a half. In a meditation the glowing white disc featured a purple fetus. I knew I was pregnant. I knew it was my girl. I wanted to name her Anna Brita for my great great grandmother. But I had a series of three dreams. In the first, I had the baby, in the second I saw it was a girl, in the third her name was Cicely. I didn't know or especially love the name. Yet her name was always Cicely.

Cicely Joy Elizabeth was born eleven years, to the day, after Kirsten. Kirsten said, "She stole my birthday." And I responded without thought, "Maybe you stole hers!" Whoa!

Cicely has always been with me. This being is her.

CHAPTER TWENTY-FOUR
TO TEACH, TO HEAL, TO LOVE

A number of parents, while describing pre-birth connections, have spoken of their belief that their child is in some way extraordinary. In some cases they have had a vision telling them only that a special child will be theirs; they may have no definite idea about the nature of the "specialness." Some feel that their child has unusual powers, such as healing or psychic gifts.

Sometimes it is people other than the parents who sense exceptional qualities even in an unborn child. Susan Stout spent many weeks hospitalized to prevent premature labor. She recalls:

> One of the nurses who cared for me said she felt Joshua was a very advanced being and that his energy was of a much higher vibrational level than mine which was why my body was having such a hard time keeping him inside me! She also felt that he had a purpose to being in the hospital and was maneuvering circumstances to be where he needed to be in order to do his work (whatever that was?).
>
> During this time, we had three other friends who visited and said they felt an incredible presence from Joshua and that he was a very powerful, higher being. As his parents, we had this same feeling before his birth and feel very blessed that such a special soul had chosen to live with us.

Although it seems natural to look for special qualities and signs of importance in our children, there are dangers in this way of thinking. Carried to extremes and pumped up with heightened energy, it can lead to delusions of grandeur, as I learned from my own experience.

After the birth of my first child, my mood was exalted for several weeks and at times I slipped into delusional thoughts. I described them later to my friend Alicia, herself a new mother: "The pitfall was my tendency to try to explain or figure out what was happening in terms like: this must be a very special baby, or I must be a very special enlightened person! I remember entertaining notions such as that my baby was Saint Francis reborn, and finding 'logical' reasons to think so."

Alicia replied in calm defense of her own exaltation with her newborn son: "I do believe he's special. I think his soul 'picked' Jim and me for parents and that, because he was planned and so joyously anticipated, he has a little bit of a spiritual edge."

Another woman proposes that a mother's exalted mood after childbirth might well reflect the beauty of her infant's soul. Part of the reason for our intense experiences around birth, she says, might be that our children are indeed "special," for in her view, "there is an influx now of truly developed souls into the world... Saint Francis must be somewhere," she adds, "so why not in your house?"

There are certainly many stories of pre-birth contact that suggest children may come with special gifts, or even with missions of help and healing. Some of these children seem to make their unusual nature felt long before they are born. In *Risk To Be Healed*, Joyce Vissell describes a perception that, if true, is surely a reason for hopefulness:

> With my inner eyes I have seen and felt the greatness of the souls now coming to earth. My heart rejoices at their beauty and spiritual strength. They are great peace-makers who have come to help this planet. It is a great blessing to parent one of these shining souls.

Are there children who come "with healing in their wings," and is this a time when they are joining us in large numbers? Let's look at some beliefs regarding these possibilities.

There is a belief that the times are extraordinary. Many people expect drastic earth changes, to be followed by a Golden Age. Only time will tell if these expectations come true, but they surely influence some parents' thoughts about bringing children into the world, as well as the possible roles they envision for them.

If the times are extraordinary, it makes sense that special children are called for. One view is that a group of souls now being born has the gifts we need to see us through the spiritual and ecological crises facing us. These children are thought to possess the qualities of intelligence and leadership that the situation demands.

I admit to being uneasy with the view that some souls are higher or more advanced than others. I am concerned that by seeing "specialness" in certain people, we'll miss the level of unity, the essence of what we are. I wonder too about the implications of looking at our children this way. What a burden for a child whose parents have channelled messages announcing him as a "great leader" -- if it should happen to be a delusion!

But perhaps some children *are* born with a special mission, and perhaps some even remember their purpose. After all, there is the age-old Tibetan tradition of "tulkus," spiritual teachers born again and again to help us on our way, who are recognized by certain signs even as babies. Stories of pre-birth contact make me wonder whether many souls on the way to birth are trying harder now to remember, and communicating with their parents-to-be for this very reason -- much as I might say to my husband, "Remind me tomorrow what it is that I meant to do."

Meanwhile, the belief in babies born with special gifts and identifying signs is ancient in western folklore as well, and remains powerful today, as this mother's story reminds us:

> Nicholas was born on December 28, 1991 in a birthing tub in my bedroom. My midwife, parents, brother, cousin and close friend were all there to give their support and love. It was a wonderful and magical pregnancy. I glowed with life and good health the whole time.
>
> I am a "Network" chiropractor. Network is a powerful technique which focuses on empowering the individual to release past mental, emotional and physical traumas and stresses that have been locked in the nervous system. As my pregnancy progressed, nearly everyone in my practice began to notice a change in my "energy" while I worked on them. Comments varied from my being more powerful, to more assured, to more energetic. Whatever the case, everyone seemed to agree that there was more healing energy flowing through. They were excited and referrals came so fast that by the time my son was born, my practice had nearly doubled!
>
> Early in the pregnancy I tried to communicate with the soul of this baby who was choosing to enter the world through my body. I had some meditation experience and was frustrated when I couldn't immediately "speak" with the baby. I would focus on my belly and when I heard nothing, switch to a focus somewhere in the room outside of myself. Still no answer.
>
> After a few days I began to wonder if maybe this pregnancy was not going to be the experience of psychic connection I had hoped for. I lay in my bed and began to drift off into sleep when inside my head a voice said, "Hey, silly, I'm in here!" I woke up real fast. My son's energy is so similar to mine that I hadn't even noticed he was there. I had been searching for something outside myself or localized within my abdomen, but what I experienced was more like an overlap of our two souls. It was like we shared the same body space while his tiny body was growing inside mine.

I could ask questions and receive delightful and humorous responses.

Nicky told me when he was ready to be born. My due date was January 11 and my midwife repeatedly expressed that as a first time mother I had more of a chance of going late than early, but I knew it would be early. Friday night I heard his voice say, "I'm coming." I got down on my hands and knees to scrub out the hot tub. At 3:40 A.M. came the first signs that the baby was on his way out -- I lost my mucus plug! The delivery was an experience of total and complete trust. I kept focused and breathed and knew that my body knew exactly what to do. My midwife Karena was delighted with the hour and twenty-four minutes of hard labor.

Nicholas was born completely encased in a caul or veil. As Karena gently removed it from his body she remarked at how rare this was. One in 250 births has a partial caul over some part of the body, but only one in 250,000 has a complete veil like Nicky's. Folklore says that he will have great psychic and spiritual powers. I have no doubt.

When Nicky was brought up out of the water he held his head up and looked at me. I felt more love than I ever thought possible. My cousin says he witnessed the moment Nicky's soul entered his body. He saw a flash and Nicky's black eyes filled with light. My mother says that when their eyes met there was a moment of soul recognition.

Nicky is six months old now and when I speak to him I can still hear his delightful reply. It is fainter now and from outside my body, but I still hear him and he still hears me.

*   *   *

Gail is a longtime friend, a woman of great talent and sensitivity. In the year before conceiving her son, she went through an intense energy experience that led her into healing work. At the same time, she was producing a song cycle entitled "Seedstar." With the conception of her son, she began to see how these events had been preparing her for the dynamic being who so unexpectedly entered her life.

"I Come From Beyond This Plane:" Gail's Story

I'd been feeling stuck and ready for something to change -- an initiation of some sort. On Yom Kippur in 1984 I was told in a meditation, "The next time a wild animal comes near you, you can choose to open to it and it will give you its power."

I went for a walk on the beach and was walking back in the dark when I heard a scream. Some big bird had an animal in its talons. The bird seemed to drop the animal, flew out over the water and circled back over my head. It was an eagle.

I sat down on the rock and opened myself to the eagle. It felt like I was becoming the eagle. Energy came in the top of my head and felt like jolts of lightning coming into my body for a long time. They left me vibrating and shaken up.

I was unable to sleep for months and felt victimized. It took me a long time to realize I was opening to my *own* energy. The energy was pouring out my hands. I knew I needed to bring it down all the way through my body and into the earth through my feet.

This energy infusion happened a year before Kai was born. It seemed like the Eagle experience raised my vibrational rate so I could carry Kai -- he was such a high energy being.

John showed up to help me ground the energy; we would meditate while holding hands. I conceived six weeks after we began making love. My period was late and I began wondering -- feeling bloated and empty at the same time. Lying down and relaxing I heard a voice: "Yes, you're pregnant. It's a boy."

I felt him come in and out during early pregnancy. It felt like he had tasks to do and he'd go off, and I could call him when I wanted to communicate with him. At the fourth month I felt his soul come in to stay, and he never went away again.

While pregnant, I had the image of having carried Kai before, that he had been torn from me and I had to walk into fire to retrieve him. My legs from the knees down were full of fear because of this image. My goal was to be fully grounded in my body, "incarnated" by the time he was born, but I never got the energy farther than my knees. I was vibrating a lot of the time and still afraid of having so much energy. When I fought it or when Kai would have fits of activity inside me and I would freak out, he would say, "It's just energy, Mommy!" The fear of death and the desire to die came up strongly in the pregnancy. I fantasized "sneaking out" at the time of birth by bleeding to death.

Talking with Kai during the pregnancy was easy. I would get centered and then call him or ask him a question. The words formed in my mind and I wrote them down at the same time, clearing the way for something new to come.

As I delved into my records of prenatal communication I

began to realize that it's a bigger project than I imagined. I found that I had to keep going farther and farther back. Stuff directly related to Kai began coming in 1983 and 1984, when I started writing the song cycle, Seedstar. Of course, I was completely unaware of the implications, and had, in fact, let go of ever having a child. But there he is, all written down, a year or two before he arrived. There's all this womb imagery in Seedstar, and seeds, and children and such. One Seedstar poem, which later became a song, is pretty explicit:

> I knew you
> Before Time
> Laid its heavy hand
> Upon you
>
> You grew within
> Sheltered and alone
>
> While I
> All round
> Loved you in silence
>
> When your moment came
> We parted
> And all the Light within
> Was glowing out
>
> But I knew you
> Before time

And this one, also a song, I think was about him:

> Entering
> From time beyond
> To time within
>
> You bring with you
> All we know of love
>
> Slipping through
> With Vision trailing
>
> How will we learn

To live with you?

Your beauty sings
And all I know to do
Is weep

While softly
With crazy splendor

You offer
All we know
Of love

The next thing that came was the song for Kai, about two
weeks before he was conceived (all unbeknownst to me).

You come from afar wielding light
You are a star
I salute you

Wheeling wide, you drop your brightness home
Lost in the warm night
Wrapped all in round white
You lie waiting
in forgetfulness

With the wings of my heart I surround you
Waiting
For remembrance

So small your safeness grows
Stretching blindly will you find me
A crack widens into light

I salute you
I love you
I release you
To soar free in your own deep sky
On your own new wings of beauty
Wing tip to wing tip I salute you in power

You rise slowly now with deep light glowing

Your light grows and lifts
Glows and lifts

Reaching
From what was to is to what will be
Growing stronger
In light   in love   in power

You lift lightly now
Reaching
Your power flies

I salute you

In my journal, there was a lot of imagery about a baby in my heart, waiting to be born, and there was a lot of energy, period, including sexual, so I guess something was bound to get grounded. Now we come to the actual communications from Kai. The first thing he said, when I asked him who he was, when I was about two or three weeks pregnant, was:

I am an internalization of the energy you have been experiencing -- rolled into one concentration, one point. You've experienced it flowing through you and out to transform and heal. Imagine it rolling into a ball and becoming concentrated and that's an image of who I am... My creation was like the birth of a star or galaxy -- dust swirling into a point of being. An entry point into the physical, which you both provided through your love; a gateway from beyond to within. I am born of love, of openness, of a willingness to open to the beyond.

I asked Kai what his mission would be:

To teach, to heal, to love...   In a sense what you've experienced, Gail, was the beginning of my coming -- a harbinger of my energy. You were being tuned for my entry. I will also be your teacher, in a very different way for a while. You can open to me fully, as you have, with the same benefits: expansion and grounding.

When I asked Kai, "What are your qualities?" he replied, "Healing, open-heartedness, love, reverence for all of life."
There follows some information about releasing my pain and

fear from a past life time with Kai; how this time it will be different, and the birth will be "relatively easy: just contact my qualities and you will do fine."

The next communication must have been when I was four months pregnant, because that's when he landed in his body and stuck around:

I'm pushing through, touching your mind; please listen. I love you both with all my heart and want for you to be happy... Just welcome me. Just accept me and I'll be fine. Keep singing that song to me, I like it. Yes, I'm in the body now. I'm liking it, being in here, in you. More love and acceptance will make me want to stay.

Here's another message from him in May, at four months:

Don't worry; don't take everything so seriously. Just live your lives in harmony -- that's all I ask. I get upset when you pressure yourself, Gail. (I was working two jobs but was bleeding and had to quit and take it easy.) Learn to relax. Rejoice that your jobs are ending. Now you can really take care of yourself (and me). None of it matters as much as you think it does. Enjoy it.

Your lack of sleep is due to a disturbance in your energy field. That will smooth out; will disappear. My coming will move out all the kinks -- it is a process of grounding yourself more fully, being fully in your body. The reason you resist being pregnant and becoming a mother is because of your resistance to being in the body. This experience will bring you into your body -- whether you want to be or not. So, the more you can incarnate the easier it will be for you to sleep.

I asked, Who are you?

A messenger, a companion, an old friend, intimate and vast... I come from beyond this plane to enhance it, to bring a healing influence. My healing energy spills over into you and out of you, in several ways. Might as well learn to accept it. This is your new life -- one of fullness, joy, love and humor. You chose it. You chose it all. It's just taking you a while to adjust to it.

The last message from Kai before he was born included these reassurances:

I come to heal you and you me through your mothering. I have needs too, which you can fulfill. And my love for you is great. It is true that in a way I came to take care of you, you also have much to give me... No need to worry so much or fret -- all is well and all manner of thing will be well.

Gail's due date came and went. Finally, forty-eight hours after her water broke and with toxemia of late pregnancy setting in, she agreed to induction; but the attempts failed and Kai was born by caesarean.

I asked Gail what she thought of the discrepancy between the pre-birth messages foretelling a "relatively easy" birth, and the real experience, which turned out to be an ordeal. She replied:

> The traumatic birth seems to me to be a result of my failure to ground the energy all the way down; it stayed blocked at the knees. His birth was associated for me with death, because of the past-life material that came up to be dealt with. A part of me was attracted to dying and a part of me feared it.

I shared with Gail my reservations about seeing a child as "special." Her response gave me a new perspective. Every child is special, she said; each one of us is like a sphere of light. But most of us are more or less thickly covered with obstructions of one sort or another, while some are able to show a good deal of the radiance that is our nature.

Do the communications before birth have any bearing on her relationship with Kai now that he is a real little-boy presence?

"I was afraid he would be reading my aura while I changed his diapers," says Gail with a laugh. "He's actually a very grounded, athletic, dynamic boy." She continues:

> Perhaps as a result of the pre-birth experience, I have a deep respect for him. I take him seriously, though of course I am the one who disciplines him and sets limits. In many cases he has been my teacher. Once, driving along in the car together when he was about five, he asked, "What if this life were just a dream and when we woke up we remembered we were God?"

CHAPTER TWENTY-FIVE
RECEPTIVITY

Do we have to be special people to sense connections with our children-to-be? Must we be born psychic, or practice techniques that make us unusually sensitive? Or are these experiences a natural part of the parent-child connection, something we have only to begin noticing -- amplifying little signals until we can be more available to a communication that has been going on all along?

Undeniably, many people who shared their experiences with me are attuned to subtle kinds of awareness. Some of them were perhaps born sensitive, while others have developed receptivity through various practices and life experiences.

But this is not always the case. There are parents for whom the pre-birth connection comes out of the blue and is a great surprise, something unique in their lives. It may even contradict their belief system, as a father admits:

> I've never believed in any cosmic relations between souls and spirits, but can't deny my own experiences. I sensed something of my daughter's presence before she was born -- a very vague sense that I cannot escape or ignore.

It is not necessary to be "intuitive" or "psychic." People who feel, as one mother puts it, that "I am never one for insights into anything and I imagine my ESP level to be zip" still may experience a connection and sense of communication with their children on the way to birth.

There are, however, circumstances and events that tend to increase receptivity.

But let's pause a moment and look at the word "receptivity," for it implies a little more than I intend. Words invoke assumptions about what is real, and "receptive" suggests something "out there" to be received. Do we receive these experiences or do we create them? This is a question I want to open, not close, so let us take "receptivity" to mean: openness to a sense of contact with another being or source of information -- whether the impressions come from within or beyond ourselves.

Pregnancy and childbirth themselves seem to make us more receptive. Even the preparation -- the waiting and hoping for pregnancy -- can change our awareness. Donna Kurtz suggests that while trying to conceive, we become more sensitive to other dimensions. "I think when you're open to conception, open to bringing another spirit through, you're open to a lot more of the heavenly side of earth," she says.

Some parents feel that with each birth they have become more receptive. Being in the company of babies (both before and after they are born) and attuning ourselves to their nonverbal communication seems to increase our sensitivity to subtle impressions. Sally Gartner describes how her second pregnancy and birth changed her consciousness in lasting ways:

> Pregnancy, with the constant physical connection, rehearsed me very well to feel the other connections we are capable of, as spiritual beings. Reconnecting within myself, and feeling open to the developing child within, expanded my consciousness tremendously.
>
> Once in labor I knew that all was well, that even if my birth attendants did not arrive in time my son would be born just fine and that I would be capable and in good health. The result of this awareness was stunning and long-lasting. Not only did my cervix open up, but something else in that birth process opened with me. I came to view this other "opening" like another cervix of sorts, like a halo never to be measured in centimeters. We all have it, but these haloes are dilated to different degrees. They can be dilated through the pregnancy and birth experiences, or through any enlightening endeavor. Sensitivity flows through this halo, connecting me with others, especially my children, and also with some other aspects of my own self.

The death of someone we love can awaken our sensitivity. Laurie Bolotin felt that the pain of a loss prepared her to receive a symbolic message about her next pregnancy:

> In August of 1987 my husband and I gave birth to a stillborn baby girl at forty-one weeks gestation. The pain was (and still sometimes is) unbearable.
>
> My in-laws were travelling at the time and returned several weeks later with about six rose quartz stones for me to choose from. I spent a long time deciding, and finally chose one fairly

round translucent stone that had a foggy, fluidy look to its inside and a "membrane" through the middle.

As I chose this stone I remember the clear thought, "This stone looks like a sac of waters. It looks like two sacs. Maybe twins." And the thought/image was buried in my pain.

Almost five months later we conceived again. Our physician prescribed a sonogram at sixteen weeks, and we chose to have it done, hoping it would calm some of our fears. Seconds after the picture appeared on the screen (none of which we understood at that early stage), the technician said, "Do twins run in your family?" We couldn't believe it.

I have no doubt that my pain from the loss had opened me up to my full powers of spirit and knowledge, and although I wasn't open to the *understanding* of that knowledge at the time, I know an inner guide was telling me of my future joys.

Mucbeah Robinson, who lost her mother at the age of thirteen, writes, "When one's mother dies, a part of the veil between life and death becomes thin -- and the connection continues on some level, through it."

Susan Stout also believes that her experience at the time of her mother's death contributed to the sensitivity which allowed her later to connect with her unborn child:

While my mother was dying a hundred miles away, I had a very clear message from her. (Although I knew she was seriously ill, I had no idea that she had entered her death process. But I verified later with my uncle the precise time she started dying and it was the same time I started getting her "messages.") I had been making some curtains and had thought how I wanted to show them to Mom. That's when I started getting messages. My mother told me that she did see the curtains and that she would always be able to see what I was doing. Then for the next two hours the following message kept repeating itself, "Susan, I love you. I am dying. Goodbye." It upset me terribly but I just opened myself to hear what was being said. It has always comforted me that we did have this last communication before she died. This experience led me to be more open to events outside the normal realm.

Mary Bohman passed through a near-death state herself during a delivery and she feels this has made her more aware of other dimensions:

I do believe that these experiences are unique to people who are becoming more in touch with the other side and are themselves opening to metaphysical happenings. As I open more and more to these possibilities, the experiences happen more and more often. I am honored that my children have gifted me with these experiences and I wish that more people could tune into this ability. It may be easier for those of us who have already been to the other side in out-of-body experiences as I did during Ian's birth, because there is a memory ingrained. Since then, these things come easier, while I am also consciously trying to encourage them and working at developing my skills more intentionally.

We are influenced by the attitudes of people around us. Those who care for us in pregnancy may or may not support the idea of connecting with our child before birth. Sally Gartner points out that as we rely on "professionals" for information about our child in the womb, we may be less likely to notice the information that comes to us directly. She writes:

> How we experience pregnancy and birth is deeply affected by the care we receive from others. Doctors doubt even the physical sensations of women who experience fetal movement before the textbook date indicated. How can we always appreciate the psychic, the spiritual influences?
>
> When we wake up to the very real relationships going on during pregnancy (and even before) with the unborn, I believe we will have more people acknowledging and opening up to the signals they receive. Technology and physical measurements seem to matter most in the way pregnancy and birth are currently managed. So many women need the doctor to tell them how they are doing with their routine checkups which never explore the other dimensions of the pregnancy experience. Since most births are surgical (either caesarean or episiotomy) with numerous other interventions, controlling or harmful outside influences can diminish the mother's ability to tune in to her baby.
>
> My midwife said she hears stories of spiritual contact and psychic insights all the time from other women. She experienced it herself. My doctor was very much taken aback when he said, "Well, I just don't *know* about spiritual contact!" And he is a real sweet doctor, but the idea is a new one for him judging by his reaction.

Even more crucial than the attitude of caregivers is the reaction of one's mate. We tend to mute the parts of ourselves that look foolish to our partner, as one woman observes: "My husband laughed at me when I told him, so after that I kept it to myself." Without that acceptance, it's difficult to trust oneself to the subtle, unusual experiences of pre-birth communication.

*   *   *

What are some of the conditions that help us get in touch with our unborn children? There are techniques and practices we may wish to try, if we want to be as open as possible to having such an experience. We can find helpful suggestions in parents' stories, by noting the situations that seem to facilitate pre-birth encounters.

About half of the communication experiences described in this book happened in altered states of awareness -- something other than our usual waking consciousness. These include dreams, reveries at the edge of sleep, states of deep relaxation, meditation, rebirthing and other breathing practices, hypnosis, biofeedback, and guided visualization or meditation exercises.

One surprising setting that seems to favor receptivity is taking a shower! One might assume this to be due to the falling water's sound, a white noise that we easily transmute into words, perhaps messages from our own subconscious. On the other hand, a shower can be much like a massage: relaxing, stimulating our senses, changing our mood with its negative ions and perhaps altering the state of our "field."

Walking outdoors may have similar effects. A mother recalls:

> My memory is that I sensed her more during daylight hours, especially when I was in sunlight; walking outside was the most common situation. Trying to "summon" her was very difficult -- she, like the muse, came when she pleased.

Peaceful surroundings and solitude are helpful. Most often, communication is felt when one is alone, undistracted by others. Some people find they hear inner voices or sense presences more easily while concentrating on a demanding task, or while absorbed in a monotonous, rhythmic one such as washing dishes. Both of these situations can bring an inner quieting much like the stillness of meditation.

The deep relaxation involved in bodywork, massage, yoga, and similar practices is central to many people's contact experiences. Visions and messages are received during various kinds of healing sessions. For example:

When I first learned I was pregnant, I called up a social worker who did Reiki and Mariel Healing. She worked on getting me to relax and stop worrying, and to trust that my labor and delivery would turn out fine. While Laurie would heal me, we would both pick up messages from Angela -- my unborn baby -- that everything would be fine and not to worry, and that Angela was happy and that I had labored before in past lives and everything had gone fine then.

However, many contacts come during a time of emotional stress and upheaval. Ann Wasserman recalls:

It all really began because during my first pregnancy there was a lot of emotional trauma going on; first my only uncle and then my mother died after three months of hospital and nursing home. So instead of the wonderful summer I'd envisioned, lying in the hammock reading baby books, I was dealing with doctors and funeral homes and crying a lot.

I remembered back to a session of a meditation group we'd gone to a few years earlier, where the leader counseled a pregnant woman going through some crisis to talk to her baby and tell him/her that none of the upheaval had anything to do with him/her, to just keep growing healthy and calm. So that's what I did, often, during that time. It was really cool to feel I was getting a response of relief and comfort. That sort of segued over into having little conversations sometimes. These were not in formal meditation-type settings, just being quiet enough to hear her. I imagine that having experience with meditation and visualization helps a lot in sensing this and accepting that this could happen, just being open to communication on this sort of level.

A typical setting, then, is a moment of quieting and turning inward while in the midst of a stressful situation.

There are techniques and exercises we can use with the specific intention of connecting with our unborn child. Mary, a pregnancy counselor, was only a few days from her due date when she wrote of her own experiences before conceiving this child:

We both felt we would have one more baby, even when Emily was so small that it seemed far in the future. The years passed and whenever I wanted Number Three, Jim said "not now," and whenever he wanted Number Three, I wasn't ready. Last winter

I started thinking about a baby again and feeling that if I didn't have one right away I never would.

So I kept asking Jim what did he think and want? He kept answering that we should meditate on it -- but he would forget to do it, and I wouldn't. One time when I asked for an answer after my meditation, I felt the baby's presence very strongly. There was a strong nonverbal, non-visual, intuitive communication.

Another time, I decided to do an exercise I had my clients do, in pregnancy counseling. My clients were often choosing between parenting and adoption for their babies, and I would encourage them to visualize both options from pregnancy through childhood. So I set out to visualize our life with and without a third child.

I couldn't get any pictures at all for the first option, and with the second it was more like a vision -- the pictures just came without my doing anything to create the visualization. I saw a blond haired boy, about two years old, playing in my dahlias. It was very vivid and wonderful.

I had to deal with my feelings about a boy. Being a girl myself, I'm sort of partial to girl babies/children and had hoped for another girl. But I felt so well-acquainted with this "boy" and so attached to him after feeling his presence off and on for most of six years, that it ceased to matter.

Mary's very blond baby boy was born soon after she wrote this letter. She says, "I'm sure he is the baby we were supposed to have, the one I envisioned and expected, the one who picked us before we knew for sure we would have him. He seems real familiar..."

Many practices and exercises have been mentioned in the stories; information about others can be found in the Notes at the end of the book.*

CHANNELS OF RECEPTIVITY

We each have our characteristic way of being receptive, and it seems likely that we connect with our child along the pathway of perception that is our most sensitive "channel."

Some of us normally see colorful, detailed imagery when we close our eyes; others see a dark gray void. Some receive impressions through physical feelings in the solar plexus. Some people recall vivid dreams almost every night, while others seldom remember a dream. We may become more receptive by recognizing our own natural channel, however unusual it may be. For example, Fran communed with her unborn daughter through the medium of the color of her thoughts. She explains:

> As it became closer to the delivery date, I began having a greater sense of the personality of this child. She was active and had visual thoughts very different from mine. The internal color of my thoughts has always been a part of my life, but hers were now joining mine. The differences were more of detail and complexity. Hers seemed to be endless space sorts of views. Lots of dark rose, velvety midnight, pale blue, touches of watery green... I began to see her face with more regularity and as having more expression. There were large spaces and times which were sort of hidden. I later associated them with the very different ways we each think, a sort of inability to translate, if you will.

Those of us who are primarily verbal might try listening in a different way to the things we say to ourselves when we speak in metaphors. They may be truer than we realize! Let me give a personal example. In an earlier chapter I described the profound sense of peace and beauty that came over me one night while I was pregnant with my daughter. For some unquestioned reason, I always thought of that occasion as "Roselyn's real birthday." Was this my way of "knowing" that what I felt was her consciousness becoming fully present? I'll leave it as speculation, for it is all too easy to harden a bit of poetry into a bit of dogma.

Receptivity in one area tends to go along with unusual awareness in other areas as well. Isabelle Kessler writes:

> I've been having some amazing experiences lately. I was asleep in bed -- woke and saw about six feet high and at the foot of my bed a shimmering white spiral of light which burst into a rainbow. I felt such peace from gazing at it. I think if we can open ourself to all the "unknown" that is within our world, we can communicate with our unborn children and see spiral lights of peace. It all seems to be a way of showing us what else is around, besides just what we perceive to be "reality." I'm very thankful for all. Even the frightening things.

Good experiences through one channel embolden us to explore other kinds of subtle perception. A woman compares the inner voice she heard in pregnancy with another unusual awareness that had long been familiar to her:

> I have been aware of an odd ability that I have to know certain numbers before they are said. You may find this strange and off the subject, but I think it's relevant because the sensation is identical to when I knew my child was a girl and what her name was.
>
> The number knowledge has *always* happened with me and usually occurs while I am listening to someone, either in person or on TV or radio, who is about to say a number for whatever reason. I always know the number.

The accuracy of her "number knowledge" encouraged her to be receptive when she sensed contact with her unborn daughter:

> This history of premonition (which I have shared with no one else but my husband, before now) led me to trust the voice when I heard it concerning my child. The feelings I got regarding what her temperament and personality would be like have not yet been wrong. I truly feel that either I knew her "before" (not quite sure when or how), that she was already "formed," or that I was shown a blueprint for what was to come.
>
> And that brings us to how it has all fit in with my ideas and beliefs about life, birth, and so on. The "knowledge" is my only "god." Because what I saw and heard during such an important, change-filled time in my life (which could have been a very scary time) proved to be good and true, I have come to love and trust it more.
>
> I am still wildly impatient and not often in touch with the more serene parts of myself from where this strength and guidance come. I often feel tired and helpless in ways that I didn't as a single, childless working woman (girl, really). But now I feel there is something more. Something deeper or beyond and I sometimes regret not being more of a seeker or an intellectual with ways to define or compare it. I need more time! I don't want to be cut off from the information I feel is available to me. Nothing else in my life thus far has brought me closer to that light than pregnancy -- I don't know what else will or would... I'm curious and trying to remain open.
>
> In the past year or so, I have come to a place where I can articulate and appreciate these sensations that have been secret and second nature in me for so long. Tentatively at first, I have begun to share these things with my husband, and his

encouragement and support have helped me begin to look for ways to strengthen these abilities, although I still don't know *why* I know these things.

Some speak of a conflict between their training or education and the recurrent experiences that contradict their intellectual framework. "Ever since I was a teenager," says Dr. Juliann Mitchell, "I have had premonitions about things. This is quite contrary and opposite to how I have been trained and schooled -- which has been very logical, scientific and rational. Yet I cannot deny my own experiences."

Another woman writes that she and her husband both have a love of science and so "sometimes our spiritual experiences and feelings are jarring to our logical selves. But the experiences keep happening and chasing our skepticism away. Our rational selves find these events kind of embarrassing so we deny them or change their power. Sometimes it's hard to believe the truth of my experiences. But my spiritual self seems to have a lot of patience with my overly-logical self."

THE RECEPTIVE/CREATIVE PERSONALITY

> *I wonder if artists, writers and right-brain types are more open -- therefore more inclined to hear the angels... If I had it to do over again, I would have prayed for wisdom as well as vision.*
>
> *-- Mucheah Robinson*

Although we all have our ways of being receptive, some people seem particularly likely to experience connections with their children-to-be. These are people whose lives are full of encounters with alternate realities and/or fantasies -- sensitive, visualizing people.

Many of those who shared their stories with me related that these were part of a lifelong pattern of unusual experiences. Claire Baiz, for example, says: "I had many strange experiences as a child -- flying, talking to my dead father, seeing shadows, not recognizing myself in a mirror (still have a time with that!). I learned that such experiences are not accepted in mainstream America, and I sublimated much, forgot some and rebelled against it all." Another woman writes:

You asked whether I ever had similar experiences at other times in my life. I've never had quite the intensity of that experience, never before heard a "voice." But I've always been conscious of being acutely aware, of being receptive to people, to living things, having mystical experiences in nature, and awareness of people beyond the physical level, sensing inner meaning, vibrations, moods...

Mary Halter Petersen describes a lifelong sensitivity:

> I certainly always have felt rather unusual from an early age. Since about the age of twelve or thirteen I've been rather out-of-step with most of my peers. I've meditated since I was a teenager, but even before that I always felt a very strong connection with what I call the Source.
>
> As a young child I had many instances of praying intently about something and having it happen... When my mom began reading Edgar Cayce material, UFO books and later the Seth books, she shared much of this with me and I recall many long talks with her about consciousness, reincarnation, life's purpose, and so forth.
>
> In high school I had a very influential religious education teacher. When I first met him I *knew* I had known him before and he felt likewise. Which is actually the same way I met my husband years later. I only dated about two times and that in my twenties. I was never interested in "playing" at intimate relationship. I always had a sense that when I "dated" it would be my husband. I *knew* this. And that's how it happened. He and I were camping separately on an island state park off the Wisconsin mainland. We had an instant recognition experience and were talking of marriage within a week, engaged three months later and married six months after that, and very happily too I might add.
>
> I think I *came* to earth this time more open and sensitive to such awarenesses and my experiences always have led me to supportive people and expanded ideas.

We differ in our degree of openness to non-ordinary experience, and at the far end of the spectrum are people of extreme susceptibility. While some researchers emphasize that these people are "fantasy-prone," others (perhaps more sympathetically) call them "encounter-prone." I prefer to use the term "receptive/creative" to describe these highly sensitive individuals.

How can you tell if you are a person who is unusually likely to have experiences of a mystical, psychic, non-ordinary nature?

Typically, your life has already been full of such events, beginning in childhood. Your dolls and stuffed animals were "real" to you; you believed in fairies and other beings and may even have seen and played with them. You easily submerged yourself in pretending to be someone or something else.

You have vivid memories going back to your earliest years, and can almost see, hear, smell, touch and taste the experiences you recall. In fact, you can imagine things so clearly that they seem almost real. Your body responds intensely to ideas and imagery. Images of violence can make you ill; thoughts of pregnancy can bring on convincing physical symptoms.

Along with these qualities, receptive/creative people are often extremely responsive to hypnotic suggestion and presumably to auto-suggestion as well. As Michael Murphy sums up in his book *The Future of the Body*, research indicates that some people regularly experience vivid, even hallucinatory imagery:

> Some people develop strong fantasy lives through a lifetime of imagery practice... The lifelong cultivation of imagery... appears to produce powerful imagination and memory, intense concentration, openness to unusual experience, sensory acuity, and strong somatic responsiveness to mental imagery. All of these capacities can facilitate extraordinary functioning in general.

This description of the receptive/creative person surely fits many of the most talented and sensitive among us. Such powers may seem a gift or a liability -- depending on whether they serve to enrich or to distort our perception of reality. And that throws the question of "fantasy" versus "encounter" right back into the ring where belief systems contend over what is real -- which is where we will leave it.

To make it all still more thought-provoking, some researchers identify non-ordinary experience with unstable brain function. Michael Persinger, a neuroscientist, has developed "an entire theory about the role of the temporal lobe in religious experience:"

> He pointed out that the temporal lobe and its associated structures... are involved in memory, strong emotions and in the sense of self in time and space. It is activity in these areas, he argued, that is associated with the sense of deep meaningfulness, as well as recall of early memories and even out-of-body experiences. The more unstable the activity in a person's temporal lobe, the more liable they are to have such experiences, and everyone can be placed somewhere along a continuum from very stable to very unstable.*

In other words, when I experience what feels like a contact with my unborn child, I may ask myself whether this is the touch of another soul or a slight storm in my brain.

When first learning of these issues, I found them somewhat threatening to my sense of personal meaning. With time, they have come to seem wonderfully intriguing. For all we know, if other worlds of consciousness exist, the temporal lobe may be our window to them, our receiver of their energies. Perhaps it holds our fragment of the hologram.

In any case, we need not fear that by continuing to question, we will come to the end of wonder, for it seems the mystery of things keeps on escaping from every attempt to pin it down to something finally known.

ARE WE IN RECEPTIVE TIMES?

Is sensing contact with children-to-be a more common experience nowadays than, say, fifty years ago? While it's probably impossible to know, there are reasons to think it may be so, at least in the world dominated by mass media and rapid change.

We're in a time of transforming family patterns. We've begun experiments whose effects we won't be able to see for a generation or more: single parent families, step-parents, blended families, homosexual couples with children, many forms of adoption, not to mention surrogate mothers, babies born by artificial insemination, and new possibilities with genetic technology.

Prenatal testing has created the "conditional" pregnancy -- the possibility of postponing acceptance of one's baby until it is known to be healthy, genetically normal, or even of the desired gender. We have scarcely begun to know what effects these new realities will have on us.

It seems we're looking for the essence of parenthood that will hold true through all these changes. Perhaps this is part of why many parents emphasize the spiritual dimensions of the relationship with their children. Genetic lineage seems less important now that there are so many ways of being a family.

There are other reasons why we may be growing more attentive to communication from our unborn children.

We have options in our personal lives now that mean childbearing is a matter of choice, not a matter of course. The need to make a conscious choice creates anxiety, and we look for signs that our decision is right. Anxious as well about the quality of our children's future, we may like to be reassured that they accept the situation as it is. For the times are full of danger and the future looks uncertain. Perhaps we feel weary, unable to fix the mess we've made. Longing for help and rescue, we may focus this wish on our children in hopes they will prove wiser than we.

For many, the issue of overpopulation brings an element of guilt to childbearing. (As a young woman, I sadly believed "it's immoral to have even one child now, by birth.") We may feel uneasy with the implications of our choice, and wish for a sign that someone else is making the decision.

And some of us, influenced by various philosophies, spent years trying to be free of "desires" and had to go through considerable soul-searching and change to come to the point of wanting -- or admitting that we wanted -- to have children. Like the Buddha, who commented, "A fetter is born" at the birth of his son, we feared our attachment to children would be an obstacle on the spiritual path. The resolution of this struggle doesn't necessarily make us more receptive, but it means we've thought a great deal about the decision and are attentive to signs that parenting, itself, can be spiritually enriching.

And then, our awareness has been expanded by psychedelics, meditation and other adventures in consciousness, including the basic insights of psychology. We are increasingly open to mystical experiences and more accepting of the concept of life after death -- so why not life before birth?

Perhaps the prevalence of these experiences is part of a ripening process, and we are naturally growing more receptive. Perhaps the doors between the worlds are becoming transparent. Maybe the "frequencies" of different dimensions are coming into phase with each other. When images of the dead appear on TV screens and stories of angelic encounters are legion, such speculations don't seem far-fetched.

And just possibly, the children themselves are coming with more determination to connect before birth. As Nancy Cohen observes:

> I only hesitate in thinking that couples may feel inadequate if they *can't* make connections. I know when a friend wrote to me that her baby's spirit contacted her during meditation I, who didn't even meditate at the time, felt so inadequate! I thought she must be a saint! Many children are conceived so unconsciously -- yet many seem to be coming through with a great need to communicate their love and blessing before conception.

AFTERWORD

As I come to the end of this book, the Christmas season is approaching, and once again the image of the newborn baby appears.

In my native Italy, shepherds with their bagpipes come down from the mountain villages to the cities, and play a haunting carol whose words go something like this: "You descend from the stars, O King of Heaven, and enter a cave amid the icy cold. O my divine child, I see you trembling here..."

There's something about this picture that speaks to us and holds us. A child shivering in a stable, attended by animals and angels: could it be an image of the soul's trek from the beyond into the rude world?

The soul is strong, according to the evidence of pre-birth connections. But coming to birth means taking on vulnerability. Even with heaven and nature looking on, there's no denying the harsh conditions that face the newborn baby here.

Can we change the world, making it more tender and more fit to receive a newborn soul? It is my hope that these shared stories will help to make it so.

NOTES

p. 27 APGAR
A scoring system devised by Dr. Virginia Apgar, used to evaluate the newborn's condition one minute after birth. It ranges from zero to ten, with ten being the best score. An Apgar of zero implies a newborn who is limp, blue, unresponsive, unbreathing, and without a heartbeat.

p. 32 CHAKRA
There are various systems and theories of the "chakras." Perhaps the simplest definition is that they are thought to be energy centers in the body. Seven chakras are generally recognized. The "crown chakra" is at the top of the head.

p. 87 CHOLESTASIS OF PREGNANCY
A disorder caused by the effect of pregnancy hormones on bile transport. Constituents of bile back up into the bloodstream, causing itching.

p. 123 IN VITRO FERTILIZATION (IVF)
A technique that allows some couples with fertility problems to achieve pregnancy. Eggs are removed from the woman's ovary and combined in the lab ("in vitro," literally, "in glass") with the husband's sperm. If fertilization occurs, the embryo is transferred to the woman's uterus. The success rate with this technique is about twenty percent.

p. 135 LIGHT INSTITUTE
For information, contact:
    The Light Institute
    HC 75 Box 50
    Galisteo, NM 87540
    or phone (505) 466-1975, or FAX 505-466-7217 for brochure

p. 156 HELEN WAMBACH, JOEL WHITTON, MICHAEL GABRIEL
These are among the psychologists who have experimented with hypnotic regression to memories of womb life and before. For more information on their work, see:
Life Before Life, by Helen Wambach, Ph.D. (Bantam Books, March 1979)
Life Between Life, by Joel Whitton, M.D., Ph.D. and Joe Fisher (Doubleday and Company, 1986)
Voices From The Womb, by Michael Gabriel, M.A. with Marie Gabriel, M.P.A. (Aslan Publishing 1992)

p. 157 TIBETAN VIEW
As described in *The Tibetan Book of Living and Dying*, by Sogyal Rinpoche (HarperSanFrancisco, 1992), which presents a detailed account of the soul's journey to birth, from the perspective of Tibetan tradition.

p. 163 LACT-AID
One of several models of supplemental nursing systems. A plastic bottle containing formula is worn on the mother's upper chest, with tubes leading to the nipple. The baby is able to nurse at the breast, stimulating milk production, while receiving supplemental feeding from the tube, which acts as though it were another milk duct.

p. 177 A SOUND BEGINNING
For information about this program, contact:
A Sound Beginning
5737 Kanan Road, Suite 333
Agoura Hills, CA 91301, or call (818) 889-2229

p. 178 COMMUNING WITH THE SPIRIT OF YOUR UNBORN CHILD
Audiotape is available from:
Aslan Publishing
3356 Coffey Lane
Santa Rosa, CA 95403
A book, *Communing With The Spirit of Your Unborn Child*, by Dawson Church, is also available from Aslan Publishing. Write the above address or call (707) 542-5400 to request a catalog.

p. 207 EFFECTS OF CARBON DIOXIDE
L.J.Meduna, "The effect of carbon dioxide upon the functions of the brain," from *Carbon Dioxide Therapy*, Charles C. Thomas, Publisher, 1950. Reprinted in *Dying To Live* by Susan Blackmore (Prometheus Books, 1993).

p. 236 D & C
Dilatation and curettage -- a surgical procedure in which the cervix is dilated and the inner walls of the uterus are scraped. Often performed to remove retained tissue after a miscarriage.

p. 258 CONSCIOUS CONCEPTION
Conscious Conception: Elemental Journey Through the Labyrinth of Sexuality by Jeannine Parvati Baker, Frederick Baker and Tamara Slayton (Freestone Publishing Company, 1986). A spiritual philosophy of conception; includes accounts of communicating with the unborn.

p. 262 "RELUCTANT, ANXIOUS OR RESIGNED"
See page 63, *Life Before Life* by Helen Wambach, Ph. D. (Bantam Books, March 1979).

p. 285 SPIRITUAL ADOPTION SERVICE
Denise Shaffer offers spiritual counseling during the fertility quest. She can be reached at:
263 Lafever Court, Manchester TN 37355

p. 289 MODELS OF LOVE

Models of Love: The Parent-Child Journey, by Joyce Vissell, R.N., M.S. and Barry Vissell, M.D. (Ramira Publishing, 1986). An inspiring book that includes, among many other topics of interest, experiences of connection before conception, and remarkable examples of "mood as message." See especially Chapter Nine.

p. 307 PRACTICES AND EXERCISES

Bonding Before Birth by Leni Schwartz (Sigo Press, 1991) includes a series of imaginative exercises for both parents, to help us explore the emotions of pregnancy and connect with the unborn child. An audiotape, "The Child Within: Six Meditations for Pregnant Couples" is also available from Sigo Press, 50 Grove Street, Salem MA 01970.

Communing With The Spirit Of Your Unborn Child by Dawson Church (Aslan Publishing, 1988) is a detailed guide to exploring the spiritual dimensions of pregnancy, through meditations and exercises for both parents. The revised edition (fall 1995) is titled *Birthing The Angel*.

Nurturing the Unborn Child by Thomas Verny, M.D. and Pamela Weintraub (Delacorte Press, 1991). Subtitled "A nine-month program for soothing, stimulating, and communicating with your baby," this book contains much information about life in the womb.

p. 312 TEMPORAL LOBE

For a very readable explanation of the physical correlates of some nonordinary experiences, see *Dying To Live* by Susan Blackmore (Prometheus Books, 1993), from which this quote is taken.

GRATITUDE. . . to the contributors who shared their experiences, insights, and enthusiasm. Thanks are due as well to the partners, husbands, and wives who allowed the stories to be told. This book was created through the generosity of:

Clare Adams
Claire Baiz
Lu Ann Balfrey
Susan Bassett
Ethan Bauch
Vivien Beirne
Margaret Birnbaum
Denise Boggs
Mary Bohman
Laurie Bolotin
Rebekah Bridge
Alisha Buchser
Marilyn Bunn
Jane Anne Buzana
Kristina Bystrom
Anne Calajoe
Sally Calvin
Cheri Carlson
Bunny Chidester
Patricia Chubb
Susan Clarke
Nancy and Tod Cohen
Lisa Conyers
Annemarie Demarkles
Ruthie Ervin
Jean Fejes
Deanna Finney
Gail Fleming
Sally Gartner
Judy Goodale
Diane Gregg
Trilby Malinn Hanek
Beverly Hayes
Linda Heal
Kim Ilowit
Celestia Jasper
Elyse Zorn Karlin
Doryan Dean Kasoff
Lucy Kennedy

Isabelle Kessler
Julie Klekas
Kristine Kovach
Donna Kurtz
Katryn Lavanture
Nikki Lee
Jeri Lermusiaux
Nettie Lessmann
Karin Liedtke
Liz Lipman-Stern
Diana Lorenz
Kathryn Mayton
Leigh McCune
Kathy McNeil
Nancy Mendez
Pam Millar
Sue Jo Mitchell
Juliann Mitchell
Cathie Morales
Vicki Morrison
Stacey Mott
Marion Nelson
Karen Nelson
Katy Nielsen
Kenneth Nova
Liz Nusken
Amy Oscar
Lisa Torchio Oviatt
Janette Patterson
Isadora Paymer
Monica Peabody
Dove Penn-Hamburg
Mary Halter Petersen
Lisa Ponder
Deborah Prince
Sue Pultorak
Stephanie Quinn
Raven-Wolf

Tim Richardson
Holly Richardson
Louise Richardson
Mucbeah Robinson
Lani Rosenberger
Alicia Russell-Smith
Denise Shaffer
Lynne Shank
Sheila Sherman
Barbara Sieradzki
Susan Sitler
Kamille and Al Smith
Debbie Smollen
Patricia Smuland
Vicki Stamler
Ellen Stanclift
Fiora Starchild
Susan Stout
Ginger Strickland
Carla Sunderland
Tamara Thomas
Julia Toth
Adam and Lee Tritt
Marilyn Turkle
Barbara Umberger
Diane Umile
Michele Veasey
Candy Wasser
Ann Wasserman
Larry Wasserman
Candice White
Carin Willette
Martell Williams
Teresa Williams
Barbara Wolf
Becci Wolfer
Tammy Zechman
Laura Ziemba

. . . and an additional seventy contributors whose names I do not have permission to publish. Special thanks to Rosalie Denenfeld for her encouragement, and to Dr. Marshall White, Jr. for his help. And to my husband, Nicholas, thanks. . . for everything.

ACKNOWLEDGEMENTS

The author gratefully acknowledges permission to reprint:

pp. 80 and 89-90: from *The Secret Life of the Unborn Child*, copyright 1981 by Thomas Verny, M.D. and John Kelly. By permission of Simon & Schuster, Inc.

pp. 94-95, 103, 120: quotations from Barbara Wolf, Laura Ziemba, and Vicki Morrison, from *A Phenomenological Study of the Relationship Between the First-Time Pregnant Woman and her Unborn Child*, copyright 1984 by Rosalie Denenfeld, M.A. Reprinted by permission.

pp. 105-106: from an article by Janette Patterson in Midwifery Today,1989 #12. Reprinted by permission.

pp. 127-128, 292: from *Risk To Be Healed: The Heart of Personal and Relationship Growth*, copyright 1989 by Barry Vissell, M.D. and Joyce Vissell, R.N., M.S. By permission of Ramira Publishing.

p. 136: from an article by Karin Liedtke in The Compleat Mother Magazine. Reprinted by permission.

pp. 143, 148: from *Born To Live: A Holistic Approach to Childbirth*, copyright 1980 by Gladys T. McGarey, M.D. Reprinted by permission.

p. 160: from *Take Me Home*, copyright 1994 by John Denver. By permission of Harmony Books/Crown Publishers, Inc.

pp. 168-169: from *Life Between Life*, copyright 1986 by Joel Whitton, M.D. and Joe Fisher. By permission of Doubleday.

p. 194: from *The Earliest Relationship: Parents, Infants, and the Drama of Early Attachment*, copyright 1990 by T. Berry Brazelton, M.D. and Bertrand G. Cramer, M.D. By permission of Addison-Wesley Publishing Company, Inc.

p. 202: from *The Gift of Healing* by Ambrose A. Worrall and Olga Worrall, Ariel Press edition 1985. Reprinted by permission.

p. 204: from *The Radiant Child*, copyright 1985 by Thomas Armstrong. By permission of The Theosophical Publishing House.

p. 206: from an editorial by Peggy Taylor in New Age Journal, March 1978. Reprinted by permission.

p. 207: from *Carbon Dioxide Therapy*, copyright 1950 by L.J. Meduna. Courtesy of Charles C. Thomas, Publisher, Springfield, Illinois.

p. 312: from *The Future of the Body*, copyright 1992 by Michael Murphy. By permission of Frederick Hill Associates.

pp. 312-313: from *Dying To Live: Near-Death Experiences*, copyright 1993 by Susan Blackmore. By permission of Prometheus Books, Buffalo, NY.

INDEX

324

ABOUT THE AUTHOR

A lifelong passion for the mysteries of the mind has led Elisabeth Hallett to explore psychology, nursing, and yoga. More recently, she has pursued her interests through independent research/writing projects. Her first book, *In The Newborn Year* (1992) provides an in-depth look at the transformations of consciousness that parenthood may bring.

Elisabeth lives with her husband and two children in the Bitterroot Valley of Montana.

✳   ✳   ✳

Your responses to this book, and your experiences of connecting with an unborn child, are welcomed. Please direct them to Elisabeth Hallett, in care of

Light Hearts Publishing
P.O. Box 705
Hamilton MT 59840

If you have enjoyed this book, you may also wish to read *In The Newborn Year: Our Changing Awareness After Childbirth*. Intimate stories unveil the mysteries of the bonding time: new emotions, altered senses, and psychic and spiritual awakenings reveal that the parent-and-child connection has power to open and change us.

Ask for **In The Newborn Year** or **Soul Trek** at your bookstore, or order directly from

Light Hearts Publishing
P.O.Box 705
Hamilton MT 59840

__ *Soul Trek* $14.95
__ *In The Newborn Year* $10.95

Please add $1.00 shipping/handling for each book ordered.